ROOSEVELT'S ROAD TO RUSSIA

Roosevelt's Road to Russia

by
GEORGE N. CROCKER

HENRY REGNERY COMPANY CHICAGO 1959

Library of Congress Catalog Card Number: 59-13049
Copyright © 1959 by Henry Regnery Company
Manufactured in the United States of America

First printing September 1959
Second printing November 1959
Third printing February 1960
Fourth printing August 1960
Fifth printing December 1960

CONTENTS

Earth is sick
And Heaven is weary, of the hollow words
Which States and Kingdoms utter when they talk
Of truth and justice.

WORDSWORTH

INTRODUCTION

RANDOLPH BOURNE, one of the critical commentators of the Woodrow Wilson period, once wrote that war is like a wild elephant: it carries the rider where it desires, not where he may desire. Perhaps the historian predilected to spare Franklin D. Roosevelt an unfavorable judgment at the bar of history will find in this simile his best expedient for divesting Roosevelt of responsibility for the tragic epilogue which followed World War II. By conjuring up the vision of the savage beast uncontrollable by the man, one can reduce to irrelevancy the qualities of the man. In the psychological climate thus engendered, a bald assumption that the man's intentions were virtuous, his motives pure, and his competence abundant becomes easy to propagate. History bows to a legend.

There is no longer any doubt that World War II led to consequences so at variance with the purpose of the war as proclaimed by President Roosevelt that some explanation must be produced and made plausible to multitudes of baffled and disillusioned people, for it will be remembered that Roosevelt sold the war, or at least American participation in it and his own indispensability for conducting it, with the avidity and cocksureness of a huckster.

The explanation can be realistic or it can be fanciful. The demagogue, of course, is tempted to offer one which will meet the empiric test of mass acceptability; the sentimentalist will embrace the one which is least disturbing to his memories, which, in turn, have been shaped and colored by his emotions; the participant, in his memoirs, strains to shield his own reputation and that of those with whom he has been linked. It remains for the historian, or rather many historians, each in his own way, to cull the truth from a mélange of fact, fancy, and propaganda. To do this, he must, of course, be unawed by the ephemeral glamour of popular heroes and undismayed by the disparity between the words and the deeds of men, for he will know that the guises of guile are many and that the words used by men of power are often chosen to conceal rather than to reveal the truth.

It is "the secret motives," wrote Élie Faure, "which, in men's intentions, determine historical events and by that fact make history half unintelligible to us." The same thought impelled Napoleon, in the wane of his brilliant career, to complain that historical truth "is too often merely a phrase ... a story that has been agreed to tell."

Perhaps psychoanalysis will rewrite history. It will, eventually, predicts Dr. Raymond de Saussure in his contribution to Géza Róheim's symposium under the title *Psychoanalysis and the Social Sciences*. While the task is an enormous one and methods of investigation will need to be greatly improved, psychoanalytic understanding of the motives that spur men to action will throw new light on events whose cause and meaning have otherwise been obscure. It is banal to say that only a psychoanalytical approach can explain Hitler's appeal to the German people. Is it not as likely that the roots of Franklin D. Roosevelt's curious relations with the Soviet Russians abroad and their minions in this country will be reached through similar psychological explorations? Of Roosevelt, Harold Ickes once said that it was "impossible to come to grips with him." Indeed, his mind was a perfect exemplification of the "feeling" and "intuitive" types of extroversion described by Jung and van der Hoop, so his analyst will not expect to find logical consistency as he follows the threads of motivation through a tortuous course of behavior that is at once masterly and preposterous. In the case of the intimate assistant and confidant, Harry Hopkins, a more transparent man and one whose brooding antipathies and wanton enthusiasms were as passionate as they were often fatuous, the psychopathology is already dimly visible to the observant layman.* Later generations of savants, far removed from the political considerations which now discourage such projects and aided by the testimony of secrets yet untold, will undoubtedly write of these "cases" in books which men now living will never have an opportunity to read.

Randolph Bourne's simile of the wild elephant will not do. The story of World War II and its aftermath is a drama of human will. The denouement, so full of irony, was not fortuitous. It is too easily forgotten that conscious, deliberate choices between specific alternatives were made time after time. While armies were clashing all over the world, important men met and made decisions and compacts. In varying degrees, these men were either clothed with legal authority to do what they did or they arrogated the power to themselves. The lives and fortunes of millions of living human beings and the futures of those yet unborn were admittedly to be affected by what these high personages decided to do or not to do. The legality of their actions

* General John R. Deane, head of the United States Military Mission in Moscow during the war, writes that Harry Hopkins carried out the Russian aid program "with a zeal which approached fanaticism." Hopkins' "enthusiasm became so ingrained that it could not be tempered." (John R. Deane, *The Strange Alliance* [Viking, 1947], 90)

under national and international law is perhaps now academic; the results are not. The travail and violence that must inevitably be faced in order to undo much that these men did remain the burden of the present and the future.

In August, 1941, while war was raging in Europe but before the United States formally became a belligerent, President Roosevelt met with Prime Minister Winston Churchill on a battleship off the coast of Canada. The Atlantic Charter was pronounced at the end of this conference. Later, when the United States was at war with Germany, Italy, and Japan, Roosevelt left American soil to engage in conferences with Churchill, Chiang Kai-shek, Stalin, and others at Quebec, Casablanca, Cairo, Teheran, and Yalta. The finesse of master politicians in dramatizing their movements, the subtle art of press-agentry, and the natural susceptibility of most human beings to the appeal of the spectacular all united to glamorize these parleys. Roosevelt's treks across the world led him closer, ever closer, to Russia until finally, at Yalta, Stalin received him on Russian soil.

Stalin received much at Yalta besides the effusive company of a still garrulous, though ill, American President—as the world was later to learn. Harry Hopkins was, of course, in Roosevelt's entourage when the President met with the Soviet dictator in the winter palace of the Czars on the shores of the Black Sea; he busied himself passing little notes to Roosevelt, prompting him. Also there was Alger Hiss, as a special adviser from the State Department. One can imagine his inner jubilation.

After each conference, communiqués were issued. They seldom told the story fully. It would be presumptuous, indeed, for this volume to purport to do that. Fragments yet unsuspected are undoubtedly locked in the memories or files of persons still alive, or may be written down in papers hidden in the vaults of the heirs of men now dead, not to be brought forth until still later generations have come upon the scene. The political party of Franklin D. Roosevelt remained in control of the State Department and its files for seven years after his death. Much material that found its way to Hyde Park during the Roosevelt and Truman regimes has been seen only by a few trusted eyes, and its disclosure has been stubbornly refused. The line that must be drawn between private papers of a President, on the one hand, and papers of public interest which come into a President's possession but which in good faith belong to the nation, on the other, is a tenuous one at best, and it is not to be expected that a family as politically minded as that of the late war President will always draw such a line in a manner to please inquisitive historians.

As a result, many details concerning Roosevelt's foreign conferences have never seen the light of day. This volume will have served its purpose if it can marshal, in some clear form, the tangled mass of facts which have already become known and if it can help to dissipate the fog with which propaganda has shrouded these important historical events. Enough has come to light to warrant some inescapable conclusions.

It is a sad, at times a sordid story. The United States had no Talleyrand—learned, philosophical, combining adroitness with a passionate patriotism for his country—to send to Cairo, Teheran, Yalta. Or if it had a Talleyrand, it did not send him. Nor was there a Woodrow Wilson to blush with shame at the mass dislocations of helpless populations, the sugar-coated acquiescence in slave labor, the secret agreements, the hypocritical communiqués; nor a Theodore Roosevelt ever to call a spade a spade, in talking to Stalin or in talking to the American people.

Writing of the cause of the Peloponnesian War, Thucydides said: "The real cause I consider to be the one which was formally most kept out of sight." Obliquity on the part of rulers of nations is not a lost art two and a half millennia later. That Franklin D. Roosevelt was a master of it, his champions even

boast. To them it was simply his clever way of outflanking political opposition. One is struck by the nonchalance with which
Professor Thomas A. Bailey of Stanford University, in his book
The Man in the Street, a generally sympathetic work, writes that
"Roosevelt repeatedly deceived the American people during the
period before Pearl Harbor," going on to say that "if he came
out unequivocally for intervention, he would be defeated in
1940."[1] Perhaps in the view of the good professor this would
have been a terrible calamity. In any event, if a bit of skillful
duplicity was needed, Roosevelt was equal to it, both before and
after Pearl Harbor.**

** Professor Bailey's assertions that "Roosevelt repeatedly deceived
the American people during the period before Pearl Harbor" and that
if he had not done so he would have been defeated in 1940 drew no
dissent, even from that ardent biographer of Roosevelt, Harvard Professor Arthur M. Schlesinger, Jr., who reviewed the Bailey book for
the *New York Times.* Said he, with approval: "If he [Roosevelt]
was going to induce the people to move at all, Professor Bailey con-
cludes, he had no choice but to trick them into acting for what he
conceived to be their best interests." (*New York Times Book Review,* May 9, 1948) He also used this review to scold Charles Austin
Beard for having laid Roosevelt's deceptions out on the table for all
to see, grumbling that this was "in the manner of a prosecuting at-
torney."

It was frightening to observe that the pretension of omniscience
and the usurpation, by "trickery," of the power of making vital decisions by the chief executive of a democratic country aroused no moral
indignation in many educators in the United States, for this reflected
a widespread, basic contempt for the democratic concept in academic
circles; and, as Beard had pointed out, it was a symptom of the intellectual chaos of the times that self-styled "liberals" were so often found
to have this fundamentally reactionary bent.

In subsequent national political campaigns in which Professor
Schlesinger co-worked with Mrs. Roosevelt and in which he served
as a top adviser and ghost writer for the candidates, the subject was
dropped. A study of his later writings finds no indication that he
would accord to *all* Presidents the prerogative of perpetuating themselves in office and moving the country into war by "tricking" the

Whatever we may think of the ethics of this tactic in a democracy, at the least it precludes the historian from ever taking Roosevelt's public attitudes at face value. In the perspective of time, we know now that his words and his deeds often galloped off in opposite directions. An editor of the *Saturday Evening Post* was once moved to remark that when listening to Roosevelt's speeches, he was reminded of two people going through a revolving door in opposite directions without touching. For a man of Roosevelt's mental habits, semantics is more than just an interesting branch of the science of philology; it is the arsenal from which the practical politician procures his sharpest weapons.

For this reason, a broad view and an uninhibited inquisitiveness are necessary when one approaches the foreign conferences of Franklin D. Roosevelt. They cannot be understood if sealed off from the stream of history, and they are utterly incomprehensible if one overlooks at any point in the narrative the psychological characteristics, in particular the inordinate political ambitions, of this man who ran successfully for the Presidency of the United States four times.

Accordingly, Part One of this book will touch upon some of the more general aspects of the subject. These, it is felt, are essential in preparing us to see in truer proportion and to integrate the details of the conferences when they are examined individually. It may prove helpful to look at the canvas as a whole before studying the brush strokes.

One more word as prelude. . . . It will be said, in a critical vein, that this is an unfriendly, opinionated book. The author does not pretend that his researches have hatched no convictions. Nor

---

people. As the record now stands, one could do no more than to infer that Professor Schlesinger accords the prerogative to Presidents whose re-election Professor Schlesinger would favor and with respect to wars which Professor Schlesinger would wish the United States to enter.

would he deem it a literary virtue to be insensitive to hypocrisy and misprision when they are uncovered in the search for facts.

Truth is always the first casualty in war. In later years, there are always those who stubbornly resist its resurrection. Among them are the hero-worshipers, intellectually supine or sentimental, but many have a gnawing sense of guilt, for they either participated in the thought manipulation of the war period or were its dupes. People who scrambled onto the propaganda bandwagon like jack rabbits do not enjoy having their own folly shown up, even to themselves. Let anyone seek to correct the historical record, by dredging up what William James called "the irreducible brute facts," and they will quickly brand him as "one-sided" or "biased" or "extreme." They have a vested interest in the delusions of the past.

In the post–World War II period, this phenomenon has, in some academic and literary circles, approached the level of Orwellian farce. Squirming in a dilemma, these people resort to a characteristically twentieth-century device with which to extricate themselves: semantics. Impervious to revealed facts which they cannot controvert, retreating not an inch, they arrogantly—and in chorus—appropriate to themselves a word to use as a shield. This word is the adjective "impartial." They—they would have it known—"see both sides." They wish to hear no more.

Obviously, the truth does not flourish in such a climate. World War II is not exempt from the impulse of inquisitive researchers to probe and to set the record straight; nor is Franklin D. Roosevelt, unless we have already been catapulted into the forced conformity of George Orwell's *1984* or the nightmarish scientific dictatorship of Aldous Huxley's *Brave New World*. Revisionism has been going on ever since Lorenzo Valla (1406-1457) exposed the forged *Donation of Constantine*. But the job is never done by those genial purveyors of the pleasantly orthodox, who write histories and biographies with one eye on the currently fashionable sources and the other on the book of etiquette.

Oscar Wilde strained for his epigram when he wrote: "A man who sees both sides of a question is a man who sees absolutely nothing at all." But he had a point. The man who sees nothing at all is, with perverse frequency, the man who prides himself on seeing both sides of a question. In history-writing, impartiality is sometimes a pose, sometimes a cover for obtuseness. If a reader wishes really to dig into a subject, he must

> Beware the middle mind
> That purrs and never shows a tooth.

Who are they who lay such pompous claim to impartiality? Actually, we should suspect them. This has never been better said than by Gaetano Salvemini, who, while teaching at Harvard in 1954, published a book entitled *Prelude to World War II,* which he dedicated to his colleagues and students. It dared to challenge some of the pithless platitudes which had been passing as "objective" history in those hallowed halls. Anticipating, no doubt, a charge of bias, he wrote in the Preface:

There are certain historians and critics sincerely convinced that they are unbiased, impartial, "scientific," who reject as "biased" any opinion that clashes with their own bias: they are fools endowed with a God Almighty complex. A second group consider themselves "unbiased" because they understand all principles and have none themselves; opportunism is no more admirable in historiography than in daily life. Then there are the wolves in sheep's clothing—the propaganda agents who boast of their lack of bias. Finally, there are those who frankly admit their bias, but do their utmost to avoid being blinded or side-tracked by it. *Impartiality is either a delusion of the simple-minded, a banner of the opportunist, or the boast of the dishonest. Nobody is permitted to be unbiased toward truth or falsehood.*

PART ONE

Two Men and a Secret

> ... for that nothing doth
> more hurt in a state than that cunning men
> pass for wise.
>
> SIR FRANCIS BACON

Chapter I

"...AND BY ME."

Lord Acton's famous dictum that power corrupts and absolute power corrupts absolutely may have come to the minds of many Americans as they sat before their radios on March 1, 1945. President Roosevelt was addressing Congress, reporting on his trip to Yalta. Poland had been partitioned, and the Lublin Committee, the coterie of Polish Communist puppets, coached by Stalin, had in effect been made masters of the remnants of that unhappy country. To veil this outrage, Roosevelt pretended that what had occurred was a harmless compromise by men of good will. But in expressing this thought, he gave his listeners a glimpse into the workings of his mind by means of a peculiar choice of words, carelessly ad-libbed (and later expurgated from the authorized Roosevelt Public Papers). The solution to the Polish question, said he, had been "agreed to *by Russia, by Britain and by me.*" Explaining further, he added that "we couldn't go as far as *Britain* wanted to go in certain areas, as far as *Russia* wanted in certain areas, and as far as *I* wanted in certain areas."[1]

L'état c'est moi! Had a creeping megalomania eaten into the mind of this failing man, who was now in his thirteenth year as President of the world's mightiest nation and who had been giddily consorting with kings, potentates, and dictators? Had the plenitude of power which had been entrusted to him to distribute vast American resources throughout the world led him gradually to identify himself personally as the source of this largesse and to project this conception to the whole field of foreign affairs? Or was he trying to be meticulously Constitutional, being aware that treaties may be entered into by the sovereign United States only with the consent of the Senate?

Roosevelt did not then, or ever, present the Yalta agreement to the legislative branch of the government as a treaty.[2] He obviously did not care to treat it as such. What was it, then? An "executive act" within any Constitutional area of jurisdiction of the President? It was never made clear what Roosevelt considered it to be from the legal standpoint, either under national or international law—if he ever gave the matter a thought. In essence, it was a personal agreement by Roosevelt with the Prime Minister of Great Britain and Stalin of Russia changing boundaries of Poland and other nations and determining the nationality of some millions of unconsulted human beings. Manifestly seeing neither the comedy nor the tragedy in such a performance and as unabashed as he would be if announcing a plan for the exchange of some grain and timber, Franklin D. Roosevelt had it within his nature to say to the world that all of this had been agreed to by Russia, by Britain, "and by me."

It was this agreement that Arthur Bliss Lane, our Ambassador to Poland, branded "a capitulation on the part of the United States." Horrified and saddened, he resigned and wrote a book entitled *I Saw Poland Betrayed*.[3] A secret document concerning the Far East had also been signed "by me" at Yalta. Of it, William C. Bullitt, who had been American Ambassador to Russia and to France, later wrote: "No more unnecessary, disgraceful and potentially dangerous document has ever been signed by a President of the United States."[4]

The "by me" spirit pervaded all of Franklin D. Roosevelt's

conduct of foreign affairs. With the pushful Harry Hopkins at his side and with a powerful government war information agency under his thumb, he made foreign policy his private province. His Secretary of State, the conscientious Cordell Hull, became a figurehead. Both the President and Hopkins, who saw alike on all important issues, including the desirability of getting Franklin D. Roosevelt re-elected ad infinitum, were pertinacious men and were not tolerant of opposition or interference. When Hull resigned his cabinet post right after the election of 1944 (Roosevelt having persuaded him to stay until the election was over), James F. Byrnes was a possible choice to succeed him. Hopkins opposed Byrnes on the ground that Roosevelt was going to be his own Secretary of State, particularly in direct dealings with Churchill and Stalin, and Byrnes (who had once told Hopkins to "keep the hell out of my business") was not one to fit himself placidly into the role of a mere mouthpiece. So the obliging Edward R. Stettinius, who already had a perfect record in taking orders from Hopkins as Lend-Lease Administrator and as Under Secretary of State, was selected to be the "mouthpiece."[5]

At the close of World War I, Woodrow Wilson had gone abroad to negotiate a treaty of peace. Franklin D. Roosevelt, both before and during World War II, traveled far and wide as no American President had ever done before. On those trips he made vast commitments of a military and political nature, some of which were long kept secret. The Congress, first on his pretension that he would keep the country out of war and later on his assurance that his policies would "win the peace," made available to him, for disposal at his almost unlimited discretion, billions upon billions in dollars and resources. No President of the United States ever exercised such enormous powers nor in so autocratic a manner. Therefore, a heavy responsibility must inevitably overshadow his memory. The tragic consequences which have followed so many of his acts, and so many of his almost incredible omissions, cannot justly be laid at the door of fate or charged alone to the wickedness or intransigence of other men.

It was Roosevelt who impetuously blurted out the "unconditional surrender" ultimatum at a press conference in Casablanca, to the surprise of Winston Churchill, who was sitting at his side and who had no alternative but to nod approval.[6] This ill-considered policy has been branded by Hanson W. Baldwin and other sober authorities in this country and in England as one of the blunders that prolonged the war and lost the peace.[7] It was Roosevelt who, at Quebec, put his initials to the barbaric Morgenthau Plan for the pastoralization of Germany, a scheme which later years were to prove so unfortunate and which had to be abandoned for the good of all Europe before it was ever fully implemented. When Roosevelt returned to Washington from Quebec, he confided to his shocked Secretary of War, Henry L. Stimson, that "he had evidently done it without much thought."[8] But this is not a very convincing disclaimer, for the Morgenthau Plan meshed too well with the rest of the Roosevelt-Hopkins pattern for Europe.

It was Roosevelt who obstinately blocked Churchill's plan for attacking Germany through the Balkans and insisted instead upon the Russian-favored strategy of the Normandy invasion. This was another decision that had disastrous consequences for the future, delivering eastern Europe to the Communist terror and making another war virtually inevitable.[9] It was Roosevelt who would brook no stint in the lavishing of Lend-Lease upon the Russians and who exacted no conditions to safeguard the future security of Russia's neighbors or of this country itself while the power to do so was still in his hands. And it was Roosevelt—personally and willfully and with the ominous shadow of the world's next great threat already plain for such as he to see—

who took such men as Harry Hopkins and Alger Hiss with him halfway around the world to the suburbs of Russia, in the year 1945, to talk to Stalin and to bribe the Soviet Union to enter the war with Japan just in time to pluck the fruits of victory.

As the record unfolds and as events come to be seen in the perspective of time, it becomes more and more difficult to exculpate Franklin D. Roosevelt. Even the men who were of his official family have, in later days, either given up the attempt or have drifted into a morass of mutual contradiction. Stettinius, last Secretary of State, who was at Yalta with the President, felt impelled to produce, four years after Roosevelt's death, a lengthy apologia for the Yalta Conference. Although by that time it had become apparent to all the world that the fruits of Yalta were sour indeed, Stettinius was unabashed to write in his book that it was, "on the whole, a diplomatic triumph for the United States and Great Britain."[10] James F. Byrnes, who was also at Yalta and who succeeded Stettinius as Secretary of State under President Truman, chooses to wash his hands of most of the ill-fated agreements made at that conference and takes pains to point out that the secret protocol promising Russia certain Japanese territory and important concessions in China was signed by Roosevelt the day after Byrnes, thinking the conference was over, had left for home. The impression that Roosevelt, or those who had his ear at the time, did not want Byrnes to know about this deal is irresistible. It was not until some time after Roosevelt's death that a safe in the White House yielded the astonishing document.[11] General Patrick J. Hurley, Roosevelt's wartime Ambassador to China, has characterized this secret agreement as a "blueprint for Communist conquest of China." With a lingering loyalty, perhaps, to his old chief, he explained that Roosevelt was "a sick man" at Yalta.[12] Farley, Stimson, Hull, and others have said or implied the same thing. Even Robert E. Sherwood, one of the White House ghost writers and certainly never one to tarnish the memory of his idol, is constrained to say that when Roosevelt agreed to the provisions concerning Manchuria (which he did in China's total absence from the conference, and clandestinely) he was "tired and anxious to avoid further argument."[13] Perhaps this appeals to Sherwood as a felicitous explanation of what happened at Yalta. The moral monstrousness of diplomacy, touching the fate of millions of people, being conducted on such a basis seems not to have occurred to him.

One tragicomic facet of this illicit bargain was that it would be Russians, not Americans or Chinese, who would accept surrender of Japan's Kwantung Army. That Army's huge stores, the Mukden Arsenal, and the industrial facilities of Manchuria were to be handed on a platter to the Russians, who were to arrive on the scene in American-made jeeps, tanks, and trucks, uniformed, booted, and armed out of the supplies pledged by President Roosevelt at Yalta, to be carried on a hundred American ships across the Pacific Ocean to Vladivostok.

The "blueprint," to use General Hurley's metaphor, served its purpose well. The next five years saw the carrying out of the Communist conquest of China, followed by the embroilment of the United States in war in Korea in a belated and costly move to stem the tide of Russian expansionism.

When Joseph C. Grew, the prewar Ambassador to Japan, learned about that secret Yalta deal, he wrote a grave memorandum which the State Department promptly locked up out of sight. Once Russia is in the Japanese war, he predicted, "Mongolia, Manchuria and Korea will gradually slip into Russia's orbit, to be followed in due course by China and eventually Japan."[14]

Time has not yet run out on that prediction. For Japan, the word was "eventually." There is no mystery about why, year after year, the East China Sea and the Sea of Japan must bristle with American warships and planes patroling in battle readiness.

Nor is there any mystery about how the Soviet empire expanded during and soon after World War II to the point where 800,000,000 people were under its rule instead of the prewar 170,000,000. Estonia, Latvia, Lithuania, half of Poland, a chunk of Finland, a big slice of Rumania, pieces of Manchuria, the Japanese half of Sakhalin, and all of the Kurile Islands were annexed. Mongolia was torn from China and practically incorporated into Russia's Siberian hinterland. Poland, Hungary, Rumania, Bulgaria, Czechoslovakia, East Germany, China, and North Korea became satellite states. Of these gains, the industrial areas of East Germany (Silesia) and Czechoslovakia were the most valuable asset in modern resources. In Asia, Manchuria was the key to enormous industrial potentials, while China as a whole represented an inexhaustible source of manpower for almost any purpose—agricultural, industrial, or military. This vast Eurasian storehouse, workshop, and labor pool, all to be put to the service of Russian foreign policy, was the prize Stalin sought and won.

That Roosevelt was "a sick man" at Yalta—in truth, a dying man—is hardly to be disputed in view of the evidence concerning his physical condition which has subsequently come to light. His extraordinary statement to Congress on March 1, 1945, in his report on the conference, that "I was well the entire time" and "I was not ill for a second until I arrived back in Washington" can only be taken as an example of the duplicity to which he so frequently felt free to resort in order to allay public suspicions. There is pathos in the picture of this pale and shaking man, with sagging jaw and cavernous eyes, addressing the Congress and feeling it politic to say, in a speech broadcast to his country and to the world, that he had just returned from his trip "refreshed" and that he had not been ill "for a second." It is shocking to reflect that he could treat the truth so casually and to be reminded by so glaring an example that the half-truth or, if need be, the plain prevarication came so easily to his lips whenever political repercussions unfavorable to him might ensue from honesty.

However, to blame the Yalta debacle on Roosevelt's state of health or to shield him from culpability on that ground is to take too easy a way out. Yalta followed the pattern of statesmanship— if it can be called that—which Roosevelt, Hopkins, and the other favored Presidential intimates, "advisers," and "experts" had already established in their handling of the foreign affairs of the country. It was a natural extension of the habitual procedure of abject and reckless appeasement of the appetites of the Soviet Union. If that was Roosevelt's policy when he was sick, it had also been his policy when he was well. From the Atlantic Charter through Quebec, Casablanca, Cairo, Teheran, and Yalta, as well as by his instructions to the emissaries he sent to other meetings in London and Moscow, the role he played in this respect was always the same, as the following chapters of this book will show. By intention and deed he not only built up the power of the Soviet Union and made it a high-priority project but also fanatically devoted himself to bringing about a state of affairs in Europe and Asia in which there would be no neighboring powers capable of offering any check to Soviet ambitions. His "unconditional surrender" ultimatum and his insistence upon keeping American and British troops out of the Balkans and eastern German areas were but parts of this general design; and he overrode with inflexible stubbornness the efforts of Winston Churchill to look to the future and guard against the threat of a colossal Communistic hegemony casting its dark shadow over all of Europe and Asia.[15]

Churchill had the historical perspective to know that the military defeat of Germany and Japan could not alone be the cure for the violent tensions of the Eurasian continent or bring freedom from the fear of war to an unhappy world. He was also realist enough to know that conjuring up a new League of Nations and bestowing upon it the euphemistic name "The United Nations" could not be expected to accomplish such a miracle. Therefore, although he was willing to indulge good-humoredly the penchant of political leaders like Roosevelt for making stirring speeches that dripped with hope and confidence and was not above giving forth some very sanguine rhetoric himself and exchanging loving toasts with the Russians at vodka-flushed banquets, he knew the importance of getting the right troops to the strategic places before it would be too late. The right troops in his mind were British and American, not Russian.

Roosevelt must have known all this, too. There is ample evidence that he did. Yet he did things which made both peace and justice for Europe and Asia impossible, and he concealed from the American people information which could have put them on notice of the perils into which they were being steered by their leaders. The onus cannot be shifted to the generals and the admirals. The President too often vetoed or ignored their suggestions. They were expected to execute policies made for them on the political level. Even Harry Hopkins became a dilettante military authority. When he spoke to generals or admirals, they were not unaware that they were facing the alter ego of the Commander-in-Chief himself. We know from the writings of General Deane, General Mark Clark, General Wedemeyer, Admiral Leahy, Admiral Zacharias, and others and from the information which has been permitted to leak out concerning General Patton's show of recalcitrance that there was grave apprehension in Army and Navy circles concerning the Russians at the very times that Roosevelt was pretending to the world that relations were excellent. Such fears were not allowed to be publicized.

"While our armed forces were fighting with superb skill and courage," William C. Bullitt has written, "our foreign policy was being handled with ignorant and reckless disregard of the vital interests of the American people."[16] This is not political invective. It is the serious judgment of a man who had served by the appointment of Franklin D. Roosevelt himself as an Ambassador to Russia and to France but whose deep patriotism revolted at the spectacle of folly approaching downright treachery which he observed.

There is no doubt that Roosevelt was, throughout the war, determined that the truth about our relations with Soviet Russia should not come out. In the government and in the armed services, he rewarded those who helped him conceal it, and he promptly punished all who sought to reveal it. Looking back over the public effusions of the Roosevelt official family, it is hard now to suppress a smile at such flights of oratory as that of Edward R. Stettinius, then Under Secretary of State, who said in a radio broadcast in January of 1944 that the end of the war would find Soviet Russia to be America's biggest, strongest, and warmest friend. It has been widely said that Stettinius was well meaning but a man of considerable naïveté, but there is nothing to justify the belief that he was so naïve that he believed that prediction. The Soviets had shown their real hand long before that in innumerable ways, as Stettinius well knew (not to mention the historical and ideological factors which made the prophecy so unlikely).

Nor is it credible that by such statements it was hoped to cajole the masters of the Kremlin away from unfriendly attitudes and plans which were basic to them and which had already been plainly manifested to American representatives in high and low posts both at home and abroad. One has only to read the reminiscences of General John R. Deane, head of the American Military Mission in Moscow during the war, to realize how belligerent to their "allies" the Russians really were during the entire war and how impervious they were to cajolery. The General titled his book *The Strange Alliance*.[17]

No, when Stettinius spoke in January, 1944, to his radio audience, he was merely parroting the theme which at that time, an election year, was of the gravest concern to the political fortunes of the Roosevelt clique. The President and Harry Hopkins and the others had crawled too far out on the Russian limb to allow the limb to be sawed off. Stettinius was rewarded for this and similar public professions by being promoted to Secretary of State. In that post, one of his closest advisors was Alger Hiss, the revelation of whose *sub rosa* activities was to shock the country a few years later.[18]

To those who retort that hindsight is better than foresight and that Roosevelt, Stettinius, and others should not be condemned for not having seen the future as in a crystal ball, the simple answer must be given that statesmen of any competence are presumed to have a reasonable appreciation of the probable consequences of the policies they chart. As a matter of fact, the handwriting was on the wall, in legible terms. Many Americans saw it; courageous ones pointed to it publicly and were usually savagely attacked by the Rooseveltian propagandists.

If our statesmen read such honest analyses as Dr. David J. Dallin's *Soviet Russia's Foreign Policy*,[19] it was their policy to ignore their practical implications and even to resent angrily the expression of any views that Soviet Russia might be something less than a "peace-loving democracy." "We must not annihilate either Germany or Japan," Professor Nicholas Spykman of Yale warned in a book shortly after Pearl Harbor, "lest we leave Europe or the Far East open to domination by Russia." And he was bold enough to stress that our foreign policy "should be designed not in terms of some dream world but in terms of the realities."[20] To Rooseveltians, this was heresy. No professor escaped from his placid campus to land a lush job in wartime Washington with that kind of talk. The Russophilism of the Harry Hopkins coterie of White House favorites was of almost pathological intensity. These men were unmoved by logical considerations bearing upon the security of the United States in the years to come. General Deane, who watched the flow of American resources to Russia from his vantage point in Moscow and attended conferences dealing with it, writes that Hopkins carried out the Russian aid program "with a zeal which approached fanaticism." Hopkins' enthusiasm "became so ingrained that it could not be tempered."[21]

Meanwhile, the public was treated in the spring of 1943 to such balderdash as Joseph E. Davies' *Mission to Moscow*,[22] which would have been on the level of the moronic if it had not been conceived as sheer propaganda. This book was filmed in Hollywood with great fanfare and did much to condition the American people for the vast benefits to be conferred upon our Soviet "allies." Stalin was pictured as a sort of combination of Pavel Milyukov, Harry Emerson Fosdick, Bernard Baruch, and Jane Addams. People who called themselves "liberals" were deserting reason in droves, as though struck by what Aldous Huxley calls "herd-poisoning." But not all were struck. Norman Thomas went to see the movie *Mission to Moscow* and came home disgusted. It was dishonest, and he was a man of intellectual integrity. The next day, he organized a protest petition and found fifty-two fellow anti-Communist Leftists to sign it. The statement asserted that the film "falsifies and glorifies dictatorship . . . creates the impression that the methods of Stalin are not incompatible with genuine democracy." But Norman Thomas, in spite of his prominence, met difficulty in getting his protest to many newspapers or on the air. *Mission to Moscow* went its dizzy way through the theaters of America, and so cleverly had its Hollywood contrivers and their "special advisers" from Washington done their work that millions of Americans could not separate the 90 per cent of fiction from the 10 per cent of fact.

Sparked by the President and his indefatigable wife, whose

political shrewdness was of such a subtle character that it escaped the perception of most of her admirers, by the fanaticism of Harry Hopkins and the covey of strange birds which he gathered in the government, and by the Communist agents in this country operating either openly or surreptitiously, all of the modern techniques of propaganda were put to work to sell the American people what may best be described colloquially as "a bill of goods." A preposterous delusion was foisted upon the electorate of the United States. Why?

And why, as victory mounted upon victory, did a strange uneasiness grip so many patriotic Americans? Why was there, to people of discernment, a foreboding mystery about so many things that were happening, a hollowness in so many of the fine words that were spoken?

The reason was that the President of the United States had a secret.

Chapter II

THE SECRET IN THE CLOSET

THE SECRET which Franklin D. Roosevelt guarded so obstinately could not, from his point of view, be allowed to come out. He had too much at stake. And public suspicion of it had to be stifled.

It was not a small secret, like those which often burden politicians, such as a departmental scandal or some shady vote-trading deal or petty personal graft. Roosevelt's robust genius far transcended these lesser stratagems. This man did everything in a big way; even his secrets were gigantic. This one was as big as a war. In fact, it was a war.

But it was not the war with Germany and Italy, the war which found Great Britain, France, Russia, the United States, and other countries lined up in resistance to the aggressions of Adolf Hitler and Benito Mussolini. That war involved the demands of Germany and Italy, spurious or otherwise, for *Lebensraum,* the arrogance and brutality of their ruling regimes, and the general problem of preponderant German power on the continent of Europe. Everybody knew about that war.

Nor was it the clash which Japan precipitated by her insistence upon creating what she liked to call the "Greater East Asia Co-Prosperity Sphere," which would have put China and South-

14

east Asia, at the least, under the economic aegis of a bloated Japanese Empire. Everybody knew about that war, too.

But there was also a third war, one which Franklin D. Roosevelt was determined should be hidden from the masses of the American people by a camouflage which was to be his chef-d'oeuvre. That war involved Soviet Russia, the fount of Communism. In it, Russia was the aggressor. It was she who was on the march, both literally and figuratively. She waged her offensives with a perseverance and cunning probably never before equalled in the annals of warfare.

This secret war must not be confused with the others mentioned, although they overlapped. Thus when Hitler turned his divisions east in the summer of 1941 and invaded Russia, Stalin, who had theretofore been on the prowl in Poland, Finland, Rumania (Bessarabia), and the states of Lithuania, Latvia, and Estonia and who had tried to reach a deal with Hitler for carving up the Middle East, was, of course, put temporarily on the defensive himself.* He had to meet this development, and his other plans were contingent upon his success in doing so. But the war which was dearest to his heart and which was implicit in his ideological credo had started long before Hitler's *Panzers* rolled into the Ukraine and was to continue long after *der Führer* was a charred corpse under the rubble of Berlin and his Third Reich nothing but a memory. It was destined to prevent the return of peace and security to the world for many years after what was popularly thought of as World War II had come

---

* It is probable that Russia would have turned on Germany at a propitious moment if Hitler had not struck first. The Soviets were planning to attack Germany in the autumn of 1941, according to General Alexei Markoff (see his article in the *Saturday Evening Post* [May 13, 1950], 175). Most opinions are that Stalin would have waited to see America committed and his prey weakened by Allied bombing.

to an end. World War II was really three wars. Two of them ended in 1945. The third one did not.

Against whom was the Soviet Union waging this war, the concealment of which from the American people was the cornerstone of President Roosevelt's foreign policy? The more immediate victims slated for conquest were, of course, Russia's territorial neighbors: Finland, Estonia, Latvia, Lithuania, Poland, and Rumania on the west; Turkey, Iran, and Afghanistan on the south; and China and Japan on the east. Near-neighbors on the list were Hungary, Bulgaria, Czechoslovakia, Iraq, and Tibet. Indochina, India, Burma, Malaya, and the Dutch East Indies, chafing restlessly in colonial or semi-colonial status, loomed like rich, unripe plums for later plucking. On a broader scale, but with equal intensity of purpose, the war was being waged against all of the capitalistic countries of the world, by military attack or threats of attack, subversive conspiracy and infiltration, economic debilitation, or by a combination of these means. True to Lenin in this regard, Stalin charted a course of flexibility and opportunism, and wherever possible he would have others fight his battles for him.

The United States and Great Britain, as the major bulwarks of democratic capitalism, were, of course, archenemies whose ultimate downfall was essential. That this project was not to be easy was apparent to such cool plotters as Stalin, Mikoyan, Molotov, Voroshilov, Vishinsky, and the lesser-known, behind-the-scenes zealots of the Politburo; so the most subtle indirections were reserved for its long-term accomplishment. Germany and Japan, the two great buffers against Communist expansion in Europe and Asia, were first to be removed from the path in two simultaneous wars. England, France, and the United States would help Russia crush Germany. The United States could vanquish Japan singlehandedly; there was no doubt about that. The Soviet Union would not have to dissipate her strength fighting Japan, but only manage to swoop in at the surrender.** A new chaos would be precipitated in China, and into the power vacuums thus created in both Europe and Asia, Soviet Russia would then step.

Through his sources of information in the United States, some of whom were in high places, Stalin knew that Franklin D. Roosevelt could be relied upon to see at least this phase of the program through. He was not mistaken.

Does this mean the American people had elected a crypto-Communist as President? Or that this President, by shunting the third war, the secret one, out of sight, consciously intended harm to his country? It does not. No such inference is intended. To make it is to misapprehend the Roosevelt mentality.

Here we touch a delicate point. Roosevelt was no more a Communist than he was a Jeffersonian. Conversely, he was no more a Jeffersonian than he was a Communist. Ideologies were not the stuff of the cerebrations that took place in that handsome head. Here was no furrow-browed zealot for a system, no Karl Marx, no Adam Smith. In the presence of an argument between a socialist and a capitalist, he would be likely to steal the show with a charmingly put evasion. To Harold Ickes' wistful plaint that it was "impossible to come to grips with him," James F.

** A war between Japan and the United States was a consummation which could only have favorable consequences for Soviet Russia because for half a century Japan had been a check to Russian expansionism in the Far East and her defeat in a war with the United States was inevitable. It is well known that pro-Soviet influences in Washington discreetly fomented an outbreak of hostilities. Nor was Moscow indifferent during the months that preceded Pearl Harbor. In January, 1941, Sir Stafford Cripps, then British Ambassador to Russia, wrote in his diary: "At the moment the Russians seem more sphinx-like than ever and I doubt if even the Germans know what they are thinking. There are indications of something being on the tapis with Japan; I think an attempt to encourage Japan to go to war with America and so get Japan defeated and that danger out of the way."

Byrnes has added that "Franklin Roosevelt was not the same to any two men."[1] The man who, as we shall see, clandestinely obtained the recommendations of Earl Browder, the head of the Communist party, in the crucial months of the war, wore a different collar than the man who discussed affairs with Byrnes.

That a web of subversion was spun over Washington in Roosevelt's administration is now beyond question. J. Edgar Hoover's *Masters of Deceit* is but one of many authoritative sources which verify that the government was infiltrated by both Communist sympathizers and Soviet agents and that U.S. policies, plans, and official attitudes were not only influenced by these infiltrators but also promptly reported to Moscow. In Washington, however, some people were spiders in the web and some were flies. Some were strange hybrids. Most were none of these.

If Franklin D. Roosevelt became, as the war went on, Stalin's favorite fellow-traveler, it was not necessarily because any ideological conversion had occurred. Byrnes observes that his "stamp collection was often referred to as his hobby, but politics was really his hobby," while one of his cabinet officers, Jesse Jones, put politeness aside to describe him as "a total politician." Here it is that the psychobiographers of the future will probably start in their quest for the "Why?"

Historian Charles A. Beard, a man of vast human perspective, when looking for Roosevelt's war motivations, saw "only conceit, dreams of grandeur, vain imaginings, lust for power, or a desire to escape from our domestic perils and obligations." More magnanimous is the hypothesis that in his obsequiousness toward the Kremlin, Roosevelt was simply carried away by the hopeful expectation, implicit in the Dale Carnegie philosophy, that if you offer people a friendly smile and a warm handshake they will reciprocate in kind. The flaw here is that Roosevelt always used this technique, or abandoned it, as it suited his other plans. He did not practice it on the Germans (even the anti-Nazi underground), Italians, or Japanese, and he was never one to embrace it out of sheer innocence or credulity.

General Wedemeyer recalls that when he came back from China and told the President that he felt certain the Communists would cause trouble as soon as the war ended, the President "did not seem to understand what I was talking about" and quickly terminated the interview.[2] This had happened to others before. It is possible that Roosevelt was so constituted psychologically that he could easily insulate his mind against jarring facts and that his egocentricity was such that what he thus excluded from himself he deemed unfit for assimilation by the public.

In the present narrative, we are not concerned with the smiling, debonaire Roosevelt as a private person but with his deeds as a powerful public functionary. Robespierre, in his private life, was a man of culture, honest and kind; in his public life, he was a different kind of man. Vengeance was not the Lord's, but his. Under his leadership, the bloodletting that followed the French Revolution became a travesty on justice that went down in history as the Reign of Terror. We shall see, as we follow Roosevelt through his foreign summit conferences with Churchill and Stalin, that he permitted himself to become a tacit accomplice to, and abet, a terror on so broad a scale that the excesses of Robespierre's day are dwarfed by comparison.

Some believe today that Roosevelt's mind was possessed by a myth. Thus Arthur Koestler writes that Roosevelt "sincerely believed that Stalin's regime was a kind of uncouth, Asiatic New Deal" and that he could be sympathetic to its enhancement because he was under this illusion. This is too facile. It was the same regime that his successor, President Truman, denounced on Washington's Birthday, 1950, as "a modern tyranny far worse than that of any ancient empire." From its bloody inception it had been the antithesis of a democratic state. The fascist theory of the "elite" and the rejection of parliamentarianism had al-

ways been dominant with Stalin, as with Lenin. As Franz Borkenau, the leading authority on international Communism, says,
"it was Stalin who regarded democracy as the worst enemy."[3]

This dictator had shown his venomous hostility toward the
Western democracies time after time. In all of them he maintained apparati of subversion and sabotage, and, viper-like, he
had snapped at them in an interview given to *Pravda* on November 30, 1939, saying: "It is not Germany who has attacked England and France, but England and France who have attacked
Germany."

The postulate, so often stated and so widely accepted on sheer
faith, that Roosevelt showered American largesse on Russia only
to defeat Nazi Germany crumbles under the weight of the facts.
His beneficence to the Soviet regime and to Communist factions
elsewhere went too far beyond such a limited objective.

When Alcide De Gasperi, the non-Fascist premier of postwar
Italy, told a press conference in Rome on February 24, 1954, that
Italy was not entirely to blame for her failure to uproot Communism because "the evil plant . . . was born and prospered in the
Roosevelt climate," he was speaking of a country which had
surrendered in 1943, only to find Palmíro Togliatti rushed to
Naples from the Soviet Union in an American ship and almost
the whole of the local matériel and political favors assigned by
the Allied command to Communists in Italy, Dalmatia, Monte-
negro, Slovenia, and, indirectly, Croatia, with enormous political
consequences. His rueful remark about "the Roosevelt climate"
is amply verified by Borkenau's detailed researches on European
Communism.

Of Poland, for example, Borkenau reminds us: "From the
beginning Stalin had fought a battle of extermination against
any conceivable non-communist Polish leadership; a battle starting with the extermination of many thousand captured Polish
officers in 1941 (in Katyn and other camps), continuing . . . to

the prompting and subsequent sabotage of the Warsaw rising of the Polish underground army in July 1944 (which led to the extermination of the best Polish forces, as was Stalin's intention), and to the kidnapping of all available Polish underground leaders in March 1945. . . . Between the Lublin committee and the Polish government-in-exile which enjoyed the loyalty of an overwhelming majority of Poles, there ensued a fierce struggle. Wherever the NKVD went, it exterminated the Home Army forces within its reach, *while simultaneously Roosevelt preached to the Polish leaders in exile the virtues of Stalin's Russia. . . .* Thus the men of Lublin became the rulers of Poland."[4]

When Roosevelt told Chiang Kai-shek at Cairo in November, 1943, that he would have to coalesce with the Chinese Communists to hold his, Roosevelt's, favor after Japan's defeat, he was stepping out of the American-Japanese war and into another one.[5] In this third war, which was to be the longest and most crucial one of the twentieth century, we find Franklin D. Roosevelt almost invariably charging ahead on the side of Soviet Russia. In fact, his support was the *sine qua non* of its successful launching. His mission, which he performed implacably, was to put weapons in Stalin's hands and, with American military might, to demolish all of the dikes that held back the pressing tides of Communist expansion in Europe and Asia. Meanwhile, everything was done to prevent the average American citizen from becoming conscious of this war; his mind was kept preoccupied hating Hitler and Tojo. And since Roosevelt was concealing the war itself, a fortiori he did not reveal his own sympathies in it.

Gullibility was widespread but not universal. Actually, the secret could not be kept indefinitely from any alert observer of world affairs endowed with reasonably good powers of analysis. However, it must be remembered that many Americans were riding the crest of the wave in their personal careers, as was the

President himself, and were content not to probe too deeply under the surface appearances. Like Cinderella, they took their moment of revelry and asked the fairy godmother no questions. The government, in particular, was swarming with such individuals. But there were others, patriotic, disapproving people, both in and out of the armed services, who, under conditions of war hysteria, were cowed into a discreet silence.

So perverted did the dominant mores become—in the press, the pulpit, the schools, and the clubs—under the impact of Rooseveltian propaganda on all subjects pertaining to the war that truthful objectivity concerning "our gallant ally," Russia, was actually associated with disloyalty. In those irrational days, one courted ostracism if he was bold enough to bring up Lenin's very plain words:

> We are living not merely in a state, but in a system of states; and it is inconceivable that the Soviet republic should continue to exist for a long period side by side with imperialist states. Ultimately one or the other must conquer. Meanwhile a number of terrible clashes between the Soviet republic and the bourgeois states are inevitable.

Although Hitler's *Mein Kampf* was everywhere pointed to with horror, it was made to seem rather unpatriotic, or at least bad taste, to quote in public from Stalin's comparable call to action, his *Problems of Leninism,* or from the bellicose resolutions of the Congresses of the Third International, dominated first by Lenin and later by Stalin. Yet the design of ultimate world conquest, through the combination of Soviet military power with revolutionary action outside Soviet frontiers, is, and was when Roosevelt was President of the United States, one of the most open and undisguised conspiracies of historical record.[6]

If Mr. Roosevelt had cared to call J. Edgar Hoover over from the F.B.I., he could have heard an earful about Stalin and the world-wide Communist mechanism to subvert and wreck the capitalist nations.[7] Hoover and those around him had no illusion that the writings of Marx, Lenin, and Stalin were mere intellectual exercises. They saw in them a battle plan for conquest. The tactics might shift, they knew ("We must resort to artifices, evasions and subterfuges," Lenin had prescribed), but the grand strategy was unshakable. These men of the F.B.I. were coolly efficient but necessarily silent.

Mr. Roosevelt sometimes had the *New York Times* brought to his bed. In that newspaper he could read such items as the report of Cyrus Sulzberger's trip to Russia. In the *Times,* Mr. Roosevelt could also enjoy with his morning coffee a series of slippery articles by the Soviet writer Ilya Ehrenburg which stressed the "community of aims" of America and Russia. But for five cents he could have read the accurate premonitions of the *New York Daily News*. That tabloid may not have been the President's favorite newspaper, but it has been able to boast in a postwar editorial: "Begging nobody's pardon, this newspaper never did get suckered into believing that Bloody Joe was fighting for anything but eventual Communist domination of the world." The boast was largely true.

In addition, there were ample overt warnings from within Russia. The drums of war were beating there long before Hitler attacked. The predatory intentions of the men in the Kremlin were certainly known to the President of the United States, who had an ambassadorial staff and military attachés on the spot to make constant reports to him. Surely they heard and saw as much as did the American press correspondents in Moscow, with whom they naturally exchanged information. In the latter part of 1940, there were only two American reporters left in Moscow, for the atmosphere was very belligerent and the censorship was stringent.[8] One represented the United Press, the other the Associated Press. An interesting report made at that time has come to light, a copy now being in the possession of the Hoover Institute and Library at Stanford University. This was a confidential, sealed report made to Hugh Baillie, president of the United Press Associations, by Virgil Pinkley, then United Press manager for Europe, after a swing through Europe, including Russia. It is dated November 28, 1940, and was transmitted through the diplomatic pouch from Switzerland. *(This was a full six months before the German attack on Russia.)* In it, Mr. Pinkley said:

Virtually all Soviet Republic enterprise is now devoted to building a gigantic military machine. Many competent observers believe that the idea of world revolution through propaganda has been shelved, and that emphasis is now being placed on building a tremendous military machine which will enable Soviet diplomacy *to take over territories and countries by demand,* and if requests are rejected, then objectives will be obtained through military force. Looking around Europe, Russians have observed the game of power politics and have proved apt pupils. [Italics added.]

This definitely connotes aggressive, offensive, predatory intentions on the part of the Soviet Union, not mere preparations for home defense. Of Stalin's government, Mr. Pinkley wrote:

Russia has swung a long way back from the left and is rapidly becoming a completely military dictatorship conducted along absolute totalitarian lines. . . . All decisions of any import in Russia are made by Stalin: in this respect he is far more absolute than either Hitler or Mussolini and entrusts his assistants with far less authority than other dictators.

These observations were accurate. They are supported by everything that transpired both before Hitler was defeated and after he was defeated. Further confirmation of Russia's greedy demands in the days before Hitler attacked came to light later in documents captured in the ruins of Berlin. The transcript of the conversations between Russian Foreign Minister Molotov and German Foreign Minister von Ribbentrop a few weeks before the attack came as a shock to many of the gullible people who had supinely succumbed to the love-our-ally-Russia propaganda. This document proved that Molotov went to Berlin from the Kremlin to offer Germany a full military alliance and that he failed only because the Russian demands for territory in Europe and in the Middle East were too rapacious for Hitler to concede. It was simply a case of two bandits being unable to agree on how to divide the loot.[9] The idea that President Roosevelt, with so many sources of information at his command, did not know of this background is, of course, incredible.

In July, 1941, but a few weeks after Molotov had failed to sell Stalin's plan for pillage to Hitler, the exuberant Harry Hopkins flew to Moscow to see Stalin and to promise him vast supplies of weapons and matériel from the United States. The Russian dictator, calm and cool and implacable, knew then that the Europe and Asia he had envisioned and plotted for might become a reality—with American help. He had an ally—at the least an unwitting one—in his war, his long-term crusade for the destruction of capitalism and the domination of the world by militant Communism. With cunning and deceit and every expedient, he would press his advantage. As for Hopkins, he came home enthralled and wrote a magazine article in which he showed a childlike reverence for Stalin's every word, gesture, and mannerism. He obviously thought him a great man who talked "straight and hard." He was charmed when Stalin, in saying good-by, "added his respects to the President of the United States."[10]

So Stalin's war, which was Roosevelt's secret, proceeded victoriously, and eventually it became very difficult to conceal the fact that there was more up Stalin's sleeve than the defeat of Hitler. But to the bitter end, Roosevelt kept up the show.

On the same day in January, 1944, that Edward R. Stettinius took to the radio to make his fatuous prophecy that Russia would be America's warmest friend after the war, Karl von Wiegand, foreign correspondent for the Hearst press, wrote in an article published in the Hearst newspapers that if Washington's policy of unbounded help to and blind enthusiasm for Soviet Russia continued without safeguards, it would be the logical, natural development of history that Russia would be America's greatest, strongest, and most formidable foe at the end of the war and would seek to become the dominating power in Europe and the world. The Hearst press was much despised and maligned by the most vociferous segment of the literati, the pseudo-intellectuals who danced, as if they were in a trance, around the flame of what was called "one-worldism" and echoed the prevailing slogans of the day with little or no regard for the underlying historical forces which were at work in the world. It was not fashionable among the sycophants and poseurs to read the Hearst press and certainly not to be caught agreeing with what was advocated in it. It was *démodé* to see any scoundrels outside Germany, Italy, and Japan. Fawning over Soviet Russia was the mark of a new type of snobbery among that large group of people who are given to following intellectual fashions. Naturally, in those circles the warnings of such publicists as Karl von Wiegand, or Senator Robert A. Taft or Herbert Hoover, fell on deaf ears.

On February 13, 1944, when the pro-Russian propaganda sponsored by the Roosevelt administration was at its raucous height, von Wiegand had the courage to write in his column: "The next war—the coming war is showing its horrible face before this war is ended—will be the first of the wars between the East and the West and will be led by Russia. By strange irony of destiny, America and Britain are clearing the way for Russia." On October 4, 1944, in answer to a letter from Vice Admiral William A. Glassford, he wrote: "As you so clearly indicate, the end of the shooting and bombing this time will not be the end of the war. Through the smoke and dust of the battlefields there already is visible the outline of World War III. It can come in fifteen years. . . . Its character at first will be mainly economic and ideological." This was three months before President Roosevelt went to Yalta and participated in making what his own envoy to China has referred to as "the blueprint for Communist conquest of China" and gave his benediction to the westward extension of Soviet power to the heart of Europe. It was also before the secret connivance that triumphant American troops should be held back to permit the capture of Berlin and Prague by Red armies.

Von Wiegand and the handful of other writers who dared speak out were merely trying to illumine for the American people a picture which the Roosevelt regime strove desperately and with a remarkable measure of success to keep in darkness. Although both political parties in the United States were infected, in varying degrees, by the same psychological disease, which dulled their critical faculties and distorted their perspective, it was the Roosevelt regime which set up and controlled the censorious and propagandistic Office of War Information, and it was Roosevelt himself who locked the secrets of his machinations with foreign potentates securely away from the ears and eyes of the masses of the American people.

The OWI was "stacked." There sat Owen Lattimore as a deputy director, and there were many like him. It was easy for an Adam Tarn to get a job in the OWI (after the war, this man switched his citizenship to Communist-governed Poland). James F. Byrnes, who as a Supreme Court Justice, Director of War Mobilization, and later Secretary of State, knew the Washington bureaucracy from many angles, put it mildly when he wrote: "Many of the people in OWI, admittedly a propaganda agency . . . were sympathetic with Soviet ideology."[11]

Roosevelt himself knew the truth about the Soviet dictatorship.

The evidence to that effect is overwhelming. He knew to a certainty that the intentions of Stalin and his Politburo did not fit the pattern of the postwar world as envisioned by the American public. He knew that Stalin's show of adherence to the principles of the Atlantic Charter was just a hoax.

He was familiar with the outrages already committed. From Ciechanowski, Mikolajczyk, General Sikorski and others, he received unimpeachable evidence of what was taking place and being planned in eastern Europe. The gruesome facts of the Katyn massacre, which had wiped out fifteen thousand Polish officers who had been taken prisoner by the Russians in 1939 and whose whereabouts had been shrouded in mystery, had been laid on his desk; he was silent when the Kremlin angrily broke off relations with the Polish government in April, 1943, because the latter had appealed to the International Red Cross to investigate the Katyn murders.

Premeditated and organized savagery, this pogrom will likely rank in history alongside the slaughter of the French Huguenots in the Massacre of St. Bartholomew in 1572. The diabolical purpose of Stalin had been to obliterate at one stroke the flower of the Polish army, literally to bury the entire trained officer corps. Scheming to impose Communism, he wanted no potential guardians of Polish freedom to live to resist.[12]

When the piles of corpses were discovered by the Germans in April, 1943, the Polish Red Cross reported to the International Red Cross in Geneva they were satisfied the massacre had taken place in March or April of 1940 (a time when the Germans were not within hundreds of miles of Katyn Forest). Stalin screamed to Churchill that the free Poles under General Sikorski, prime minister of the exiled Polish government, who wanted an investigation, were "Fascists." Prompted by Roosevelt, Churchill replied to Stalin on April 23, 1943, that any International Red Cross probing was unthinkable. "We shall certainly oppose vigorously any investigation. . . . Mr. Eden is seeing him [Sikorski] today."[13] When a special intelligence report and documents and pictures attesting Russian guilt in the cold-blooded atrocity were brought to Roosevelt in the White House, he reacted with anger, not at the Russian murderers, but at those who had collected the facts, and he clamped the lid down tight.

The Congressional committee which in 1952 investigated the Katyn Forest massacre declared that the suppression of information about it was a product of the "strange psychosis" of the Roosevelt administration. However, the case can be put more simply: whenever there is a big secret, there must be many little ones, too. Katyn was one of the many little ones.

The popular delusion that Russia, our "gallant ally," was a freedom-loving, non-aggressive democracy anxious to co-operate with the United States was insidiously nurtured, although Roosevelt could not have believed it himself. His own experiences at the conference table put him on notice that the opposite was true. The predatory government that had, in December, 1939, been expelled from the League of Nations for its cold-blooded attack on little Finland, had swallowed up Estonia, Latvia, and Lithuania and had, in concert with Hitler, carved up Poland and erased that nation from the map could not and did not undergo a metamorphosis. Its leaders were not miraculously purged of international banditry when another bandit, Adolf Hitler, turned on them. They never specifically recanted; they showed no penitence. They never told Roosevelt they would free the Balts and the others, nor did he ever require them to say so. On the contrary, they continued to whet their appetites as war raged. He was aware of this, even if the American people were not.

The idea that Roosevelt, not a naïve man, was fooled is unbelievable. The camouflage, not the exposing, of Soviet imperialism was the expedient that best fitted his own political plans. Friendly critics who write magnanimously of what they call Roosevelt's "Great Design" for luring the Reds into co-operative, peaceful ways,[14] a design which they say somehow miscarried, are merely spinning a yarn. Some of these people know better. For the rest, the sentiment is father to the thought. They do not really know their man.

To becloud the issues whenever glimmerings of truth seemed to be reaching the public, it pleased the sycophants to have Russia spoken of, semi-romantically, as a great mystery and Stalin as a strange enigma. What Russia wanted was no mystery.[15] What Stalin was determined to do and to take was, as John T. Flynn picturesquely puts it, "as plain as the mustache on Stalin's face." That these intentions did not square with the Atlantic Charter was equally plain. But even Mr. Flynn falls at times into the error of presuming that Roosevelt was "taken in," that he "completely deceived himself" about Stalin. He states that Harry Hopkins and Averell Harriman and Joseph E. Davies were completely taken in (even to the point of not considering Stalin a Communist at all) and that they, in turn, "passed on their deceptions to Roosevelt, who swallowed them without salt."[16] This interpretation would make Roosevelt more the fool and less the hypocrite, and it is not entirely consistent with Flynn's analysis of Roosevelt's character from other aspects.

Generally, men are puzzled, mystified, as they look back at Roosevelt's dealings with the Soviet leaders and reread his eloquent words. A distinguished former university president makes the not uncommon comment that "the reason for our encouragement of Soviet Russia . . . is one of the historic enigmas of our time." But it ceases to be an enigma when one casts aside all false assumptions of Roosevelt's integrity, while the riddle must otherwise remain forever insoluble.

Robert E. Sherwood, at one point in *Roosevelt and Hopkins,* speaks of Roosevelt's "incomprehensible character."[17] From one who writes of Roosevelt in the honey-dripping manner of Mr. Sherwood, this is probably meant to be a compliment. It is like speaking of the mystery of God. The remark is significant. To his worshipers, there must perforce be an element of incomprehensibility in Franklin D. Roosevelt's character. The wide gulf between his words and his deeds, the manifold contradictions in his avowed policies, can most felicitously be bridged if the workings of his mind remain somewhat inscrutable. A curtain is then more easily drawn over the troublesome facts that might otherwise mar the picture, and this is psychologically necessary in the process of rationalization.

Diverse as Roosevelt's personal traits were, naïveté was not one of them. Not a student or reader of books,[18] his talents lay in the field of direct human relationships, in which his activities were always marked by a keen perceptivity and the extraordinary shrewdness which is the politician's special gift. A scholarly academician with his head in the clouds, such as Woodrow Wilson, might conceivably have been deceived about the true motives of someone with whom he was in contact over a number of years, but not Franklin D. Roosevelt. He knew people far too well. To use a pithy colloquialism, people were "his dish."

And his man Friday was the amazing Harry Hopkins. Harry knew the secret, too.

Chapter III

HIS MAN FRIDAY

GENERAL HUGH JOHNSON, a key man in the early New Deal, once wrote of Harry Hopkins, that "he has a mind like a razor, a tongue like a skinning knife, a temper like a Tartar and a sufficient vocabulary of parlor profanity . . . to make a muleskinner jealous."[1] This is a description of the man President Roosevelt sent to have private chats with Winston Churchill and Joseph Stalin. This is the man Roosevelt always brought along with him to the big international conferences. There, as the great men sat around the table, Hopkins would scribble and pass over to the President intimate and gossipy little notes.

That these two men, Roosevelt and Hopkins, reveled in the glamorous roles they were playing on the world stage and that they were particularly susceptible to the lure of the power and adulation which vast international manipulations offered to them is obvious upon the least study of their characters. But it is quite another matter to say that they were ever really "taken in" by the blandishments of Churchill or of Stalin.

At Casablanca, at a dinner attended by the Sultan of Morocco, Hopkins, arrayed in black tie, was seated next to the French Governor, General Noguès. His comments about this dignitary are characteristic. General Noguès, he wrote in his notes, "is the bird that De Gaulle wants pitched out of here. . . . He lives in a big palace and is the big shot in this part of the world. . . . I wouldn't trust him as far as I could spit." At the same dinner, "a smart British Marine walked in about the middle of dinner with a despatch." But, noted the suspicious Hopkins, "I have a feeling Churchill cooked that up beforehand."[2] This attitude is typical. Cynical and worldly, something of an epicure in his tastes, and a man of extraordinary political shrewdness, Hopkins was a sophisticate in whom one does not find the weakness—if it be that —of credulity. If he was compliant to Soviet interests most of the time to the point of servility, it was not because he could not see behind the Soviet mask; it was because he saw only too well, liked what he saw, and found that it coincided with his own objectives. His influence on the President of the United States exceeded that of any other person during most of the long regime. That the President, in turn, chose this man as his intimate helps us to understand the character of Franklin D. Roosevelt himself.

It is, of course, impossible to study the story of the foreign conferences of Franklin D. Roosevelt without perceiving at the outset the enormous power which was wielded, in the open and behind the scenes, by the ubiquitous Harry Hopkins. His finger was in every pie. Consequently, his character becomes of great importance to students of the Roosevelt period.

It is unfortunate that the voluminous notes and private papers of Harry Hopkins, who died early in 1946, were turned over to his close friend Robert E. Sherwood, the playwright, rather than to an impartial biographer or made available to serious historians. During the war years, Hopkins, Sherwood, and Sam Rosenman had collaborated in the writing of Roosevelt's speeches, as Mr. Sherwood candidly admits. When Hopkins died, Mr. Sherwood was asked by the Hopkins family to write the book which Hopkins was prevented by death from writing himself. So we have from the pen of this able dramatist a book which is a running narrative of the war years, a quasi-biography, an eclectic publication of notes, letters, and extracts, and a potpourri of reminiscences and hearsay which one must accept on faith, all put together under the title *Roosevelt and Hopkins: An Intimate History.*

When Mr. Sherwood was called in by the Hopkins family to undertake this work, he found that "there were some forty filing cabinets packed with papers in the Hopkins house, and a great many more in a warehouse." For eight months an assistant employed by Hopkins had been going over the papers.[3] Obviously, a big job of selection and editing was done before any of the private papers of Harry Hopkins saw the light of day in Mr. Sherwood's book, and it is doubtful that for this job there could have been chosen anyone more friendly to the reputations of both Roosevelt and Hopkins than Robert E. Sherwood. Nevertheless, the book contains a vast amount of interesting information. In extenuation of its errors, which are more conspicuously those of omission and misinterpretation than of misstatement, it should be mentioned that Mr. Sherwood quite frankly avows in his first chapter a friendship for Harry Hopkins "which," he says, "must color everything I write about him and for which no apologies are offered." Such loyalty to a departed friend is commendable, but it is not conducive to objectivity in the writing of history.

As a professional and successful writer of fiction for the stage, Robert E. Sherwood had a keen sense of the dramatic. The playwright must above all else possess the ability to make a sharp emotional impact upon an audience. Using the tools of imagination, he fashions an illusion of reality which can evoke sorrow or laughter, anger or good humor, hatred or love. He deliberately creates sympathy for this character, antipathy for that. The end he is striving for may be clear enough, but his means to achieve it are professional tricks or, if one prefers, special techniques of the art. These are recognizable by experts in the field of the drama; other people are generally unconscious of the clever devices which have been used to evoke their emotional responses to the play. It was not because of his knowledge of economics or world affairs that Robert E. Sherwood occupied a compartment in Roosevelt's own car in the Presidential train which toured the country during the election campaign of 1940, when Roosevelt was running for a third term. Nor was it for such reasons that he slept in the White House so much of the time during the next four and one-half years. His plays *Idiot's Delight* and *The Petrified Forest* had been smash hits on Broadway but certainly his qualifications as an expert on the affairs of state were rather inconspicuous, to say the most about them.

In that same Presidential Pullman car in the fall of 1940 were also Harry Hopkins and that ghostliest of ghosts, Sam Rosenman. By this time, as even some of Roosevelt's staunchest admirers now concede, the President was determined that the formal entry of the United States into the war was only a matter of time, yet he knew that if he bared his real intentions to the public, he would be defeated in the election. There was much suspicion in the country. Mothers wanted to be assured that if they voted for Roosevelt, they would not be voting to send their sons into battle. A strong anti-war statement had to be brewed for the important speech in the Boston Arena near the end of the campaign. Roosevelt knew this, and so did the triumvirate of Hopkins, Sherwood, and Rosenman, who were strongly pro-war but who also wanted above all else to have their illustrious friend and benefactor re-elected. As the train sped through the night, there were some worried heads in the President's car, for disquieting reports had come from the party politicians in the hinterland. At this point, we learn, there came from the fertile mind of the playwright the famous phrase: ". . . again—and again—and again. . . ."[4] Roosevelt, who could recognize a good punch line as well as the crustiest journalist, grabbed the words avidly. And from the Boston Arena there went out over the air to an anxious people, in sonorous tones and studied cadences, the promise that sealed his election:

> And while I am talking to you mothers and fathers, I give you one more assurance.
> I have said this before, but I shall say it again and again and again: Your boys are not going to be sent into any foreign wars.

The playwright had earned his fare. Embedded in the President's words, of course, was a sly quibble. The average American thought he was talking about wars on foreign soil when he used the words "foreign wars," whereas Roosevelt (who knew perfectly well how the words would be taken by the public) really meant nothing more than wars not involving the United States. By the latter interpretation, no war would be a foreign war, no matter where fought, if the United States were in it. Thus the all-important question of whether or not the country would be led into a war, or an attack upon us provoked, was completely begged. The clever word-spinners of the President's private car knew that the President had pledged nothing. That this campaign coup was a monstrous piece of chicanery is now, in the light of facts since revealed, hardly deniable. Even Sherwood admits that his conscience bothers him. "I burn inwardly," he writes, "whenever I think of those words 'again—and again—and again.'" That his conscience may have had moments of elasticity we gather from his confession that "unfortunately for my own conscience, I happened at the time to be one of those who urged him to go the limit on this, *feeling as I did that any risk of future embarrassment was negligible as compared with the risk of losing the election.*"[5]

The ghost of Machiavelli must have been stalking the President's car as it rolled on toward Boston in that campaign of 1940. It will be perceived that what was really involved in this incident, and others like it, was the deceiving of the people of the nation with regard to the most vital issue of the day. That must be why Sherwood's conscience later stirred, why he "burned inwardly" when he thought of the matter.

Sherwood declares in his Introduction that he tried, in writing of the Hopkins period, not to be influenced by subsequent events. This is not surprising, for he finds "the present" (the book was published in 1948) not only "appalling" but also "inexplicable."[6] One is tempted to suggest that the reason the present is "inexplicable" to him is that he is afflicted with a bad case of historical myopia. The causative factors which lie in the past of which he writes escape his vision. It is shocking to reflect that one who pleads guilty to such a lack of historical perspective should have been for years a member of the inner White House circle and a writer of speeches for the President.

To the volatile characters for whom Franklin D. Roosevelt seemed to have a strong affinity and who made up his entourage, the heady wine of war and the fast action of high-level diplomacy and politics on a world stage were an exhilarating adventure. This produced mental phenomena which, as Sherwood describes them, appear not entirely unlike the symptoms of intoxication. Referring to his work on his book, he writes that it was a privilege to escape back into the days "when, as Herbert Agar has written, 'Good men dared to trust each other,' when 'the good and the bad, the terror and the splendor, were too big for most of us,' when 'our spirits and our brains were splitting at the seams, which may be why so many are today denying that life was ever like that.' "[7] One suspects that the gifted playwright never did know what "life" was "like" in those ecstatic days, as far as the realities of world affairs were concerned, and one is therefore not surprised that later events, which followed as the night the day, were "appalling and inexplicable" to him.

This discussion of Robert E. Sherwood's book is important to the purpose of this volume for the reason that *Roosevelt and Hopkins: An Intimate History* is the repository, for good or ill, of so much "Hopkinsiana" and is bound to influence academic as well as popular thinking about the man who was, says Mr. Sherwood, "the second most important individual in the United States Government during the most critical period of the world's greatest war."[8]

What manner of man was Harry Hopkins? A sinister figure, a Rasputin, a backstairs intriguer? Or a selfless man of deep human compassion? Was he a blunderer in a world he was not qualified to understand, or a paragon of judgment? As in the case of Roosevelt, the psychoanalyst must explain to us his inner springs of motivation, those drives of conscious or subconscious prejudice, fear, envy, and ambition which were so adeptly masked from view. One thing is clear: Hopkins was an aggressive, pushful man with overweening personal ambitions.

Misconceptions have arisen from the fact that he was a "social worker" when he first cuddled under the wing of Franklin D. Roosevelt while the latter was governor of New York. He had never been anything but a social worker—a professional one.

As he moved up the ladder, from Christadora House to the Association for Improving the Condition of the Poor, to the Board of Child Welfare, to the Red Cross, to the Milbank Fund, to the New York Tuberculosis Association, more and more dollars came to his pockets: $40 a month, $60 a month, $3,000 a year, $8,000 a year, $15,000 a year—in pre-inflation dollars. The career of a welfare worker, says Robert E. Sherwood, is "uncomplicated by the profit motive."[9] He does not give us his definition of the profit motive.

After Hopkins entered the government, his financial emoluments became incalculable. One must consider not only his salary but also the many things he no longer had to pay for. Free trips abroad, suites at Claridge's, weekends at Chequers, Hobcaw Barony, and Hyde Park, cars and chauffeurs, theater parties with Mrs. Roosevelt and her favorites, and a thousand other luxuries were his as he basked in the Presidential aura. It is not recorded that a bill for room and board was ever presented to him during the long years he resided in the White House. Whether the hospitality be considered that of the Roosevelt family or of the taxpayers of the country, Harry Hopkins was indubitably one of the most successful house guests in American history. Nor has any attempt ever been made to evaluate, in monetary terms, the ministrations of Dr. McIntire, the White House physician, or the advice of the Surgeon General of the United States Navy, or the sojourns for weeks and months at the Naval Hospital, with the medicines, facilities and experiments that were made freely available to this friend of the President. For Hopkins, who had serious ailments requiring expert treatment and much rest during most of these his years of glory, these gratuities saved tens of thousands of dollars. In short, there are at least two ways to obtain the luxuries of life that money can buy. One way is to earn the money to pay for them; the other is to manage to be the No. 1 man in the palace guard of a President like Roosevelt and not have to pay for them. The second was Hopkins' way. This is not to imply any corruption or even impropriety on his part, but merely to challenge the notion that Harry Hopkins was a sort of selfless humanist who sacrificed his all for public service.

It was not only for money that Hopkins was greedy. It was for power. This was attested to by his behavior in social-welfare work and later in government. Through his relationship with President Roosevelt, he achieved great power, even to affect the course of world history, as these pages will show. But he failed in his ambition to be President. Perhaps that was because the idea of Harry Hopkins being President was, as General Hugh Johnson called it, "ineffable nonsense," or perhaps it was because it so happened that an insatiable lust for power was not left out of the character of Franklin D. Roosevelt and he was budged from the Presidency only by death. However that may be, Mr. Sherwood tells us that Hopkins thought for a long time that Roosevelt would retire in 1940 and that he, Hopkins, might succeed him. As far back as December, 1937, it appears, this rosy dream had already come to him. His biographer writes: "Hopkins did take himself seriously as a candidate at that time, and one of the last requests that he made before his death was that, if anything should be written about him, there should be no attempt to disguise the fact that he once had ambitions for the highest office and that he worked and schemed to further them."[10]

There is something rather pathetic about this "one of the last requests" of Harry Hopkins. It was not enough that he thought himself big enough to be President; he wanted the world to know—posterity to know—that he thought so! It is as though, with his devious mentality, he believed on his deathbed that by binding his probable biographer to make this strange posthumous revelation, he could raise himself, in the eyes of history, to a higher stature.

The cream of the jest is that apparently, Roosevelt—if we are to believe Hopkins' handwritten notes of a private conversation with the President in the spring of 1938—led Hopkins to believe he was his, Roosevelt's, own choice for the Democratic nomination in 1940.[11] The ironic appointment of the soaring social worker to the Cabinet as Secretary of Commerce was supposedly part of the "build-up" which followed. Since Hopkins had never had any experience as a part of the American business and industrial system and was known to be unsympathetic to it, it seemed logical that the exigencies of politics should demand such a maneuver. To make a show of re-establishing a residence in his native state of Iowa (which he had abandoned immediately after he finished school), Hopkins even took a lease on a farm there in 1939. He never lived on this farm and visited it only once.[12] But if Harry Hopkins was a sly fox when it came to politics, in the big house on Pennsylvania Avenue there lived a slier one. While Roosevelt was nurturing this happy hope in the breast of his crony, he was giving very different ideas to others, as the memoirs of Cordell Hull, Frances Perkins, and James A. Farley disclosed after Roosevelt had passed on to his reward.

Serious illness in 1939 dampened Hopkins' ambition to be President, and the growing realization that Roosevelt intended to seek a third term squelched it entirely. He was sure of the truth long before Cordell Hull was. Hull was being told by Roosevelt right up to the month of the Democratic convention of 1940 that he, Hull, would be nominated.[13]

The practical maneuvering of the nomination at the convention was handled by the trusted Hopkins, who had resigned himself to the not uncongenial fate of being the good man Friday of the President of the United States in the exciting war years ahead. From a suite in Chicago's Blackstone Hotel, with a direct wire to Roosevelt at his hand, he directed the sham proceedings which "drafted" Roosevelt for a third term. The faithful biographer Sherwood, unable to escape what he calls the tawdriness and vulgarity of this notorious display of high-powered practical politics, would have us believe that Roosevelt and Hopkins both had great distaste for this sort of thing, although evidence of such delicate sensibilities on their part seems conspicuously lacking. We are expected, apparently, to share the assumption, which Mr. Sherwood takes for granted, that "the job that Hopkins had to do . . . had to be done."[14]

It is not surprising that Mr. Sherwood takes pains to bring Harry Hopkins out of this episode unscathed. Throughout his book, the dramatist draws him as a man of finer mold. He had "lyrical impulses," we learn, and was even known to have written poetry. Experiencing such a "lyrical impulse," he said after a look at the English countryside: "It's only when you see that country in spring that you begin to understand why the English have written the best goddam poetry in the world."[15] Whether he had ever heard of Sophocles, Virgil, Li Po, Dante, Goethe, Heine, or Verlaine is not recorded. Nor are we told whether or not Boss Kelly's infamous "voice from the sewers" at the Democratic convention in Chicago in 1940 should be considered one of Harry Hopkins' "lyrical impulses."

With the re-election of Franklin D. Roosevelt for a third term, the star of Harry Hopkins climbed high in the heavens. He, a dilettante in the field, was catapulted into the inner circle of world statesmen. Lend-lease, which followed after the election, resulted in his wielding almost dictatorial powers over the giving of billions of dollars in American resources to Britain, Soviet Russia, and other recipients. In Washington, London, Teheran, Moscow, Yalta, on the high seas, and in the air, as he breezed through the war years like a boy at a country fair, he was, with his illustrious chief, one of the co-architects of the most terrifying "peace" ever to follow a great war.

History, it is safe to predict, will be less kind to the memory of Harry Hopkins than is his adulatory friend, collaborator, and biographer, Robert E. Sherwood. It will not soft-pedal the "subsequent events."

Chapter IV

WHOSE CRUSADE?

IN A CORNER of Amiens Cathedral there is a wreath of Flanders poppies dedicated to the memory of the British soldiers who perished in France in World War I. An inscription reads:

> Went the day well or ill?
> I died, and never knew.

The most poignant tragedy of war is perhaps the fact that those who fall in battle know not for what they died. Subjectively, a man fights for those ends which he is told and believes will follow a victory. Objectively, however, he fights for the consequences which actually will ensue in a compassionless world of cause and effect. If his leaders have misinformed him or if they betray him at the council table, the quintessence of irony may be brought to pass: a man may forfeit his life for the exact opposite of that of which he dreamed.

General Dwight D. Eisenhower's war memoirs were published under the imposing title *Crusade in Europe*. The war ostensibly ended in complete military victory. Five years later, the good General was still—or again—crusading, only now he was crusading *against* the forces he had previously crusaded *with*. On September 4, 1950, in a nationally broadcast address launching a movement called the Crusade for Freedom, he said: "The people behind the Iron Curtain have no conception of a free press or of free discussion. . . . This is what the Soviet planners contemplate for all the world, including America. . . . How depressing it is to realize on this Labor Day, 1950, that one-third of the human race works in virtual bondage. In the totalitarian countries, the individual has no right the state is bound to respect."[1] In 1952, General Eisenhower was elected President of the United States. His most serious task was to fend off the consequences of World War II.

What, one must ask, was the great crusade of 1941-1945 meant to accomplish? Just the defeat of Hitler? Or was it a crusade to bring the Russians to the Elbe? To partition Poland again? To lop off one-fourth of the arable land of overpopulated Germany? To make Königsberg, German since its founding by the Teutonic order seven hundred years ago and the home of Germany's greatest philosopher, Immanuel Kant, a Russian city? To hand Stalin the keys to eastern Europe and eastern Asia? To uproot and cast upon the open roads ten million people whose homes were bartered away at a conference table? To put eight hundred million people under the yoke of Communism? To make the eighty million people living on the tiny islands of Japan dependent upon the United States for their economic survival? To put the whole world under fear of Soviet aggression?

Actually, all of these things, and more, were accomplished. A crusade with such multifarious results should be suspect. Whose crusade was it? Was there one crusade, or could it be that there were several, contemporaneous but irreconcilable in purpose?

The intellectual climate of America during World War II, writes William Henry Chamberlin, was "a depressing compound of profound factual ignorance, naïveté, wishful thinking and emotional hysteria."[2]

The disillusioning results followed inexorably. In the Introduction to his war memoirs, Winston Churchill gloomily looks at the world and observes: "The human tragedy reaches its climax in the fact that after all the exertions and sacrifices of hundreds of millions of people and of the victories of the righteous cause, we have still not found peace or security, and that we lie in the grip of even worse perils than those we have surmounted."[3] On four separate occasions since the war, Churchill has said that only the possession of the atom bomb in American hands kept the Red Army from invading western Europe after the war.

The war aims of the United States, as proclaimed by President Roosevelt, were grandiose. They went far beyond the mere military defeat of Germany, Italy, and Japan. Months before Pearl Harbor, Roosevelt took pains to identify himself in the public mind as the harbinger of spectacular reforms, which were to be the fruits of the war and which would accrue to all of the peoples of the world, victor and vanquished alike. The United States was still technically at peace with all nations when, in August, 1941, he staged his dramatic meeting with Winston Churchill on a battleship in the Atlantic. For the Prime Minister, the occasion served but to hasten the entrance of the United States into the war, but for public consumption, chiefly in the United States, there emerged a windy document that was promptly hailed as the Atlantic Charter. Roosevelt had long since determined upon war.[4] If men needed causes for which to fight and die, here they were. Here was the vision of a world of justice, liberty, and abundance for all men everywhere.

On December 15, 1941, eight days after Pearl Harbor, President Roosevelt took to the radio on the occasion of the anniversary of the adoption of the Bill of Rights in 1791. Over a nationwide hookup, he said in a stirring peroration:

We covenant with each other before all the world that, having taken up arms in the defense of liberty, we will not lay them down before liberty is once again secure in the world we live in.[5]

This pledge was intended for the ears of all the people of the world, and it was rebroadcast across the seas. It obviously did not mean liberty only for Americans; it meant liberty for Poles, for Lithuanians, for Manchurians, for sad, regimented men and women in Dresden and Budapest—all people who had become the pawns of tyrants. It was a covenant "before all the world," and it brought upon Franklin D. Roosevelt the prayers and blessings of humble people wherever tyranny existed. Naturally, its leavening effect upon the American audience was very important to Roosevelt. He wanted no misgivings about the moral rectitude of any phases of the global struggle he had championed so vigorously and into which American men and resources were to be thrown on a prodigious scale. The war would not be over in 1944 when he would run for his fourth term.

The crusade was on. Roosevelt, although never a student, knew something of history; he knew very much about the psychology of his countrymen. No doubt he was aware that Americans have a habit of idealizing the wars in which they become engaged as almost holy crusades. "As He died to make men holy, let us die to make men free." *The Battle Hymn of the Republic* gave emotional satisfaction to the armies of Grant and Sherman, just as, half a century later, the slogan of World War I, "To make the world safe for democracy," fired the imagination of a half-reluctant people and made acceptable to them a conflict the issues of which were far from clear. Now, a generation later, we were embarking upon an even more heroic crusade, this time allied with a semi-Oriental dictatorship which rested upon ideological foundations repugnant to most Americans and which had only two years before been expelled from the League of Nations for brutal aggression upon a small, peaceful neighbor. This phantasmagoria set in motion, Roosevelt took it upon himself to pledge to the world on our behalf that we would not lay down our arms "before liberty is once again secure in the world we live in."

This promise, in addition to the alluring, if ill-defined, quix-
otisms of the Atlantic Charter, put upon the project, or projects,
the stamp of self-righteousness. Nor did Roosevelt overlook the
fact that religion is a cause for which men have often fought.
He took pains to sanctify the struggle long before the United
States was in it. In his message to Congress in January of 1939,
he asserted that the United States was menaced by "storms from
abroad." These storms, the President said, challenge "three institutions indispensable to Americans. The first is religion. It is
the source of the other two—democracy and international good
faith."[6]

To be sure, there were religious persecutions occurring in
Germany and Austria, to which Roosevelt was referring, but
religion was dealt with roughly in other countries, to which he
was not referring and which he then and later condoned. The
Nazi cruelty was indeed deplorable. However, since the nations
of the world were not at that time lining up on a religious basis
(nor did they later), this statement of his was merely an oversimplification of a tangled skein of issues.

Not all observers were willing to grant the purity of President
Roosevelt's solicitude about religion in his message of January,
1939. The historian Charles A. Beard was moved to comment,
with dripping sarcasm: "Evidently he was clearing a way to
make the next war a real holy war."[7] (Coincidentally with the
end of the "holy war" some years later came the brutal obliteration of religious freedom in vast areas of eastern Europe.)

At the end of November, 1939, the Red war machine invaded
little Finland. Since the Roosevelt administration had for years
been very cordial with the Soviet dictatorship (one-sided though
the cordiality had been), this was naturally embarrassing to the
President, just as the German-Soviet pact of the preceding August
had been. In the United States there was a potent bloc of voters

of Scandinavian descent. They were irate at Soviet Russia. Sympathy for the Finns was widespread throughout the world, and on December 14, Russia was expelled from the League of Nations for her ruthless aggression, which had been initiated, with dramatic cruelty, by the bombing of Helsinki. But it was the impact upon public opinion in the United States which particularly disturbed President Roosevelt. Within a matter of months, a Presidential election campaign would be starting. He was never one to be insensitive to any political wind that was blowing at such a time. Although he had never previously expressed any particular abhorrence for the Soviet system of government and had not appeared shocked by its religious practices, he now deemed it expedient, in a speech to the American Youth Congress on February 10, 1940, to call Russia a dictatorship and to say that he detested "the banishment of religion" from Russia.[8]

However, this sudden moral upsurge was temporary, for after the election of 1940 was safely passed and the dictator Stalin was locked in mortal combat with the dictator Hitler, none of Roosevelt's plenteous supply of righteous wrath was reserved for Soviet Russia. If Marxian dialectic materialism had no room for God, that was never again mentioned. On the contrary, when Roosevelt started pouring lend-lease into Russia in 1941, he told skeptical reporters at an amazing press conference that they should read Article 124 of the Russian Constitution; the provisions concerning religion, said he, are "essentially what is the rule in this country; only we don't put it quite the same way." Since the Russian Constitution with its Article 124 had been adopted in 1936, why had he not mentioned it on February 10, 1940, when he had momentarily deplored "the banishment of religion" in Russia? Could it be that his research experts had simply overlooked the fact that Russia had a constitution, or was it because he and they knew perfectly well that the Russian Constitution was mere window dressing and that Article 124 was not to be taken seriously as giving a true picture of religion under the Soviet system?

The plain truth is that at that time it had served a temporary purpose of Roosevelt to appear perturbed by the pugnacious atheism of the Soviet regime. Now, in 1941, he had another purpose: to give Russia a clean bill of health on religion. It was purely a matter of political tactics. Nor was Roosevelt in the least deterred by the fact that Article 124 of the Russian Constitution contains several jokers and is heavily weighted in favor of anti-religious forces in the Soviet Union.[9] His bald statement would be published in all newspapers, and who would bother to check its veracity by seeking out a copy of the Russian Constitution and analyzing its tortuous phrases? None but a few inquisitive souls. The soporifics administered by the efficient Roosevelt propaganda machine had already begun to dull the public's consciousness of the realities of world affairs.

So godliness was added to the virtues at stake in President Roosevelt's great crusade. The details were a bit hazy, perhaps, but most people were inclined not to quibble about them. They felt rather exalted following the plumed knight from Hyde Park, who promised to bring about a Utopia on earth.

These grandiose aims all converged in the beloved concept of freedom. That was something an American could understand and would fight for, would pour out his wealth for. Franklin D. Roosevelt well knew this. But from former President Herbert Hoover, there was a stern warning. He said on June 29, 1941, one week after Germany attacked Russia and while Roosevelt was preparing to give all-out aid to the Soviets: "Joining in a war with Stalin to impose freedom is a travesty." He called it a "gargantuan jest."[10] But Roosevelt never let it be thought of as anything but a war for universal freedom, and such was the alchemy of mass propaganda that he largely succeeded in implanting that fallacy in the public mind. As we have seen, there

were really three wars being waged simultaneously, one of which
was kept secret from the American people and was to continue
to rage long after the termination of the other two.

How Roosevelt—by means of an oil embargo which would
stall the machines of Japan and reduce her people to starvation
and by means of other measures—deliberately, and over Navy
objections, goaded the Japanese into their rash attack on Pearl
Harbor is now a revealed, thoroughly documented story.[11] After
that attack, the theme of self-defense was joined with that of the
crusade for universal freedom. We now had to fight.

The crusading spirit was infectious. For one thing, the President had much to offer to those who would jump on his bandwagon. The flighty Wendell Willkie, after losing in his try for
the Presidency in 1940, suddenly "got religion" and became an
ebullient emissary for Roosevelt, traveling to London, Moscow,
and Chungking in an Army transport plane, emotionally over-
come by his precipitate arrival in the upper regions of international fame. His much-publicized slogan, "One World," served
well to help cover up the real state of affairs. In a speech in
Toronto, he gushed: "This war is either a 'grand coalition' of
peoples, fighting a common war for liberation, or it is nothing!"[12]

This, of course, was meaningless jargon, just as "One World"
was. With Stalin as a partner, did Willkie think he was going to
liberate the Lithuanians? Who was going to liberate the millions
of Poles Stalin had captivated in 1939 and whom he still claimed
as his subjects? What did he think were Stalin's plans for Manchuria, for Rumania, for Bulgaria? Was the great liberator in
the Kremlin going to give back to Finland what he had just
stolen from her? Did he think the Red Army of Communism
was going to bring to the lands it overran things never tolerated
in Soviet Russia—such as free speech and free elections?

Whether other Republican leaders, such as Hoover and Taft,
and dissident Democrats, such as former Secretary of War

Harry H. Woodring, looked upon these antics of Wendell Willkie as those of an opportunistic hypocrite or an impressionable dupe, we know not. They themselves had no hallucinations about "a 'grand coalition' of peoples, fighting a common war of liberation." Where did Willkie get this idea? There was nothing in the array of forces at battle to suggest it. He got it from his new host and promoter, President Roosevelt. Where did the President get it? From his own fecund imagination. It was an ipse dixit, a supercilious pontification, a self-serving dictum, never anything more. Its promulgation was the Atlantic Charter.

This remarkable document was the fulcrum of Franklin D. Roosevelt's herculean feat of embroiling his country in war, hypnotizing its people into what the war was about, and winning for himself a third and a fourth election as President of the United States. It was never carried out. It was never intended to be carried out. In the rush of time, it has never yet been held up to more than superficial scrutiny, although it has an import far greater than historical. For a people who profess to be self-governing, there are lessons now to be learned.

The children of 1941 are adults of our day. What do they know of these techniques? More than their parents did? Perhaps. Yet in the intensity of men's craving for the peace and justice which World War II made impossible, traps will be laid again, and words—bewitching words—will again be the bait. "Behind the shallow truism that 'history repeats itself,'" Arthur Koestler gloomily remarks, "hide the unexplored forces which lure men into repeating their own tragic errors."

PART TWO

The Atlantic Charter: Platform for a War

Decipimur specie recti.

HORACE

Chapter V

FROM SHOUTS TO WHISPERS

WHEN THE Atlantic Charter was proclaimed to the world on the fourteenth of August, 1941, wild cheers and hosannas arose in certain quarters. A state of mind bordering on ecstasy seems to have possessed the editorial room of the *Atlanta Constitution,* for example. That newspaper hurried to rank the Roosevelt-Churchill declaration with Magna Carta and the United States Constitution, an evaluation which the Roosevelt sycophants through the country proceeded to echo with alacrity. The *New York Times* saw "the beginning of a new era."

So moved was the president of Chicago's Zionists that after reading the words Roosevelt and Churchill had put together at their battleship rendezvous, he looked back as far as the dawn of human history and then pronounced this conference to be "the most momentous meeting in the history of the world." This hyperbole prodded the magazine *Christian Century,* which still preserved its balance, to quip: "One thinks immediately of a certain meeting that is supposed to have taken place on Mount Sinai, or of a number of others that might be mentioned."

Of course, not everybody was enthusiastic. Some people were distinctly less so when such newspapers as the war-minded *Louisville Courier-Journal* gleefully crowed that "America stands committed." And not a few eyebrows were raised when the Left Wing *New Republic,* which had been in paroxysms of anxiety ever since Soviet Russia was attacked the previous June, now came out flatly on its front cover for a declaration of war. Many people who carefully studied the words of the Charter made a wry face. It was, they said, just a piece of rhetoric and a rather fuzzy one at that. The *Los Angeles Evening Herald & Express* called it "a prelude" to taking the country into war and was skeptical of any other import.

Not only was the Atlantic Charter hatched in a setting of carefully contrived theatrics, however, but it was broadcast to the entire world as no other document ever had been before. Sumner Welles, who was no mean phrasemaker even before his post-graduate course at the knee of Franklin Delano Roosevelt, has called it "the beacon." It was "held aloft." It was to light the way "forward to peace, to human progress and to a free world."[1] In the United States, every propaganda medium was used to glorify it. People who swallow words with the same abject trust with which they swallow a pill saw no abracadabra in its phrases; they saw only shining truth and virtue.

The Atlantic Charter was posted on the walls of public libraries. It was praised in pulpits in awed tones. Teachers celebrated it in elementary classrooms for the edification of children barely able to read a comic book. The ladies' clubs throughout the country were descended upon by an army of lecturers, including an unusual proportion who had irresistibly attractive English accents, who told them that the great Charter was the harbinger of the millennium on earth. (First the United States had to get into the war; then would come Utopia.) Plausible pundits could not take up their pens fast enough to dash off articles and books in which they assumed that the Charter must mean something, and presumed to know what it meant. They took it for granted that whatever it meant would be honored in fact and deed, at least by President Roosevelt.

This remarkable document was eventually subscribed to by

the representatives of more than thirty nations, including Soviet Russia, with great pomp and ceremony. Soviet Russia, then on the receiving end of Mr. Roosevelt's bounty, vowed allegiance to it in St. James's Palace on September 29, 1941, and again later in Washington, D.C. In this country all the disciples of the administration, the fantasists and the word-worshipers, applauded as one, apparently taking it all quite seriously.

When Prime Minister Winston Churchill set out from the shores of Britain to attend the Atlantic Conference, he, as an old trouper on the world stage, was well aware of the dramatic possibilities of the episode. There was to be no risk that an insufficiently glowing account of it would be written. He took with him on the battleship *Prince of Wales* two "literary men," as he called them. One was a writer of travel books; the other wrote best-seller novels.

The traveloguist, H. V. Morton, was naturally deeply moved by his presence at this meeting of the two great leaders, Churchill and Roosevelt, "far from the haunts of man," as he put it (although the meeting took place in a landlocked bay within rowboat distance of both Argentia, a large American seaplane base, and the town of Placentia, which had a population of three thousand and was on a railroad). In his book *Atlantic Meeting,* he predicted that "the Atlantic Conference will take its place among the great meetings of history." Strangely, his treatment of the eight points of the Charter consisted only of printing them in the appendix of the book. About the meeting, however, he wrote:

Seen against the tremendous events of 1939-41, it will live in the history books of the future and will arouse the interest and the curiosity of generations yet unborn. Men will ask what it was like to cross the Atlantic with Winston Churchill in war-time. It may be that a dramatist, an artist or a writer of films will wish to picture Churchill upon the admiral's bridge gazing through the mists of early morning towards the shores of the New World. Time may prove that such a picture was one of the great symbolic moments of the war. And should this be so, the writer and the artist will have many a question to ask. What did he wear? What did he look like? Was he well and in good spirits? Was he ill? What did he talk about? How did he spend his time as the warship carried him across the ocean?[2]

Such was the exuberance of the moment. Actually, the conference meant to the English mainly one thing: President Roosevelt had virtually committed his country to war. American and British warships had churned the waters of Placentia Bay as one armada. As for the Charter, Robert E. Sherwood, writing with Harry Hopkins' notes before him, tells us that the officers of the British government "never regarded it as a formal State Paper; it was, to them, not much more than a publicity handout."[3] Churchill wired his cabinet on August 11 from the *Prince of Wales* that Roosevelt was set on issuing it because "he believes [it] will influence the whole movement of United States opinion," and he tipped off the cabinet that it would be "most imprudent on our part to raise unnecessary difficulties."[4] The eight points were not taken seriously in England (as a study of contemporary British opinion clearly shows). They were food for American consumption, which is probably why they ended up rather ignominiously in the Appendix of Mr. Morton's book.

As for President Roosevelt, he appeared at Placentia Bay cozily surrounded by two of his sons and Harry Hopkins, as well as the faithful Sumner Welles and W. Averell Harriman. These could be relied upon to hear nothing they should not hear, to report nothing which it would be indiscreet to reveal. He allowed no representatives of the press to accompany him. But when he came home, his administration, which harbored more publicity (or "public liaison") experts than any prior President had ever dared dream of, got busy. It set in motion, in the press, on the screen, and on the air waves, a glamour drive which was meant to capture the imagination of the American people, who, whatever else may be their virtues and faults, do indubitably love a good show. Mr. Roosevelt's wife also loaned her not inconsiderable talents to the glamourization of the Atlantic Conference and its eight-point offspring, the Charter. Less than four months later the United States was in the war officially. The Atlantic Charter was supposed to be its platform.

During the next five years, two things happened. First, before Franklin D. Roosevelt's death in April, 1945, the Atlantic Charter was torn to shreds and thrown into the trash pile of discarded nostrums. Second, its memory was almost expunged by new *divertissements*. Those who had sung its praises most lustily had cause to forget the melody. They gave it the treatment of silence.

A decade and a half has now passed. The Atlantic Charter is seldom spoken of any more. Its very mention is an embarrassment to all who were in any way connected with its spectacular origin or who once glorified its maker. Shy at appearing ludicrous, friendly biographers, and even many historians, are found to skirt around its phrases and avoid serious consideration of it. Schoolteachers and professors have little, if anything, to say about it to their students. A sampling of college students today will disclose that the majority cannot even identify this strange international compact, which at its birth was heralded as one of the most memorable in the history of the world and the beginning of a new era. Not one in twenty has more than the vaguest knowledge of its contents.

To Rooseveltians, the most disconcerting fact is that the death of the Charter occurred during the lifetime of Franklin D. Roosevelt, and his own finger marks were on the throat of the corpse. It was a plain case of infanticide. An examination of the writings and speeches of the voluble Eleanor Roosevelt from 1943 to the present discloses a marked reticence on the subject, as compared with her earlier effusiveness. The Atlantic Charter has indeed become the forgotten prodigy. The cynosure of hundreds of millions of human beings at its birth, violence and oblivion were its destiny. It was never given a decent burial.

When Elliott Roosevelt wrote his book, published in 1946 under the title *As He Saw It* (the *He* being his father), he had to say something about the Atlantic Charter. After all, he was writing about the various international conferences at which he had accompanied his father, and his memory was purported to be so precise that he could quote, verbatim, choice little confidences that came to him from the lips of his father over several years. Yet about the Atlantic Charter, Elliott seems to have decided that the less said, the better. He wrote that it had "a peculiar and bitter historical interest" and then proceeded to dispose of the celebrated eight points with a few flippant evasions, all in less than a page. For example, of the important fourth point, which deals with access to the raw materials of the world, his treatment was: "Pass over the fourth point; its mysteries are too deep."[5] Of course they always had been too deep; his father and Churchill had purposely made them that way, although this uncomplimentary thought finds no expression by Elliott.

Whom did Elliott blame for the sad fate of the more explicit points of the Charter? Never Franklin D. Roosevelt. Nor the Russians. In 1946, Elliott was apparently still under the spell of the Russophilism which had infected his father's administration, even to the point of his rhapsodizing over Russia so much in this book that one would gain the impression that Russia saved the skin of America in the war, not vice versa. Russia's "mighty contribution" to America's victory in the war, he wrote, was "the greatest single fact in our lifetime."[6] If the reputations of Franklin D. Roosevelt and of the Soviet Union were sacrosanct, that left the British to blame. So Elliott placed the blame, at least by insinuation, jointly on "British imperialism" and on those Americans who eventually, after the war, decided to stand up to Com-

munist expansionism. The waywardness of this logic, or lack of
it, is hardly worthy of remark. What one reads between the lines
is that at least as early as 1946, Elliott Roosevelt knew that the
Atlantic Charter was "a dead duck" (to borrow a metaphor he
seems fond of). He played it down, just as his mother had been
doing for a long time. In a sense, it had served its purpose, for its
real purpose was propagandistic and therefore ephemeral.

The Atlantic Charter may indeed be unimportant now, as is
any cadaver, but the story of it is not unimportant. The corpus
delicti is all but forgotten, but the lesson of the crime should
never be. Franklin D. Roosevelt is not the last mortal who will
present himself as a savior to the world. The Atlantic Charter
is not the last "beacon," as Sumner Welles called it, that will be
"held aloft" just before men are asked to die.

The tale does not unfold easily. One must start far enough
back and carry it well forward; otherwise the real gist of it is
never found or is lost in sheer fantasy. The politician, if his scru-
ples be flexible, plays a constant game to outwit his contem-
poraries. If he is extraordinarily clever, he will do more: he will
outwit the historians. "We cannot escape history," said Lincoln,
but a Franklin D. Roosevelt would intuitively know this to be
a half-truth. Much that men such as he do and think escapes at
least the conscious record of history, and historians only too
often lose the scent in their quest for the truth. The story they
tell of an event is too pat. They make a frontal attack where only
an enveloping movement will yield the prey.

We shall begin by looking in at the White House a few days
before President Roosevelt sailed away for his secret rendezvous
with the Prime Minister of Great Britain in the summer of 1941.
It was just four months and one week before, on the other side
of the world, the upstart "land of the Rising Sun" made its most
desperate gamble: an attack on the American fleet at Pearl
Harbor.

Chapter VI

"IF I WERE A JAP...."

PRESIDENT ROOSEVELT had a particularly busy calendar on the last day of July, 1941. It was one of those days that would whet the vanity of any man and certainly that of Franklin D. Roosevelt, in whom that "sixth insatiable sense," as Carlyle called it, was by no means underdeveloped. It was a day replete with big manipulations, half-veiled by oblique announcements issuing forth from near the seat of power. These served to inform the public that the man of destiny was up to something important.

To the White House, by invitation, came two men impressively arrayed in uniforms of scarlet, blue, and olive drab, with the Soviet hammer and sickle embossed in gold leaf on their visored caps. They were Lieutenant General Filip I. Golikoff, deputy chief of staff of the Soviet Army, and his assistant, Engineer General Alexander Respin. They were accompanied by the Russian Ambassador, Constantin A. Oumansky, who introduced them to the President. As heads of the Russian military mission, it was their business in Washington to get military supplies for the Soviet army.

On that day, the United States was technically at peace. The Roosevelt administration had made no pretense of neutrality; but it had not yet dared to remove the word "peace" from its lexicon of rhetoric, for the public did not wish to enter the war.

The Nazi blitz on England had failed; in turn, bombs had been dropped from hundreds of Royal Air Force planes on Hamburg and Berlin, with telling premonition of devastation yet to come. Hitler's legions, now in the sixth week of their unhappy gamble in the east, had been checked on the approaches to Leningrad, Moscow, and Kiev, and a Soviet counteroffensive was actually underway in the crucial Smolensk sector of the long battle front. German peace feelers, looking toward a *rapprochement* with Britain, were being put forth in the neutral capitals of Europe.[1] Communism, the Germans were insisting, was the real menace to Western civilization.

After a lengthy visit, the Russians emerged from the White House, obviously pleased. Whatever Mr. Roosevelt had said to them had been music to their ears. General Golikoff told inquisitive reporters that he found it very "easy" to talk with President Roosevelt on military matters. Perhaps General Golikoff had not anticipated that Mr. Roosevelt would say yes to him with such gusto or without attaching any strings to his commitment. It was not so long ago that the League of Nations had expelled General Golikoff's government for aggression against little Finland or that his boss, Stalin, had joined with Adolf Hitler to wipe Poland off the map. So he may have expected a more mitigated enthusiasm on President Roosevelt's part. Under the circumstances, it is not surprising that the adjective "easy" should have come to his mind in describing the conference.

It so happened that on this same thirty-first of July, in faraway Moscow, the President's perennial message-bearer and intimate, Harry Hopkins, was having a three hour tête-à-tête with Marshal Joseph Stalin. He was promising Stalin all possible American aid. He had spent three hours with the Soviet dictator the previous evening. Stalin was coolly confident. The Germans, said he, had underestimated the strength of the Russian army, which could mobilize three hundred and fifty divisions.

Stalin wanted American guns and other things, both immediately and over the long run, but he made it plain that there was more on his mind than just the defense of the soil of Russia. Germany must be completely crushed, and to do that, America would have to come into the war. He wanted Hopkins to give Roosevelt that personal message. (Hopkins marked this part of his report "For the President Only.")[2]

Hopkins did not ask Stalin what the Soviet Union intended to do in the heartland of Europe after Germany was crushed, a question which anyone with a perspective of European history and an elementary understanding of geopolitics would have known to be important. The excuses he proffered for some of the delays which would be inevitable in furnishing Stalin the vast quantities of supplies and equipment he wanted savored of apologies. He offered even more than was asked for. "In return for the offer of such aid," writes William C. Bullitt with consternation, "he asked nothing."[3] Sherwood's account, from Harry Hopkins' own notes and report, bears this out.[4]

On this same day, the Germans had something dour to say about the visit of the American Santa Claus, in the person of Harry Hopkins, to the Kremlin. While it ill behooved the Nazis to speak of outrages and to don the robe of moral indignation, they had not lived in uncomfortable propinquity to the fountainhead of international Communism since 1917 without learning some things about it which many Americans were to discover, with painful embarrassment and at great cost, in the years to follow. The authorized German spokesman, as quoted the next morning in the *New York Times,* tossed out a ball which Franklin D. Roosevelt did not dare try to catch. He charged that Hopkins' offer of support to Soviet Russia made the United States a party to the Soviet Union's efforts to thrust Communism into the heart of Europe.

The implicit prediction in this German comment, though

prescient, was not just a case of clairvoyance, for it rested upon a knowledge of Marxism and of Soviet imperialism. "The United States is perfectly informed about the conditions of terror imposed by the Soviet in the territory Russia recently occupied," the spokesman continued. "By supporting such efforts any third party of course makes itself equally responsible for this assault on civilization."

The kettle was no less black because it was the pot that was calling it so. But in those days it was a tactic of the Roosevelt administration to scorn, as Nazi propaganda, anything said in Berlin, regardless of any amount of truth contained in it.

The police state which was spawned by Bolshevism as an ugly sequel to the Revolution of 1917 and which has ever since drawn its vitality from a weird fusion of idealistic pretensions and brutal terrorism could logically commemorate the thirty-first day of July, 1941, as one of the most auspicious dates in its history. The assurances given on that day to the Red Army by Franklin D. Roosevelt, the President of the United States, and by Harry Hopkins, the creature and mouthpiece of Roosevelt, to Stalin in the Kremlin virtually guaranteed that the Soviet Union would be built up to be a monstrous military power that would cast a lengthening shadow over Europe and Asia throughout the following decades.

Naturally, the average American citizen knew little of the import of what was occurring. He was being agreeably diverted (although unemployment recorded in August, 1941, was 5,620,-000, or one-tenth of the total labor force). His resistance to the idea of going to war, for ends which were dubious at best, was slowly being chipped away. Mr. Roosevelt saw to that personally.

For example, on that eventful day when the President was receiving the Russian generals at the White House, the American people—or at least those who were reading their newspapers —were being regaled with accounts of a visit by one Alvin York to the White House the day before. Alvin York was the heroic Sergeant York of World War I. The Hollywood interventionist set,[5] close political allies of the President, had reached back a whole generation to resurrect the almost-forgotten Mr. York. They had made a motion picture with the title *Sergeant York*. It was a clever piece of jingoism which was calculated to make many an adventurous youngster yearn to get a gun in his hands and be a hero, too. President Roosevelt then arranged to have Mr. York brought to the White House, where, with much publicity, he praised the new picture and told Mr. York that he thought it would do much "to rouse our people." This gratuitous Presidential plug for a motion picture was in the newspapers at a timely moment.

Later in the day, after Generals Golikoff and Respin and the Soviet Ambassador had left the White House, another foreign visitor arrived for an appointment with the President. It was the British Ambassador, Lord Halifax. Naturally, one of the prime duties of this suave diplomat was to keep a sharp watch on President Roosevelt's humors, with the object of accelerating, however possible, the tempo of American participation in the war. Mr. Roosevelt, in turn, had opened his arms to Lord Halifax and was a willing collaborator in the job of putting an innocent face on the British cause in the world power struggle then raging. This, of necessity, involved a liberal touching up of the record of history and so came within one of Mr. Roosevelt's special aptitudes. He liked to refer to Lord Halifax's homeland as a "peace-loving nation," in spite of the fact that since the foundation of British nationalism in the eleventh century the doughty Englishmen had never let a single generation pass without engaging in warfare somewhere away from their own soil.

On this occasion, Lord Halifax did not come to the White House empty handed. He brought as gifts to Mr. Roosevelt a portrait of the President by Frank Salisbury, a gold medal from the Royal Society of Arts, awarded by its president, the Duke of Connaught, and a diploma from Oxford University attesting that Mr. Roosevelt had received its honorary degree of Doctor of Civil Law.

The British Ambassador remained with the President one hour. They probably talked about Mr. Roosevelt's impending meeting with Prime Minister Churchill, which was to result in the Atlantic Charter. But that was a guarded secret. They also talked about Japan. What they said to each other on this subject was, of course, not made public. Upon leaving the White House, Lord Halifax was not explicit, but said that it was a fair assumption that the conference had touched on Far Eastern developments. Asked if future moves had been planned, he replied, "Not a great deal. We discussed various possibilities."

"Possibilities" for what? For fostering amicable relations with the Japanese government, then headed by the moderate Prince Konoye, or for prodding the Japanese to some desperate act of aggression that would touch off war with England and the United States? For playing into the hands of the war party in Japan by new belligerent moves which would force the Konoye cabinet out of power and bring in General Tojo and his militarists? For cutting the ground from under the conscientious Joseph C. Grew, our Ambassador in Tokyo, who thought, or hoped, that his government really wanted peace? For stultifying in the eyes of the Japanese people those moderate leaders who were known to desire a resolution of the China impasse and an escape from the tripartite agreement with the Axis powers? For forcing the Japanese to go south from their tiny islands to more favored lands in order to get oil, tin, rubber, and rice at gunpoint, as had the English, the Dutch, and the French before them?

The insinuation is not fanciful. In the first place, President Roosevelt wanted war.[6] And certainly the British, who were already in one in Europe, wished for nothing more than that

America be in it with them. The Far East was the back door. If the United States were to clash with Japan, she would also be plunged into the maelstrom in Europe. This was perfectly foreseeable (and, of course, is exactly what happened).

In the second place, secret and detailed war plans were ready. British and American military and naval experts, disguised in civilian clothes to conceal from the public the fact that the United States was surreptitiously entering into a military alliance, had drawn them up a few months earlier in Washington and Singapore. (This all came out five years later in the hearings of the Joint Congressional Committee on the Investigation of the Pearl Harbor Attack.)[7]

Third, President Roosevelt had just initiated a series of highly provocative actions which were almost certain to lead to war with Japan. The Panama Canal had been closed to Japan's ships, and her oil had been cut off.[8]

The President was not one to eschew an indirect means to an end when the direct one was denied him. During the early summer of 1941, his Secretary of War, Stimson, conscious of the fact that in a democracy the people have a right to candor on the part of their public officials, was urging Mr. Roosevelt to come out boldly for intervention in the war in Europe; but now, in July, he came to realize that political considerations based upon what was "palatable" to the people had so firmly committed the President "to his own more gradual course that nothing could change him."[9] It is obvious that Henry L. Stimson, who had never been elected to a public office, was temperamentally incapable of comprehending the *modus operandi* of a virtuoso politician such as Franklin D. Roosevelt. The squire of Hyde Park had not won his third term campaign by being candid, nor was he going to reach his fourth term by the route of candor.

In Roosevelt's machinations to embroil the United States in the European war, Hitler had turned out to be somewhat disappointing. The Lend-Lease Act, which the President rammed through Congress in March, had violated every concept and canon of neutrality enunciated in international law since the time of Grotius, including the Hague Conventions. And on April 21, Roosevelt had directed units of the Atlantic fleet to "trail" German and Italian merchant and naval ships and aircraft and to broadcast their movements in plain language at four-hour intervals for the convenience of British warships and planes.[10] These were but two of a list of steps which he had taken to make the United States, for all intents and purposes, a belligerent, though a non-official one. He was waging an undeclared war. (Admiral Stark wrote in a private letter a month before Pearl Harbor: "Whether the country knows it or not, we are at war.")[11] In short, Mr. Roosevelt had put a chip on his shoulder and had dared the Nazi dictator to knock it off. The latter had not obliged. Although American warships were plowing the Atlantic and helping the British navy and although American military aid was of such a nature and the attitude of the Roosevelt administration so pugnacious that Prime Minister Churchill was able to tell the House of Commons on July 21 that the United States was "on the verge of war," the Germans were careful not to accommodate Mr. Roosevelt by giving him sufficient grounds to ask Congress for a declaration of war.

When American troops were sent to Iceland to relieve fifteen thousand British soldiers garrisoned there, hopes that Hitler might consider this the last straw rose high in administration circles. On July 7, when Roosevelt, after being badgered by Senator Burton K. Wheeler into making the revelation, finally notified Congress of this movement of forces, he made it appear to be purely a matter of defense of the Western Hemisphere because, as Stimson confides to us, he believed that "this was a more palatable argument to the people."[12] However, Admiral Stark, the Chief of Naval Operations, wrote a letter to Captain (later Admiral) Charles M. Cooke, Jr., on July 31 in which he said, in the more blunt fashion of the Navy, "The Iceland situation may produce an incident. . . . Whether or not we will get an 'incident' . . . I do not know. Only Hitler can answer."[13]

As it turned out, Hitler continued a cautious path. He did not give President Roosevelt the incident he was waiting for. His U-boats were instructed to keep away from American ships where possible.[14] "They're keeping out of our way, apparently," said Secretary of the Navy Knox on August 16. To be sure, the American destroyer *Greer* was sunk on September 4 by torpedoes, but under circumstances which were far from clear on the point of whether the *Greer* or the German submarine had been the aggressor.[15] This was clearly not the case for the President to take to Congress without fear of a rebuff. In fact, the Navy Department refused to submit the log of the *Greer* to inspection by the United States Senate.[16]

In the meantime, Mr. Roosevelt was not putting all his bets on one horse. If the Germans would not attack the United States, perhaps the Japanese would. The troubled waters of the Far East were full of "possibilities," to pluck a word from Lord Halifax's cryptic comment when he emerged from his private conversation with President Roosevelt in the White House on July 31. Had Mr. Roosevelt told Lord Halifax that the Navy Department had advised him in advance that the oil embargo would force Japan to make war to get oil? If they talked at all about the Far Eastern situation—and Lord Halifax said they did—this must have been mentioned, for it was the most potent fact in that situation and it is inconceivable that the loquacious Mr. Roosevelt would have been so lacking in frankness to his visitor on a matter of their common interest that he would smother the information. In those days, it was not uncommon for intelligence which was carefully kept secret from the American people, chiefly for political reasons, to be imparted freely to the British hierarchy.

Admiral Richmond K. Turner, chief of the War Plans Division of the Navy Department, had, with the general concurrence of Admiral Stark, Chief of Naval Operations, prepared for the State Department and the President an analysis of the effects of such an embargo. This report, made on July 22, set forth the Navy's official position on the advisability of imposing the embargo. It stated that an embargo "would probably result in a fairly early attack by Japan on Malaya and the Netherlands East Indies," that it would have "an immediate severe psychological reaction in Japan against the United States," that it seemed certain that if Japan should take measures against the British and Dutch, she would also include military action against the Philippines, which would immediately involve us in a Pacific war. The final recommendation was "that trade with Japan not be embargoed at this time."[17]

Of course to Franklin D. Roosevelt, who had other objectives in mind than the maintenance of peace, this conclusion was a *non sequitur*. Three days later, on July 25, from Hyde Park, he issued an executive order freezing all Japanese assets in the United States and imposing a virtual embargo on trade between the two countries.[18] Naturally, the British and the Dutch government-in-exile in England followed suit. Japan, which because of her natural deficiencies must trade or perish, was backed to the wall. Whether or not the Navy's analysis decided the issue for Mr. Roosevelt must remain a matter of conjecture, but we do know that when the Navy advised that the embargo would precipitate war, he promptly imposed it.

This move was palmed off on the public as an effort to deter Japan from a course of aggression. The official Navy conclusion that it would have just the opposite effect was, of course, kept secret. Five years later, the truth came out at the hearings of the Joint Congressional Committee on the Investigation of the Pearl Harbor Attack when Admiral Stark, who at the time the Japanese embargo was imposed was the top Navy man in Washington, frankly admitted that all high officials in Washington had known it meant ultimate war. Roosevelt had pulled the wool over the eyes of the American public but not over those of Admiral Stark. Stark did not even blame the Japanese. When Roosevelt cut off Japan's oil, Stark felt that "if he were a Jap," he would go and take oil where he could find it. At the Congressional hearings in 1946, Senator Ferguson put the question to him: "About the oil question, and your attitude toward Japan: Did you not testify before the Navy Court that after the imposition of economic sanctions upon Japan in the summer of 1941, you stated that Japan would go somewhere and take it [oil], and that if you were a Jap you would?"

"I think that is correct," Admiral Stark responded. "I stated it, and I stated in the State Department, as I recall, that if a complete shutdown was made on the Japanese, throttling her commercial life and her internal life, and her essential normal peace life by stopping her from getting oil, the natural thing for a Jap was to say, 'Well, I will go down and take it.' "[19]

President Roosevelt and Lord Halifax knew what was natural for "a Jap" to do as well as Admiral Stark did. So on that busy July 31, when the shrewd, gangling Ambassador of His Majesty's Government, armed with a portrait of Mr. Roosevelt and other touching gifts, bore down upon the President in the White House, "the various possibilities" they discussed were, it is reasonable to assume, of a distinctly bellicose nature. The term was a British understatement. "Probabilities" would have been more accurate, but it would have stirred up more embarrassing questions.

Lest the pressure on Japan be not quite strong enough, more

was now applied. Mr. Roosevelt's verve was undoubtedly inten-
sified by the realization that if Japan were kept well occupied
elsewhere, she would not be a threat to the Russian flank in Si-
beria; and the sanctity of the Soviet Union never failed to arouse
sympathy in the heart of this man, who was later to participate
in carving up at least six sovereign nations with icy aplomb. His
visitors, the Russian generals and the British Ambassador, had
hardly departed when he tossed back his leonine head and
roared again in the direction of Japan. He signed an executive
order setting up a governmental office of economic warfare,
known euphemistically as the Economic Defense Board, and
put Henry A. Wallace in charge of it. It was simultaneously reported that administration officials had prepared "an additional
blacklist" of some four hundred firms and persons doing business in Latin America and that this consisted, in large part, of
Japanese concerns.[20]

On the following day, President Roosevelt ordered a further
tightening of the gasoline and oil embargo. Comments were
heard from men in the petroleum trade to the effect that the ban
would seriously affect Japan.[21] This, of course, tended to confirm the secret advice the President had received from the Navy
that it would force Japan to seek oil by open warfare, but Mr.
Roosevelt, posing as a zealous worker in the cause of preventing
aggression, could count on a fair degree of public complacency
and feel secure politically in the knowledge that the public was
ignorant of the fact that he had flouted the recommendation of
the Navy. His mood of belligerence unabated, he also had his
Office of Production Management stop all processing of raw
silk for civilian use. This meant the cessation of manufacture of
silk hosiery, neckties, dress goods, etc.[22] Since for many years the
United States had been the greatest raw silk–consuming country
in the world and Japan the greatest raw silk–exporting nation
in the world, this was a cutting blow. In the art of incitement

of international conflict, Mr. Roosevelt was as resourceful as he was adept at screening the shadow of impending consequences from public sight.

The Japanese had moved troops into southern Indochina and had established bases there by agreement with the Vichy government of France. Indochina was a French possession toward which the Russian colossus to the north had long been casting an envious eye, just as it had toward China proper. A serious Communist-inspired revolt had occurred at Yen Bay in 1930, and Soviet propaganda and agitation had continued among the Annamite peoples throughout the decade. There are those who would scoff at any analogy between the movement of American troops into Denmark's Iceland and the entry of Japanese troops into France's Indochina two weeks later. That the Japanese, Asiatics by geography and by blood, should have exhibited a positive concern for the future status of southeastern Asia is hardly astonishing. (Nor should it later have surprised anyone cognizant of the basic problems of the Far East that chaos and war raged in Indochina for many bloody years after Japan was eliminated from the scene and that American planes and guns were eventually needed there to hold at bay an enemy far more sinister than the Japanese.)

Franklin D. Roosevelt was adamant on the point of erasing all Japanese influence on the rich continent of Asia. While the British sat smugly in Hong Kong, Malaya, and Burma, while a decadent French colonialism clung, with weakening fingers, to the rice fields and rubber plantations of Indochina, and while the Kremlin was entertaining and educating Mao Tse-tung and other Chinese henchmen who were being trained to implement the Soviet blueprint for the ultimate Communization of all China and Korea and the lush lands to the south, Japan was treated to a diet of sanctimonious preachments by the American President and his Secretary of State, Cordell Hull. One would have supposed from their lectures that if it were not for Japan's dream of her "Greater East Asia Co-Prosperity Sphere," the war lords, the bandits, and the Communist, Soviet-supported revolutionists would sheath their bloody swords and peace and amity would reign from Singapore and Batavia to Harbin. One would also have imagined that aggression and exploitation in the Far East began and would end with the Japanese.

Baffled by what they called the "lack of reality" of the Roosevelt-Hull approach, the attitude of the Japanese oscillated between propitiation and truculence, between polite amiability and explosive anger. They did have visions of empire. From their small, overpopulated islands, these energetic people saw across the Yellow and South China seas and the Sea of Japan the natural resources which they needed, not merely to achieve what they conceived to be a worthy destiny, but also to feed themselves.

But there were good reasons to hope that they could be deflected from a path of wanton aggression. These hopes brightened just one week before President Roosevelt, against the Navy's advice, cut off Japanese trade. This sequence is at least curious. On July 18, a shake-up in the Japanese cabinet had eliminated Foreign Minister Matsuoka, the proponent of close collaboration with Germany. In his place was Admiral Teijiro Toyoda, who was known to be a moderate.[23] The new vice-premier was Baron Hiranuma, who had been heading a drive to suppress clandestine German activity in Japan.[24] No pleasure was shown by President Roosevelt at these changes. He became all the more intransigent.

The American Ambassador in Tokyo, Joseph C. Grew, subsequently made impassioned efforts to arrange a meeting, in Hawaii or in Alaska, between the Japanese Premier, Prince Konoye, and President Roosevelt. Prince Konoye urgently desired the meeting. Mr. Grew, who had been at his post nine years and who understood Japanese politics and psychology intimately, believed it was the road to a *rapprochement*. His efforts, of course, were futile. President Roosevelt brushed them off with a bullheadedness which was possible only because the American public was not aware of the incident.

Across the Pacific Ocean came a fervent entreaty from Ambassador Grew. It was a cry of frustration from an honest public servant. He firmly believed that "a complete readjustment of relations between Japan and the United States" could be brought about if the United States would "use the present opportunity." The American people never heard this prayer because it was communicated, as diplomatic usage prescribed, in a long but secret cable addressed to Secretary of State Hull. It cautioned that further stalling by the President would convince the Japanese "that the United States Government is only playing for time" and would lead to the downfall of the Konoye cabinet, which, Ambassador Grew was convinced, was prepared to make great concessions for a peaceful solution.[25]

The point was not lost on the wily man in the White House, but the effect was quite the reverse of Ambassador Grew's intentions. When Mr. Roosevelt was thus authoritatively apprised of the consequences of further stalling on his part, he proceeded to stall the more and with the greater arrogance. He would not meet with the Japanese Premier to discuss anything unless the latter would surrender to all of Mr. Roosevelt's terms in advance of the meeting. This condition was, as Mr. Roosevelt knew and as Ambassador Grew had told him, an impossible one for the chief of any Oriental state to accept, particularly one faced with a delicate internal political schism.

As Cordell Hull puts it, Roosevelt refused to meet with the Japanese Premier "without first arriving at a satisfactory agreement."[26] But such an agreement was impossible without the meeting. (After such an agreement, the meetings would be unnecessary.) Grew took pains to point out this dilemma (as though Roosevelt, who devised it, were not conscious of it). The absurdity was compounded by Secretary Hull's communications to the Japanese, which were such masterpieces of negativism that their recipients could not possibly know what, specifically, they were expected to agree to.[27] The general intention, however, was clear: Japan was to be relegated permanently to the status of a third-rate power, dependent for the sustenance of her eighty million people upon the willingness of vested empires to trade with her and exposed, through a China chaotic from civil strife and Communist penetration, to the well-known and dreaded ambitions of the Soviet Union. Against anything short of this, the President was adamant. (As will be seen, he later [at Yalta] secretly connived to bring the Soviet army into the North China power vacuum which the collapse of Japan would create.)

Even so, Prince Konoye virtually begged to see President Roosevelt and make a try for peace. When he was brushed off repeatedly, the result was what Ambassador Grew had prophesied. The Konoye cabinet fell, and the only hope of peace was extinguished. The military dictatorship of General Hideki Tojo took the reins of power in Japan. The American people knew that Konoye had fallen. They did not know who had pushed him.

When Cordell Hull wrote his memoirs, he did not even mention that long, anguished cable from Ambassador Grew, although in its historical implications it is one of the most important documents of the time. This was not an oversight, for he devoted an entire chapter to what he labeled the "Roosevelt-Konoye Meeting," which never took place. By a slight concession to historic completeness, Hull grudgingly mentioned that Grew "recommended" the meeting, then hastened to say that Grew "could not estimate the over-all world situation as we could in Washington."[28] But Joseph C. Grew was a career statesman of much broader experience in international affairs than this elderly, provincial former Senator from Tennessee, to whom Roosevelt had given an office and a title but no real authority and whom Harry Hopkins always virtually ignored. The only crucial thing Ambassador Grew did not know was that Franklin D. Roosevelt and his aides wanted war, not peace. If Hull had set forth the Grew cable in his memoirs, its contents would have demolished the structure of words which he was building to exculpate himself.

Most apologists for the Rooseveltian diplomacy of the period conveniently also omit all reference to it. It is too embarrassing. It evokes a vision of the what-might-have-been, if there had been a different President in the White House. An exception is that indefatigable Roosevelt infatuate, Professor Basil Rauch of Columbia University. In his *Roosevelt: From Munich to Pearl Harbor*,[29] he makes bold to meet this troublesome point head on. Remembering that Professor Rauch's major prior historical effort was an almost ecstatic *History of the New Deal*, one is not surprised that he rallies to the cause in this emergency. His solution has at least the virtue of simple directness. Ambassador Grew, says he, was wrong. The Roosevelt-Konoye meeting would have been futile because previous Japanese communications had not fully met the American terms.

If this logic is less than inexorable, it is at least faithful to the line which Secretary Hull set for loyal historians to follow when he wrote his memoirs. But the Grew plea, which Hull omitted, specifically and persuasively answers it; that was its very purpose. Grew was convinced that Konoye, at a personal meeting with the American President, could go much farther than had been possible in formal communications. Professor Rauch, to parry the obvious retort that since war and peace hung in the balance, President Roosevelt should at least have tried to have a successful conference with the Japanese Premier, reaches into the blue and brings forth the startling excuse that Roosevelt would have been guilty of bad faith "had he then refused to sign an agreement with Konoye to implement United States cooperation with Japan in aggression."[30] Not even Roosevelt had thought of this one, much less Cordell Hull. But Professor Rauch apparently finds it comforting.

The latter author has been selected for mention here chiefly because he typifies a certain dwindling but still clamorous band of academicians and journalists. Having a penchant for facile categorization, which permits them to capture complex and even diverse ideas with a single word or slogan, they, in effect, divide all Americans of the 1938–45 years into two groups. In one group are all of those who believed that almost everything Franklin D. Roosevelt did in the conduct of foreign affairs was wise and honest; in the other are "isolationists." Naturally, these latter are dolts, intellectual pariahs, and they make up in malice what they lack in ignorance. There is no third group. There were thoughtful citizens in all walks of life who were skeptical of what President Roosevelt was up to and what it would lead to. Among them were men of broad backgrounds in international trade, diplomacy, and cultural intercourse, such as Herbert Hoover, Felix M. Morley, Hugh Gibson, and similar figures whose careers betokened the very antithesis of provincialism. No matter; they are all "isolationists."

It was, of course, Mr. Roosevelt who isolated himself when the Premier of Japan desperately sought a conference with him to try to work out a solution, other than war, to the Far Eastern imbroglio. It was he who had isolated Japan from oil, rubber, and a score of other materials vital to a modern nation's existence. It was Roosevelt who, by a flourish of his pen, had isolated the silk industry of Japan from its American market. The word has infinite applications. Its noun compound, "isolationist," is a shotgun word that hits fifty wrong marks for each right one. Its use as an epithet verges on the puerile.

"Facts," said Huxley, "do not cease to exist because they are ignored." That Franklin D. Roosevelt wanted war, invited war, and provoked war is no longer seriously disputable. The biographical remembrance of Jesse Jones, who sat in President Roosevelt's cabinet during that historic period, to the effect that Roosevelt was a "total politician" who was "eager to get into the fighting" to perpetuate himself in the Presidency[31] is surplusage to the mass of carefully documented evidence which has already been brought to light and which points unequivocally to that conclusion. There remain, of course, the hero-worshipers, but today, only those who are blinded to the facts by partisanship or sheer idolatry can fail to admit that the Stanford University historian, Thomas A. Bailey, said a true, if shocking, thing when he wrote, in *The Man in the Street,* that "Roosevelt repeatedly deceived the American people during the period before Pearl Harbor."[32]

Returning our thoughts to that summer of 1941, we find that on August 16, the Japanese Ambassador in Washington, Admiral Nomura, called on Secretary of State Hull. A maddening negativism on the part of Mr. Hull pervaded this meeting, at which Nomura again pleaded for negotiations which would get beyond platitudes. But by this time Nomura was able to read between the lines. That same day, he cabled his estimate of the political situation to his government in Tokyo:

I understand that the British believe that if they could only have a Japanese-American war started at the back door, there would be a good prospect of getting the United States to participate in the European war.[33]

This was not propaganda. Here was a Japanese diplomat reporting, in code, to his superiors. Was Admiral Nomura just seeing hobgoblins under the bed? Well, we know that when the war finally did start at the back door with the attack on Pearl Harbor, the Prime Minister of Great Britain was delighted. In fact,

Mr. Churchill confesses in his memoirs that he was full of "the greatest joy."[34] Two months later, he gloated in the House of Commons that the vast resources and power of the United States were now in the war on the side of Britain all the way and to the finish. Then, perhaps letting his ecstasy overwhelm his good taste, he paused to give his next words extra punch, and with a roguish glint of triumph in his eyes and a tremor of emotion in his voice, he confided to his enraptured audience:

This is what I have dreamed of, aimed at, and worked for, and now it has come to pass.[35]

It would seem that the hobgoblins Admiral Nomura saw under the bed had real flesh on their bones.

The cat slipped out of the British bag again three years later when Captain Oliver Lyttelton, production minister in Churchill's war cabinet, speaking on June 20, 1944, to the American Chamber of Commerce in London, asserted that "America provoked Japan to such an extent that the Japanese were forced to attack Pearl Harbor. It is a travesty on history ever to say that America was forced into war."[36] Obsessed as he was with the British point of view, Captain Lyttelton probably meant to pay his American listeners a compliment. He later apologized when he learned that he had blurted out a truth that was embarrassing on the other side of the Atlantic.

As for Franklin D. Roosevelt, the Pearl Harbor disaster on December 7, 1941, was a great fulfillment. His wife saw him shortly after he was informed of it. She tells us that he was more "serene" than he had been for a long time.[37] At the cabinet meeting that evening, Frances Perkins found that he had "a much calmer air." Naturally; he had accomplished his purpose. "His terrible moral problem had been resolved by the event," wrote Miss Perkins.[38] She spared her benefactor by choosing the word "moral." It was his political problem that had been resolved by the event. He no longer had to pretend. (Perhaps that is what she meant by his "moral problem.") Neither of these ladies say he was surprised, although at the time he let the public draw the impression that he was. In fact, Mrs. Roosevelt later let her guard down so far as to write: "We had expected something of the sort for a long time."[39] Actually, American intelligence had cracked the Japanese secret code[40] and many things were known, including almost the precise time when war would begin. Only the American people were surprised. They were led to believe that their lovable President, innocent as the dew, had been lolling about in his shirtsleeves, preparing to spend a nice homey Sunday working on his stamp collection, when the terrible shock came to him.[41]

At one time the stamp collector had expected the Japanese attack to come a little sooner. At a meeting with Hull, Knox, Stimson, General Marshall, and Admiral Stark in the White House at noon on Tuesday, November 25, he had predicted—secretly, of course—that the United States would be attacked, "perhaps as soon as next Monday [December 1]."[42] Later information had indicated that the blow would not come until the weekend of the seventh. One might have supposed—if one knew what Mr. Roosevelt apparently knew on that Tuesday, November 25—that if he were going to send a direct appeal to Emperor Hirohito in a dramatic effort to stave off war, he would have sent it immediately on that day. But he did not. He waited until 9 P.M. on December 6, which would assure its arrival, Tokyo time, much too late to have any effect. The message reached the hands of the Emperor twenty minutes before the bombs fell on Pearl Harbor.[43] It was sent only "for the record," as Hull later remarked.[44]

It would also be good "for the record" for Mr. Roosevelt to be found blithely working on his stamp collection on Sunday, December 7. The people would naturally assume that the President and Commander-in-Chief of the armed forces would have been occupied doing something more useful to the country if he had known that war was imminent. So the show of idle composure bolstered the myth. Actually, to the President, the day was to be memorable not for any progress in philately on his part but as the happy ending to his devious machinations to maneuver the Japanese into firing the first shot.

This disaster was the coming event which cast its shadow when Lord Halifax walked up the steps of the White House on that last day of July, the same steps which the jubilant Generals Golikoff and Respin had descended a little earlier. The American people were only vaguely conscious that Japan was the back door to war. But President Roosevelt was not. Nor were the British. They were sure of it.

Lord Halifax had his duties, as had the gentle, eloquent Lord Lothian before him. The blueprint for British propaganda in the United States in this war had been prepared with thoroughness and cold deliberation. "In the next war, as in the last, the result will probably depend upon the way in which the United States acts, and her attitude will reflect the reaction of her public to propaganda properly applied." This bit of practical realism was in Sidney Rogerson's well-thumbed book, *Propaganda and the Next War,* which had been published in London in 1938 and which bore an Introduction by Captain Liddell Hart.[45] Both of these writers were men of high repute in British diplomatic and military circles. "Propaganda properly applied." They were candid. "Applied" on—or to—whom? Obviously, the American people, whose susceptibility to English blandishments was not an unknown quantity, having been tested before.[46] Sidney Rogerson had not belittled the task of getting the United States into the coming war, for too many Americans still remembered bitterly the last great crusade which had sent them to Europe "to make the world safe for democracy." But he had seen new avenues of approach. Thus: "The position will naturally be considerably eased if Japan were involved and this might and probably would bring America in without further ado." The choice of words is revealing. The involvement of Japan—meaning a clash with Japan—would not be a calamity to be avoided; on the contrary, it would "ease" the situation.

Those gossipy but occasionally perspicacious columnists Drew Pearson and Robert S. Allen had hinted, as far back as April 24, 1940, in their "Washington Merry-Go-Round," that if the United States entered World War II, it would be through "the back door of the Pacific." This was not taken seriously, for most people took it for granted that a President who professed so vehemently to "hate war" could at least manage to keep the country out of war with Japan.

The intentions of President Roosevelt, of course, were otherwise. By the time Lord Halifax visited him on July 31, the course of events was mapped out. Mr. Roosevelt knew as well as Admiral Stark did "what a Jap would do." He was in the process of doing those things on his own part which would make "a Jap" do the things the Navy had told him "a Jap" would do under the circumstances, namely, go on a rampage and start a general war.

So the United States was to be at war, not only with Japan, but all over the world. But for what? Americans were to be asked to give their lives on four continents and on all the oceans of the globe. To what end?

Every war must be holy. Its stated objectives must not be prosaic, especially if its origins are at all questionable. They must be lofty, poetic, idealistic. A novice in mass psychology would know this, and surely a master such as Franklin D. Roosevelt did. He was one to put first things first, as he used to like to say. This was his next immediate job, when August came. The war had to be made holy.

Chapter VII

DEMAGOGUERY WITH A
GROTON ACCENT

To MAKE THE WAR HOLY—or even to give it some consistent moral character—was not easy, particularly with Communist Russia in it as an ally. It would take what Kipling called the nerve of a brass monkey to talk about democracy *versus* totalitarianism or about fighting the anti-Christ. We were to be linked in this great endeavor with a semi-Asiatic despotism which had already shown an incorrigible bent toward international piracy, an utter contempt for human freedom, and an ideology of which atheism was a natural end product.

This did not abash Franklin D. Roosevelt. The nerve of a brass monkey was exactly what he did have. He knew that we live in a propaganda age. In our time, public opinion is largely a response to propaganda stimuli exerted on a vast scale by the new techniques and instruments of the twentieth century. Nature had bestowed upon him some rare gifts, including a magnetic personal charm and a mellifluous voice, and he had assiduously cultivated the subtlest, if not necessarily the noblest, arts of politics. If any man could make red seem white, he was surely the one to do it. Thanks to the fortune of birth, he could give demagoguery a Groton accent.

In the second week of July, 1941, Wendell Willkie lunched with President Roosevelt at the White House. Willkie was a renegade Democrat who had, in 1940, ingratiated himself into the Republican nomination for President and, after being defeated, had leaped onto the Roosevelt bandwagon with the agility of a sophomore doing a broad jump. He had not yet invented his fatuous slogan, "One World," which was to help seduce the Western peoples off on a calamitous false premise, but he had cozied up to the President and put himself in position for some spectacular globe-trotting and world-wide publicity. He came out of the White House all smiles.

Two days before, the President had revealed to Congress that American naval forces had occupied Iceland. The ebullient Willkie now told reporters that he even favored American bases in Ireland and Scotland. A newspaperman reminded him that pollsters had found the people of the United States overwhelmingly opposed to war. Willkie smiled and said that "leadership" would win out in the end.[1]

He had just lunched tête-à-tête with the man who was going to do the leading. He did not reveal what was said over the lamb chops. But one story about this long conference reached the press as Willkie was leaving. According to Willkie, Roosevelt told him that friends had advised him to retain the foremost psychiatrists in the United States "to work out ways of correcting and influencing public opinion." Willkie grinned. "Mr. President," said he, "have you heard of the first meeting of your fifth cousin, Theodore Roosevelt, and Albert Lasker, the advertising man?" The President had not. Willkie told how Lasker traveled to Oyster Bay, how Teddy, all smiles, teeth, and outstretched arms, burst in to greet him, crying out, "Mr. Lasker, I've been told that you have the master advertising mind in the country." Said Lasker hastily, "It would be presumptuous for anyone to claim that in your presence." "And so," said Willkie to his luncheon host, "I think it would be presumptuous for any psychiatrist to tell you how to influence public opinion." Willkie could call it "leadership." (Rather maladroitly, he smiled as he said it.) It had different names in different parts of the world. Whatever it was, it was to be laid on thick, with a heavy trowel.

The objectives of the international Communist movement, under the aegis of Soviet Russia, were as obvious as the sun at noon. As early as 1936, the American Ambassador in Moscow had cabled to Washington: "We should not cherish for a moment the illusion that it is possible to establish really friendly relations with the Soviet Government, or with any Communist party or Communist individual."[2] This cable was not made public by the State Department until May, 1952, sixteen years later. However, the caveat should have been redundant to anyone who had ever troubled to read Karl Marx's manifesto. The virus was endemic in Communism; its fetid breath was its own ill omen to the world. There was no room for illusion. So it is that the American apologists and court historians of the 1950's, bent on whitewashing the Roosevelt record, were in so many cases either the fools or the faithless of the 1930's and 1940's.

As General Douglas MacArthur has reminded us, "Long before even the second World War, the Soviet was known to plan suppression of the concept of freedom and the advance of Communism throughout the world, as rapidly as conditions would permit."[3] In the summer of 1941, the United States, egged on by Franklin D. Roosevelt, was about to mold those conditions to the Soviet plan. An historic apostasy in the camp of Western Christendom, even more startling than Hitler's pact with Stalin in 1939, was about to take place. Bolshevism, now stricken, was to be put under an American oxygen tent and saved; then it was to be launched on conquest and its enemies disarmed. The next generation was to wrestle with the consequences.

Lord Lloyd, in his *The British Case*,[4] which was published in

1940 under an American imprint with a Foreword and official blessing by none other than Lord Halifax, had said the German-Soviet pact was "Hitler's final apostasy. It was the betrayal of Europe." He also had said that "Russian agents and Russian money were busy all over Europe." Sir Victor Sassoon, the British banker and a man of wide knowledge of the world, had confided to newspapermen upon arriving in New York that "Russia would be found to be the real enemy of Great Britain before long" and that the elimination of Hitler would leave that problem unsolved.[5]

Now in the summer of 1941, Hitler had bowed out and Franklin D. Roosevelt was bowing in as the collaborator with Stalin. However, the people were not to see the historical import of what was taking place. President Roosevelt would divert their attention by talking only about Hitler and Mussolini and their sins, and Tojo would be cast as the only bad man of Asia. "Practical politics," Henry Adams had said, "consists in ignoring facts."

Even before there was the added embarrassment of a Communistic ally, the war faction in the United States found that it had a difficult product to sell. The people were not sure what the war was all about. Hitler and his Nazis were generally despised for their chauvinistic antics, their arrogance and cruelty, but cool heads could admit the possibility that the international mayhem committed at Versailles had left Germany with some just grievances. The British themselves were not amateurs at the power game. Did an empire which sprawled over six continents have a right, and particularly a moral right, to denounce aggression? The British and the French, for all their obeisances to international morality, were perhaps just as cutthroat as the Germans. The only difference was one of timing; wars and pillage had satisfied their ambitions earlier. Both of them had grabbed more territories in the first World War and were exploiting them with a finesse developed in three centuries of imperialism. What had America to gain by getting into the power struggle?

Americans were in a mood to take wars with a grain of salt. In April, 1937, exactly twenty years after the United States had plunged into a war "to make the world safe for democracy," 71 per cent of those polled by the Gallup Institute believed that America's entry into World War I had been a mistake. Were they going to dash forth again in the trappings of angels and run the risk of having their children laugh at them as dupes some twenty years later? The mirages of one generation are dispersed by the revisionism of the next. Perhaps this war would spawn more problems than it would solve. Perhaps, ironically, it would beget still another war to undo the consequences of this one.

Such sentiments were not pro-Hitler. They were heard from the most divergent sources, from the National Association of Manufacturers to Norman Thomas, the perennial Socialist candidate, and such respected publicists and scholars as Harry Elmer Barnes, Stuart Chase, Quincy Howe, Oswald Garrison Villard, Sidney Hertzberg, and C. Hartley Grattan, who were as anti-Fascist as they were anti-Communist. Former brain truster and columnist Hugh Johnson said bluntly what many were thinking: "I despise Hitler and I like England but in any international war situation I wouldn't trust our fate to either of them as far as I could throw a bull by the tail."[6]

Men such as these naturally shunned any sympathy with the self-styled *Amerikadeutscher Volksbund,* which avowed its devotion to Hitler. The *Bund* members were poison to their own cause. Their inept, loutish organization was repulsive to almost all Americans of German descent, who disowned it. It did *der Führer* more harm than good. More effective for the German cause was that high priest of American anti-Semitism, the Reverend Charles E. Coughlin. His racist overtones were obnoxious to the great majority of people, but his barbs at the Allies often touched a sensitive point. At times history seemed to be irrefutably on his side, in spite of the obfuscation and imagery with which he embroidered his tirades on the radio and in his weekly magazine, *Social Justice*. Father Coughlin preached that the "advance of Red Communism into Christian Europe is even a worse threat to civilization than was the rise of Hitler." He was an early prophet—if an unwelcome one—when he wrote in *Social Justice* on October 23, 1939: "No one condones the persecutions of Hitler, nor his pact with Stalin, but when Hitlerism has been destroyed, Communism will possess Germany—Communism at the very doors of Paris and London." The passing of Hitler, he said, would not bring tranquility to Europe, and he warned his listeners against being deluded by the politicians into believing that it would. Naturally, the Rooseveltians hated him, and the feeling was mutual.

The United States was a maelstrom of conflicting propagandas.[7] Protagonists of the German cause were, however, doomed to a chilly response in the long run. The Roosevelt administration put every possible legal obstacle in their path and threw the full weight of its own propaganda facilities against them. Moreover, Adolf Hitler was too unpalatable a morsel to appeal to the American taste. As for Mussolini, only too easily could he be caricatured as a comic-opera buffoon, and the basic dilemma of overpopulated Italy slurred over. If the public was confused about the real causes of Europe's malaise, which erupted in such violent symptoms, it was also somewhat apathetic about determining them.

As for the British and the French, they sent a virtual expeditionary force to the United States, the promised land. This mobile corps invaded the drawing rooms, the lecture halls, the women's clubs, the colleges, the industrial plants, the fashion shows, even the bars. (Lucius Beebe complained in the *New*

York Herald Tribune that he could no longer "jerk a quick one" without hearing some "British Sir Somebody Something" declaiming on "what you Americans should understand.") One battalion of the invaders was erudite, another was glamorous. In Hollywood, the Anglo-French forces scored some of their most effective advances, with such shock troops as Ronald Colman, Sir Cedric Hardwicke, Lawrence Olivier, Vivien Leigh, Charles Laughton, and Basil Rathbone in the front line. Filmland hummed with pro-Allied activity. Charles Boyer was thought to be away in the French army when, early in the war, he suddenly arrived back in New York on his greater mission. Eve Curie was also sent over. She made charming talks about springtime in Paris, delicately interspersed with world politics. Léon Blum's brother, René, was on hand with a dossier on Americana and a Gallic ingenuity in probing for soft spots in the armor of American neutrality. With Alfred Duff Cooper came his wife, Lady Diana Manners, who had played the Virgin in *The Miracle* and who informed reporters that her trip to America was "my war work."[8]

This phalanx had only a limited success. Too many Americans were still unimpressed with the holiness of the Allied cause. One could not just slough off all the facts. After all, the population of Danzig *was* 99 per cent German;[9] the checkered area of central and southern Europe *was* "an economic nightmare," as Hitler called it; the French, English, Dutch and Belgians *did* have rich colonies, while Germany had none; the rise of Hitler and Mussolini *was,* in a sense, a reaction to chaos and despair and Marxist violence in Germany and Italy. These and a score of other incontrovertibles kept popping up in spite of the barrage of invective. They made the issues seem much less simple than they were described in the winsome pleadings of a Lady Diana Manners or in the ingratiating rhetoric of the British Ambassador. The majority of the American people had, it is true, a preference for an Allied victory, but the majority also wanted the United States to stay out of the war. Every poll confirmed that.

When the German *Wehrmacht* wheeled into Russia late in June of 1941 and it became clear that the defeat of Hitler would be but one face of a two-sided coin, the victory of Stalin being on the other side, the holiness of the war was even less apparent. However, the radical labor movement, whipped up by the Communists in their ranks, made a sudden flip-flop and abandoned their anti-war stand overnight. With the mother of Bolshevism at bay, the war became, for them, a crusade. From top to bottom, the Roosevelt administration became feverish with the desire to help Russia. In other circles, there was more skepticism than ever.

Herbert Hoover, sensing what President Roosevelt and Harry Hopkins were up to and foreseeing what the consequences would be, warned against "a gargantuan jest" at the expense of America. "Joining in a war alongside Stalin to impose freedom is a travesty," he said.[10] Hiram Johnson thundered in the Senate: "I will not subscribe to the doctrine that you must be a Stalinite to be an American. . . . Good God! Did we ever sink so low before as to choose one cutthroat out of two? This man was Hitler's ally. . . . Now we furnish him with weapons which may be turned upon us."[11] Charles A. Lindbergh's voice, resonating from the deep wells of courage and sincerity of this grave, studious man, foretold what lay at the end of the Roosevelt path: a Europe half enslaved and barbarized, an Asia corroded by hatred, an America bled and drained of its resources for at least a decade, perhaps two.

Well, what *did* lie ahead, at the end of President Roosevelt's path? What would Europe and the world look like? What potion was he really brewing in his bubbling cauldron? Mr. Roosevelt had not said. By the end of July, 1941, it was high time that he did say. He knew that. The country had one foot in the morass of war already, chiefly as a result of his policies. Skepticism was rife. Even England, which had declared war on Germany in September, 1939, ostensibly because the territory of Poland had been violated, had not stated its war aims with any clarity. Now that the Soviet Union, which had recently had a field day ravaging half of Poland as an accomplice of Hitler, was being welcomed into the Allied camp, no one knew what would happen to Poland after an Allied victory, much less to the rest of eastern Europe or Germany.

A powerful blast at the Roosevelt policy of getting this country involved in such a war had just been prepared for public release over the signatures of the following: Felix M. Morley, a former League of Nations functionary and a recent editor of the *Washington Post*, then president of Haverford College; Frank O. Lowden, patriarchal former governor of Illinois; Herbert Hoover; Robert M. Hutchins, precocious president of the University of Chicago; Joshua R. Clark, former Ambassador to Mexico and a powerful Mormon; Ray Lyman Wilbur, president of Stanford University and former Secretary of the Interior; Alf M. Landon; Hanford MacNider, former Minister to Canada; Henry P. Fletcher, former Ambassador to Italy; former Vice-President and World War I General Charles G. Dawes; the Pennsylvania Quaker figure, Joseph H. Scattergood; old-time opera star Geraldine Farrar; and writers Irvin S. Cobb and Clarence Buddington Kelland. The statement said: "The American people should insistently demand that Congress put a stop to step-by-step projection of the United States into undeclared war. . . . Exceeding its expressed purpose, the Lend-Lease bill has been followed by naval action, by military occupation of bases outside the Western Hemisphere, by promise of unauthorized aid to Russia and by other belligerent moves. . . . We have gone as far as is consistent either with law, with sentiment or with security. . . . It [the war] is not purely a world conflict between tyranny and freedom. The Anglo-Russian alliance has dissipated that illusion. . . . Insofar as this is a war of power politics, the American people want no part in it. . . . Few people honestly believe that the Axis is now, or will in the future, be in a position to threaten the independence of any part of this Hemisphere if our defenses are properly prepared. Freedom in America does not depend on the outcome of struggles for material power between other nations."[12]

It was not enough to sneer at such a protestation or to brush it off as politically inspired. Was not President Roosevelt himself at least as politically minded as any of these distinguished individuals could be charged with being? Was their patriotism any more impeachable than his? More was needed by way of answer. Mr. Roosevelt was astute enough to perceive that.

In reality, the gloomy prognostications of Hoover, Lindbergh, and the other critics of Roosevelt's war obsession were, both at the time they were uttered and later as reviewed retrospectively, unanswerable logically. They merely expressed what any objective analyst of the international facts of life would have had to concede. But could propaganda so becloud the obvious that the masses of the people would actually believe that Soviet Russia would be fighting shoulder to shoulder with America for freedom everywhere (or even anywhere)?

Franklin D. Roosevelt quite evidently thought this possible. It required a tour de force in the manipulation of mass psychology, which daunted him not at all. People "are governed more by feeling and sentiment than by reasoned consideration," Adolf Hitler had written in *Mein Kampf*. It is difficult not to perceive that Franklin D. Roosevelt also believed this and acted upon it. The habitual political techniques of both of these men were based on the premise that man is basically irrational. Each of them was a sensational political phenomenon in his own country, Hitler with his revival of the *Führer* legend and Roosevelt with his four terms. Each drew upon war, preparation for war, and the propaganda of war for motive power to propel himself onward and upward in his spectacular political career.

Rarely does a nation go to war without illusions. The people of the United States had not yet been given their set of illusions. This preliminary could be postponed no longer. Some beautiful war aims, innocent as the magician's fluffy white rabbit, had to be pulled out of the Presidential hat.

Chapter VIII

FISH AND CHURCHILL

On Sunday, the third day of August, 1941, a sleek 165-foot yacht slipped from its berth at the submarine base at New London, Connecticut, and headed, in the sunset afterglow, for Long Island Sound. It steamed down the Thames River, over the course of the annual Yale-Harvard rowing race, and out beyond the Race Rock lighthouse. Then it vanished into the Atlantic. Aboard was the President of the United States, ostensibly off on a fishing trip. It was to be probably the most bizarre fishing trip any angler ever took.

President Roosevelt had left Washington that afternoon in jaunty mood and with what was described as "the same old optimistic cast in his eye." Always alert to advertise himself as a lover of peace, he had taken the occasion of his departure to remark that he still hoped the United States "would not have to get in a shooting war." (Mr. Roosevelt made a habit of lapsing into a colloquial jargon, which even the twelve-year-old mentalities among the electorate could grasp, whenever he wished to strike a popular attitude upon a big issue.) A week or ten days on the *Potomac,* out on salt water, would be fine, and, as far as he could see, it was a good time to take a vacation.[1]

The country had been prepared for this the day before when

Stephen Early, the White House press secretary, had announced that the President was going to take a week's vacation in New England waters. Mr. Early's chief purpose, it seemed, was to indicate that Mr. Roosevelt desired a rest and did not wish to be bothered by publicity or routine government business. "From the time the President boards the *Potomac* until the time he returns to shore," Mr. Early said, "the movements of the ship will be a confidential naval operation and it is particularly requested that the press, radio and other media of dissemination of information so consider the movements of the *Potomac*." No newspapermen were to be permitted to accompany the party, although in the past the press had customarily covered Presidential voyages from an escort ship. Mr. Early said the President had no plans to land, even at his mother's summer home at Campobello, New Brunswick. Accompanying him would be his military aide, General ("Pa") Watson, his naval aide, Captain Beardall, and the White House physician, Admiral McIntire. Captain Beardall had been requested to send the Navy a daily dispatch, which would be released to the press. All of this, of course, was just enough to give the whole expedition a tinge of mystery.

Secretary of the Navy Frank Knox was a straight-faced accomplice. "I can assure you that it is a purely rest or vacation trip," he told reporters at his press conference, "and I ask the newspapers not to display any enterprise in attempting to follow him or speculate on his whereabouts." As though a President could not have a rest on his own yacht in New England coastal waters without enshrouding his voyage in semisecrecy, Mr. Knox added: "The man has been carrying a tremendous burden and we should let him have a week or ten days of complete rest. I am asking the press to treat the President as it would any officer of any ship." This appeal did not quite ring true, if, indeed, it was intended to. Why this uncustomary coyness? It could not be a question of safety, for surely there was no imaginable need for the President to expose himself to personal danger. There were plenty of perfectly safe places to go, in or out of the country, whether he wanted to rest, to work, or to hold a conference.

Mr. Roosevelt boarded the *Potomac* a few minutes before she sailed on Sunday. He was piped aboard as the Presidential flag was run up the mast. Sailors in summer whites stood at salute at the gangway. The President made no statement. Not even the crew knew where they were going. The correspondent of the *New York Times* wrote: "It was no more than the start of a vacation for a man who has ... longed for some sea air."

Naturally, the buzzing started soon. On Monday, the British Press Association announced that Harry Hopkins had returned to London "yesterday" from Moscow after his dramatic flight to talk to Stalin. On Tuesday, Clement Attlee, Lord Privy Seal, told the House of Commons that Prime Minister Churchill "would not find it convenient" to attend an important debate on the progress of the war. Hints were allowed to pass through British censorship that Roosevelt and Churchill had met or were to meet somewhere. In Washington, the Navy Department released a dispatch from the *Potomac*: "After a night of restful sleep the President is continuing his cruise in northern waters to an undisclosed destination. He is attired in a sport shirt and slacks and is enjoying the sea air from the fantail. . . . The President spent some time discussing affairs with the Commander-in-Chief of the Atlantic Fleet. . . . All on board well." This was a teaser. Apparently, Admiral Ernest J. King, the Atlantic fleet's commander, "had popped up from nowhere," as the magazine *Newsweek* described this development.

Meanwhile, in England, Harry Hopkins, the President's alter ego, had disappeared. London sleuths looking for him were told: "You'll find Hopkins where Churchill is." By Wednesday it was known in London that the rotund Prime Minister and the American roving wraith had left "together" for a secret destination.

White House Press Secretary Stephen Early refused to squelch the rumors of a Roosevelt-Churchill meeting. He merely said he knew nothing about it. Cordell Hull, the Secretary of State, also avoided a categorical denial, but he did say that the President had made no mention of such a meeting when he talked with him on the telephone the previous Saturday night (the night before Mr. Roosevelt's departure).

On Wednesday, the Navy released a laconic message from the *Potomac* which said that the sailors were "responding to New England air after Washington summer." It did not mention the President. Some observers viewed this omission as indicating that Mr. Roosevelt might have transferred to another ship which would speed him to a secret rendezvous. The Canadian Prime Minister was questioned, but he provided no solution to the mystery.

Washington reporters were making bets on whether Roosevelt and Churchill had met, were meeting, or would meet. The feverish inquiries of Domei's correspondent, Masuo Kato, revealed Japan's curiosity, while the German D.N.B.'s reporter, Kurt Sell, offered even money that if such a meeting were held, it would be on shore rather than at sea. (He would have come within a few hundred yards of untroubled waters in a sheltered bay of winning his bet.)

On Thursday, the Navy divulged another chatty radio report from the *Potomac*. "All members of party showing effects of sunning. Fishing luck good. . . . President being kept in close touch international situation by Navy radio." The report did not say that Mr. Roosevelt was on board or that he was not on board.

Meanwhile, the *New York Herald Tribune's* Washington bureau had been playing Sherlock Holmes. The information it ferreted out showed that "something was cooking." General George C. Marshall, Army Chief of Staff, was missing, ostensibly on a routine inspection trip to an undisclosed destination which even Chairman Robert R. Reynolds of the Senate Military Affairs Committee could not learn. Admiral Harold R. Stark, Chief of Naval Operations, was presumably on leave, but where he was, nobody seemed to know. Major General H. H. ("Hap") Arnold, Chief of the Army Air Forces, had gone "somewhere" on official business and even his wife was wondering where. On top of all this, Under Secretary of State Sumner Welles suddenly disappeared for "a short rest," and Major General James H. Burns, Hopkins' assistant in the Lend-Lease Administration, vanished without leaving a word about his whereabouts. Secretary of the Navy Frank Knox made his exodus from the capital during the week, but by Friday he had been located at York Harbor, Maine. It was now taken for granted that a momentous conference between two chiefs of state, Roosevelt and Churchill, was in progress. Washington now calmed down to await the results.

The President had, in fact, transshipped to the cruiser *Augusta* on Monday night. Elliott Roosevelt tells us in *As He Saw It* that his father "enjoyed himself thoroughly, giving the press the slip, much as a twelve-year-old boy playing cops-and-robbers will enjoy shaking a playmate who is trying to shadow him." According to Elliott, this jocular conversation occurred when he and Franklin, Jr., joined their father on the *Augusta*:

"You look wonderful, Pop. But how come all this? You on a fishing trip?"

Father roared with laughter. "That's what the newspapers think. They think I'm fishing somewhere off the Bay of Fundy." He was as delighted as a kid, boasting of how he had thrown the newspapermen off the scent by going as far as Augusta, Maine, on the presidential yacht *Potomac*. Then he told us what it was all about.

"I'm meeting Churchill here. He's due in tomorrow on the *Prince of Wales*. Harry Hopkins is with him." And he leaned back to watch the effect of his announcement on us. I guess it was big. I wasn't near any mirrors, but he enjoyed it.

Elliott takes for granted "Father's" preoccupation at the moment with "the effect of his announcement on us." To the senior Roosevelt, the "effect" of a statement or of an event, in the sense of its emotional impact, was always one of the most important things about it.

As for fishing, "Father" did fish once. It was on Thursday, in Placentia Bay, from the deck of a battle cruiser. "He caught a What-is-it, unidentifiable by anyone on board," writes Elliott. " 'Have it sent to the Smithsonian,' Father suggested, and tried no more fishing during the whole trip."

On the other side of the Atlantic, Winston Churchill left Scapa Flow on Monday, August 3, on the battleship *Prince of Wales*. His most valuable fellow-passenger was Harry Hopkins, who had been assigned the Admiral's cabin. It is generally conceded that Harry Hopkins played a large part in the genesis of the Atlantic Conference, and he was certainly the intermediary between Roosevelt and Churchill in making the preparatory arrangements. Churchill's chronicler, H. V. Morton, writes that Hopkins pressed the idea on the Prime Minister one afternoon "towards the end of July" while the two were walking in a little garden behind No. 10 Downing Street. "When Mr. Churchill reentered No. 10 he had decided to cross the Atlantic."[2] Early the following morning, President Roosevelt was called to the telephone in the White House to receive a trans-Atlantic call. It was Winston Churchill, proposing the meeting, and the President "agreed."

Of course such a meeting was in Mr. Roosevelt's plans before Hopkins had left Washington for England, as Robert E. Sherwood's account makes clear.[3] Hull states that Roosevelt had cherished the idea for some time,[4] but Sherwood does not divulge what Hopkins told the Prime Minister in order to sell the idea to him, particularly on the point of why a theatrical spectacle involving the Atlantic fleets and air forces of both nations was to be chosen as the setting for what could be more soberly accomplished at a simple meeting in Washington or Ottawa. Sherwood writes: "Most of Hopkins' conversations with Churchill on the forthcoming Atlantic Conference . . . were conducted in private and Hopkins kept no record of them."[5] But Hopkins left notes of innumerable conversations which were "conducted in private." Many of these were far less important than these talks with Churchill, which fashioned the conference at which the aims of the war were to be laid down. Yet, says Sherwood, Hopkins kept no record of them. He did, however, record in his notes that he played backgammon with the Prime Minister aboard the *Prince of Wales* and he took the trouble to describe Churchill's type of game, all of which Sherwood quotes for posterity. Sherwood states, ex cathedra, that these two backgammon players also "discussed the phraseology of the Atlantic Charter," but he goes into no details and discloses no entries in Hopkins' notes on the subject—if he made any. Here is one of those strange gaps that abound in the erratic Hopkins' "notes" as we are permitted to glimpse them piecemeal at the sufferance of his friendly biographer. The latter's historical task, it should be said in fairness, was probably not made easier by Harry Hopkins' neurotic harping upon his own intimacy with the great personages into whose company a whimsical fate had thrown him, but it is sometimes difficult to decide where Hopkins' erraticism ends and Sherwood's deft editing begins.

In his memoirs, Winston Churchill sidesteps any responsibility for the staginess of his nautical rendezvous with Roosevelt. With exquisite casualness, he writes that Harry Hopkins told him the President wished very much to have a meeting with him "in some lonely bay or other" and that he accepted.[6]

On Saturday, August 9, the *Prince of Wales* and its escort, all camouflaged, joined the American armada assembled in Placentia Bay as planes circled overhead. The battleship *Arkansas,* the cruisers *Augusta* and *Tuscaloosa,* and a flotilla of destroyers, still in peacetime gray, with gleaming brass and pine-white woodwork, rode at anchor, placed somewhat like chessmen not yet brought forward into play. Franklin D. Roosevelt, wearing a Palm Beach suit, stood under an awning that had been erected upon the forward gun turret of the *Augusta.* That day, the Atlantic Conference began.

When Secretary of State Cordell Hull, wearing his most lamblike expression, had put off inquisitive reporters by telling them that the President had not mentioned any meeting with Prime Minister Churchill when he, Hull, talked with Mr. Roosevelt on the telephone the night before Roosevelt's departure, he had perhaps spoken with literal veracity but certainly without candor. He knew about the meeting.

However, Mr. Hull had not been invited along. Under Secretary Sumner Welles, a man more consistently pliable under the Roosevelt touch, had been. In his memoirs, Hull reveals that Welles had written to him on July 28 at White Sulphur Springs, where Hull was resting (he was to be back at his desk in Washington on Monday, August 4), telling him that the conference with Churchill had been arranged for August 8, 9, and 10. In this letter Welles reported that "he intended to urge the President, if he expected to discuss more than purely military problems, to take someone with him who could keep a precise record of the conversations and of the agreements that might be reached."[7]

This was indeed a strange communication, and it accentuates

the strained relationship that existed between these two officials. Welles knew perfectly well that Roosevelt expected to discuss "more than purely military problems," for he had himself been alerted to prepare for that; there was no "if" about it. In fact, he went to the conference with a working draft of the Charter in his brief case.[8] As for his intending "to urge" the President "to take someone with him who could keep a precise record of the conversations and of the agreements that might be reached," it is difficult to credit the sincerity of this ostensible naïveté on Welles' part. One would suppose that but for Welles' solicitude, Mr. Roosevelt was going to swim out into the Atlantic Ocean to talk to Winston Churchill alone on a raft. A competent shorthand reporter would have sufficed to "keep a precise record," if that were anything to worry about. Actually, both men were to be accompanied by large entourages, and the Under Secretary must have known of these arrangements, for, as he later disclosed, he had rather detailed preparatory conversations with the President in Washington.[9] His letter to Mr. Hull appears to have been phrased to play down the importance of the impending meeting, to assuage the man who, as Secretary of State, would certainly have been a logical functionary to participate in drawing up the aims of the war but who was being left behind.

Franklin D. Roosevelt hardly needed Sumner Welles to urge him to take "someone" with him. He had a natural proclivity for showmanship. Nor did he need to be told by a Louis B. Mayer or a Cecil B. De Mille that there are three essential elements of any successful theatrical production: a good dramatic story, a colorful setting, and an impressive cast. With a war raging in the world and with all the facilities of the Army and the Navy at his disposal for use as props, his fecund imagination had had no difficulty contriving the story and the setting. As for an all-star cast, that was his at the snap of his fingers. Generals, admirals, and lords, striped-trousered diplomats and slouchhatted back-room favorites—all big names, exuding glamour and mystery—were only too happy to participate in the epic drama of the hour and could be summoned from either side of the Atlantic by a telephone call.

With the Prime Minister came his inscrutable chum and confidant, Lord Cherwell, who had until recently been plain Professor Lindemann and who is tersely described by Morton (who was also on board) as "a tall, unsmiling man"; General Sir John Dill, Chief of the British Army's Imperial General Staff; Admiral of the Fleet Sir Alfred Pound, the First Sea Lord; Sir Wilfrid Freeman, Vice Chief of the Air Staff; Sir Alexander Cadogan, Permanent Under-Secretary of State for Foreign Affairs; and their assistants, secretaries, and flunkies. England's much-cartooned newspaper publisher, Lord Beaverbrook, Minister of Supply in Churchill's cabinet, followed by air.

Even more ostentatious was the company President Roosevelt chose to surround him at the conference. Included were General George C. Marshall, Chief of Staff of the Army; Admiral Harold R. Stark, Chief of Naval Operations; Admiral Ernest J. King, commander of the Atlantic fleet; General H. H. ("Hap") Arnold, Chief of the Army Air Forces; Admiral Richmond K. Turner of the Navy's War Plans Division and Colonel Charles W. Bundy of the Army's War Plans Section; Harry Hopkins, officially the Lend-Lease Administrator, actually the President's right-hand man in all things, just back from a cabal in the Kremlin; Hopkins' Lend-Lease assistant, Major General James H. Burns; Lend-Lease "Co-ordinator" W. Averell Harriman, generally considered a traveling handy man of the President and Hopkins; Under Secretary of State Sumner Welles; General Edwin M. ("Pa") Watson, the President's military aide, and Captain John R. Beardall, his naval aide. In addition, two of the President's sons were brought into this momentous gathering.

Mr. Roosevelt had four sons. Two had put on uniforms. The

youngest, Franklin, Jr., in his early twenties, had become an ensign in the Navy. Elliott, a few years older, had been commissioned a captain in the Army. John and James were civilians. The President chose Franklin, Jr., and Elliott and had them detached from their service assignments and brought to his side at the Atlantic Conference, where they figured prominently in the photographs and movie reels taken for public display. This widely advertised the fact that two of the Roosevelt sons were in uniform.

When the battleship *Prince of Wales* hove to in Placentia Bay on Saturday morning, Harry Hopkins was at once transferred to the *Augusta*. At eleven o'clock, Prime Minister Churchill, wearing a dark blue Trinity House uniform with a visored cap, followed in an Admiralty launch. With naval ceremony and to the strains of *God Save the King* and *The Star-Spangled Banner,* he was received aboard the President's cruiser. He handed a letter to Mr. Roosevelt and said, "I have the honor, Mr. President, to hand you a letter from His Majesty the King," as the cameras clicked.

The scene was pictorially impeccable. The President, his shoulders thrown back, his head slightly cocked on one side, was handsome, impressive, and photogenic—as usual. Franklin, Jr., and Elliott had been placed in the immediate foreground. Even the veriest dolt would now see that if the world was going to be saved in its great crisis, it was the Roosevelt family that was rolling up its sleeves to save it.

Mr. Churchill stayed on the *Augusta* to have lunch privately with Mr. Roosevelt and Harry Hopkins. Elliott Roosevelt tells us that when he joined them at the end of the meal, he found the Prime Minister "draining his glass" and talking about the United States' declaring war on Germany "straightaway." We gather from Elliott's report that his father did not say to Mr. Churchill that he still hoped the United States "would not have to get into a shooting war," which was the cheerful tidings he had left with the press when he boarded the *Potomac* the previous Sunday. On the contrary, he was ruefully explaining to his guest that the temper of the American people was not yet ready. The President was thinking, blurts out Elliott, of "American politics."[10]

It would appear that this luncheon meeting on the first day of the conference provided a revelation of the basic motivations of the principals. Yet Robert E. Sherwood's account does not even mention it. Sherwood skips to the formal dinner (dinner jackets and black ties) given by the President that evening. The Americans present, he states, were Roosevelt, Welles, Stark, Marshall, King, Arnold, Hopkins, and Harriman; on the British side were Churchill, Cadogan, Pound, Dill, Freeman, and Cherwell. Perhaps it was a distaste for the inappropriate that forced Sherwood to omit two names from this list: Franklin, Jr., and Elliott. They were present, too, but the deletion is understandable, particularly since he was going on to state that "during dinner, Roosevelt, Churchill, Hopkins, Welles and Cadogan got down to business,"[11] which business, it then appears, was nothing more modest than a charter to project the future of most of the world.

Elliott, however, is not similarly deterred in his book. He gloats over his presence at the historic banquet. But from *his* ribald, eyewitness account, we gather that the "business" consisted chiefly of Churchillian eloquence on the subject of what the United States must give and do in the war. "Winston Churchill held every one of us, that night—and was conscious every second of the time that he *was* holding us." There was a reservation in "Father's" mind, however, when the Prime Minister pleaded, as Elliott puts it, "that the lion's share of Lend-Lease should go to the British lion." "Father" was thinking of Russia.[12]

The next morning was Sunday. The President, the entire

American delegation, and several hundred sailors and marines attended Divine Service on the quarterdeck of the *Prince of Wales*. They sang and prayed in unison with the British ship's company. The pulpit was draped with the American and British flags. Fifteen hundred British seamen craned their necks to see the bounteous Mr. Roosevelt, who had, the previous afternoon, sent each of them a cardboard carton containing an orange, two apples, two hundred cigarettes, and a half-pound of cheese. (Mr. Roosevelt had chosen to take personal credit for this gift, supplied by the American Navy, by having inserted in each box a card with the words: "The President of the United States sends his compliments and best wishes.")[13]

So poignant was the ceremony that Churchill's writer, Morton, recorded that it was almost intolerable in its emotionalism. There was a prayer for the President, a prayer for the King and his ministers and generals and admirals, and, lest the supplication be too personalized, a prayer for the victory of Right and Truth. *Onward Christian Soldiers* was one of the hymns chosen for the occasion. As its martial beats rolled out over the water, even the huge fourteen-inch guns of the battleship seemed beatified, and one could easily forget that some of the Allies in the great impending crusade were renegade Christian soldiers at best, with little godliness to commend them.

The propagandistic potentialities of this *mise en scène* were, of course, a politician's delight. From the standpoint of anyone bent upon wooing the American people toward greater belligerency, they were reason enough for the whole expedition. In preparation, Elliott Roosevelt had sent a Grumman plane to Lake Gander and back, a trip of almost three hundred miles, to bring Air Force photographers with both still and motion-picture film and equipment. The Navy, with its battleships, cruisers, and destroyers on the spot and its submarine base nearby, naturally had its own amplitude of such facilities, but economy

Harry Hopkins clasps the hand of Maxim Litvinov, Soviet Ambassador to the United States, after telling a Russian War Relief Rally in Madison Square Garden, New York, on June 22, 1941, that President Roosevelt sent word that the United States would aid the Soviet forces on the battlefield and that the Russian front would not fail. (At this time the United States was officially not at war.) At the left is Mayor Fiorello La Guardia of New York City. *World Wide Photos*

President Roosevelt and Prime Minister Churchill seated for church services on the forward deck of H.M.S. *Prince of Wales* at the Atlantic Conference in August, 1941. Standing behind them at the right are Admiral E. J. King, Commander of the U.S. Atlantic Fleet, and General George C. Marshall, Chief of Staff of the U.S. Army. At the extreme left are two sons of the President, Franklin D., Jr., and Elliott. In the background (center) is Sumner Welles, U.S. Under Secretary of State.

United Press International

On his way both to and from his first meeting with Stalin at Teheran, Roosevelt stopped at Cairo to confer with Generalissimo Chiang Kai-Shek of China. At Cairo Roosevelt put pressure on Chiang to take the Chinese Communists into his government and reneged on the long-promised ANAKIM operation to strengthen Chiang's Nationalist forces in China.   *World Wide Photos*

This picture shows President Roosevelt in a moment of ebullience as he poses with Joseph Stalin, the Russian dictator, and Winston Churchill, the Prime Minister of Great Britain, on the portico of the Russian Embassy in Teheran, while attending the Teheran Conference in November, 1943.

Standing (left) directly behind Stalin is V. M. Molotov, Russian Foreign Minister. Anthony Eden, British Foreign Minister, is seen standing between Roosevelt and Churchill.   *United Press International*

Stalin at Teheran.   *World Wide Photos*

Just back from the Teheran Conference, where, by agreements as yet undisclosed, a partition of Poland giving the Soviet Union 48% of the land of prewar Poland had been sanctioned and the balance of power in postwar Europe adjusted in favor of the Soviet Union, President Roosevelt is welcomed in the White House on December 17, 1943, by Rep. Joseph W. Martin of Massachusetts, Minority Leader of the House. Between them in the background is Rep. Sol Bloom of New York.   *World Wide Photos*

At the conference table at Yalta, in February, 1945. Alger Hiss is seen in the background, between President Roosevelt and Secretary of State Stettinius. He is showing something to Harry Hopkins (bending down), who is seated directly behind the President. *United Press International*

At the end of the road to Russia, a pensive Roosevelt sits flanked by Stalin and Churchill. The occasion is the final dinner of the Yalta Conference. (It was given by Churchill at Vorontsov Villa. Also present were Secretary of State Stettinius (left), Foreign Ministers Eden and Molotov (right), and three interpreters. At this dinner, Roosevelt made an important concession to Stalin on the reparations issue, over Churchill's dissent.)
World Wide Photos

could hardly be expected in exploiting this opportunity. As a promotional medium, pictures could be almost as effectual as the lofty words soon to be unloosed to the world from the unique backdrop of this trumped-up naval concentration in a bay on the coast of Newfoundland. So there was more business on hand than just praying. This, Franklin D. Roosevelt's moment of piety before going forth, like St. George to slay the dragon, had to be seen in movie theaters throughout the land, from Maine to California.

After these rapturous rites of Sunday morning on the deck of a battleship, of which a vast number of pictures were taken, Mr. Roosevelt was treated to a delectation of a more worldly kind—a gastronomic one—of which no pictures were taken. The grouse-shooting season had opened in England on August 1, and Mr. Churchill had arranged for sufficient birds to be put on the *Prince of Wales* for a luncheon party, with an extra brace for the President. This was the delight served in the wardroom to the two leaders and their staff chiefs after the Divine Service.[14] The spirit at once yielded to the flesh.

General "Hap" Arnold pronounces that "it was a good lunch."[15] The General had evidently been disporting with the British long enough to catch their habit of understatement. Yet he was sufficiently impressed to record that it started with caviar and vodka, followed by turtle soup, then grouse and champagne, tapering off faultlessly with port, coffee, and brandy. As the smoke of Churchill's long, savory cigars, passed round the table, pervaded the wardroom, it was a genial company of well-fed, well-oiled men, most of them decorated and beribboned, who sat sipping well into the afternoon, talking about the wars to be fought.

"Hap" Arnold's epicureanism, a capacity not normally cultivated by the army fare of the professional soldier, had been considerably refined during his recent peregrinations in the higher echelons of brass and might. On his visit to England that spring, the red carpet had been rolled out for him. From the many gracious references in his memoirs—such as "we had a delightful lunch at the Savoy" and "we had an interesting dinner at 'The Beaver's' [Lord Beaverbrook's] house in the country"—we gather that his "Global Mission" was not always a harrowing experience. The gates of Buckingham Palace had been opened to him. ("Then I entered a room, and there was the King.") He had also been invited for a week end with the Churchills at Dytchley Castle, where life in wartime was so far from grim that a dinner coat was still *de rigueur*. Here a guard of honor saluted his departure, in the limousine of Air Marshal Sir Charles Portal, after a luxurious visit devoted at least partly to the elaboration of Mr. Churchill's ideas of "proper propaganda" to change the thinking of the American people and bring the United States into the war.[16]

So the caviar-and-grouse feast in the wardroom of the *Prince of Wales* was not "Hap's" first experience as a gourmet, and there is no reason to believe that the vodka, the champagne, the port, and the brandy rendered him any less able to enjoy the dinner Sir John Dill gave that night "for some of us" in the Admiral's cabin. By this time he seems to have recovered from the shock of the British requests made the previous day. ("There was one item that stunned me: the British were asking for 6,000 more heavy bombers than we were then producing.") Between the luncheon and the dinner, there was, on the *Augusta,* a round-table discussion, which included Marshall, Arnold, Dill, and Freeman, on the favorite subject of expanding and accelerating the American war effort.[17] Dill and Freeman could hardly have chosen a more propitious moment to find their American military opposites in a mellow and obliging mood. By Monday, Sir Wilfrid was so pleased with "Hap" that he confided to him: "When Portal comes over, I am going to insist that he see just two people; one is the President of the United States, and the other is you."[18] (The British knew, of course, that it was Harry Hopkins who really held the key to the treasure, but as far as air-force matériel was concerned, it was important to them that General Arnold be an eager expediter, an efficient conduit.)

Elliott Roosevelt was also invited to the Prime Minister's voluptuous Sunday grouse-and-champagne luncheon. Only one incident does he record: "And there was the moment when someone rapped for quiet and cried out: 'Gentlemen, the King!' and there was a great scraping back of chairs and shuffling of feet and a moment of silence while the glasses were lifted up and then the wine sipped."

That night, and the next, too, the Prime Minister dined with the President on the *Augusta*. To these intimate meetings the brass and the braid were not invited. But Harry Hopkins was included. So were the two Roosevelt boys.[19]

On Monday morning, Churchill came over from his battleship at eleven o'clock for a two-hour conference with the President. The purpose of this meeting was twofold: to beat into shape the final draft of the joint declaration (the Atlantic Charter) and to prepare a stiff note to Japan. The State Department and the Foreign Office were represented, appropriately enough, by, respectively, Under Secretary of State Sumner Welles and Sir Alexander Cadogan, Britain's Permanent Under-Secretary of State for Foreign Affairs.[20]

One might have thought that this quartet—Roosevelt, Churchill, Welles, and Cadogan—could proceed to chart the future policy of the world (if indeed they judged themselves qualified to tackle such a project at all) as well, if not better, without the assistance of Harry Hopkins. Surely there was nothing in the background of this man that would prepare him for this role, which would seem at the least to require a developed juridical sense and a profound knowledge of history. Hopkins' recent tête-à-tête with the Russian tyrant in the Kremlin was hardly a substitute for these prerequisites. Indeed, the mantle of a sage could only look ludicrous on his shoulders. Yet President Roosevelt had him at this meeting, as he had him at most important meetings.

Harry Hopkins understood the kinetics of politics. Let such as Sumner Welles fret about punctilio; let him excite himself over the absence of a qualifying phrase in a document. If the exigencies of the moment demanded a charter, with Harry Hopkins present no nice concern over precision of meaning could long delay it. Words for the purpose would be put together and agreed upon without much ado and with little exertion required from Mr. Roosevelt. A wag in Washington had once remarked that Sumner Welles glanced in a mirror every three hours "to be sure the halo was still there." But virtue was never likely to get out of hand with Harry Hopkins in the room, which is probably one reason why he was so constantly at his master's elbow.

By the time the British sailed for home on Tuesday, "Winston" and "Franklin" had achieved a well-buttered camaraderie. This was to be expected, since both came to the conference with the same objective in mind, i.e., to hasten the entry of the United States into outright war. The Atlantic Charter was to glorify the war in the eyes of the American people. Roosevelt's eagerness to do this overrode all other considerations.

One would have supposed that in any game with the Prime Minister, the President held all the trump cards at that time, but to a surprising extent, the reverse was true. Thus on Monday, Mr. Churchill reported in a telegram to his cabinet, addressed to the Lord Privy Seal: "For the sake of speedy agreement I have little doubt he [the President] will accept our amendments." Referring to one of these amendments, he said: "He will not like this very much, but he attaches so much importance to the Joint Declaration, which he believes will affect the whole movement of United States opinion, that I think he will agree." He did agree. Churchill, it appears, was rightly confident that he had the President in his pocket, but there was the haunting doubt of whether the President yet had the American people in *his* pocket. So when the Briton asked in his telegram that the War Cabinet be summoned that night to approve what he was doing, he cautioned that "it would be most imprudent on our part to raise unnecessary difficulties" and added that he feared the President would be "very much upset" if no joint statement could be issued, and "grave and vital interests might be affected."

Implicit in this message is a recommendation that his colleagues not take too seriously all of the content of the strange declaration which he was asking them to approve. We know that they did not. As Sherwood puts it, the officials of the British government never regarded the Atlantic Charter as much more than "a publicity handout."[21]

Certain objections which Sumner Welles had raised, at the Monday-morning session, to the flabby wording favored by Mr. Churchill (on the crucial subject of the availability of the resources of the world to all peoples) died a quick death in the afternoon. Harry Hopkins had contributed the opinion that it was inconceivable that the issuance of the joint declaration could be held up "by a matter of this kind." Welles had thought President Roosevelt stood with him on the principle involved, but the President capitulated, as Mr. Churchill had known he would. Welles later wrote: "I can only surmise that afterwards Harry Hopkins persuaded him that the questions at issue would not be of sufficient importance to warrant any delay." Time was of the essence, Roosevelt told Welles. Why quibble now about the discriminatory trade practices of Great Britain and her dominions?

Churchill and Cadogan had, on Saturday evening, presented the first draft, some parts of which, according to Welles, "meant precisely nothing." Welles prepared an alternative draft which

Roosevelt edited early Monday morning. By eleven o'clock, Welles had the third draft ready for the four-man meeting in the President's quarters. The next day, the conference ended and the Prime Minister went home.

Thus was born what Churchill's accompanying chronicler, Morton, called "a new charter for Humanity." Harry Hopkins acted as a sort of midwife. The period of gestation, be it noted, was not long. However, as Morton professed to see it, it was "a splendid charter, but one that, after all, was drawn up long ago upon a mountain side in Galilee." Such plagiarism, if it be that, might perhaps explain the briskness of the literary composition that took place on the cruiser *Augusta,* although the image Morton contrives, of two master politicians dashing out to sea on warships to rephrase the Sermon on the Mount, is a bit disconcerting. The haste with which "a new charter for Humanity" was brought forth comes to mind when one reads what was said of it by the English magazine *Twientieth Century* in its next issue: "Even as a piece of rhetoric, the Anglo-American Declaration will simply not do." (As events proved, it was as a piece of rhetoric, and as that only, that the Charter did do.) This was the final text:

Joint Declaration by the President and the Prime Minister

August 12, 1941

The President of the United States of America and the Prime Minister, Mr. Churchill, representing His Majesty's Government in the United Kingdom, being met together, deem it right to make known certain common principles in the national policies of their respective countries on which they base their hopes for a better future for the world.

First, their countries seek no aggrandizement, territorial or other.

Second, they desire to see no territorial changes that do not accord with the freely expressed wishes of the peoples concerned.

Third, they respect the right of all peoples to choose the form of government under which they will live; and they wish to see sovereign rights and self-government restored to those who have been forcibly deprived of them.

Fourth, they will endeavor, with due respect for their existing obligations, to further the enjoyment by all States, great or small, victor or vanquished, of access, on equal terms, to the trade and to the raw materials of the world which are needed for their economic prosperity.

Fifth, they desire to bring about the fullest collaboration between all nations in the economic field, with the object of securing, for all, improved labor standards, economic advancement, and social security.

Sixth, after the final destruction of the Nazi tyranny, they hope to see established a peace which will afford to all nations the means of dwelling in safety within their own boundaries, and which will afford assurance that all the men in all the lands may live out their lives in freedom from fear and want.

Seventh, such a peace should enable all men to traverse the high seas and oceans without hindrance.

Eighth, they believe that all the nations of the world, for realistic as well as spiritual reasons, must come to the abandonment of the use of force. Since no future peace can be maintained if land, sea, or air armaments continue to be employed by nations which threaten, or may threaten, aggression outside of their frontiers, they believe, pending the establishment of a wider and permanent system of general security, that the disarmament of such nations is essential. They will likewise aid and encourage all other practicable measures which will lighten for peace-loving peoples the crushing burden of armaments.

The "new charter for Humanity" did bear one resemblance to Divine Writ. There were no mortal signatures affixed, no sealing wax.

Mr. Churchill also took advantage of the occasion to see to it that Roosevelt shook his fist at the Japanese again. It was now known that the imposition of economic sanctions on July 26 had put Japan in an intolerable predicament. As we have seen, this was no surprise to Roosevelt, who had been warned by the Navy that the embargo meant war.[22] Nor could Sumner Welles, with the accumulated information of the State Department at his disposal, have harbored any illusion. He could not have been unfamiliar, for example, with the Hornbeck Memorandum of January 3, 1935, in which the Chief of the Division of Far Eastern Affairs stated what must have been almost axiomatic in diplomatic circles: "It is obvious that Japan either must have access to enlarged markets for her goods and must further develop an industrialized economy or must starve. The inherent virility and vitality of the Japanese people preclude any expectation that they will passively accept the latter alternative." As for Mr. Churchill, surely no one needed to expostulate with an Englishman on the problems of Japan's insularity, and he was geographer enough to know that there was in Japan, which has meager natural resources, a population of eighty million occupying an area one-twentieth the size of Australia, which had a population of only seven million. So it is somewhat surprising to read in the Churchill memoirs: "It had not perhaps been realized by any of us how powerful they [the sanctions] were."[23] Be that as it may, it was agreed that a truculent American note would be dispatched to the Japanese. Their dilemma was to be pressed upon them. Churchill telegraphed his cabinet: "He [Roosevelt] has agreed to end his communication with a severe warning, *which I drafted*."[24] (It is no wonder, then, that when the attack on Pearl Harbor came, the exultant Mr. Churchill blurted out to the House of Commons: "This is the object that I have dreamed of, aimed at *and worked for*; and now it has come to pass!")[25]

The *Prince of Wales* weighed anchor at 5:00 P.M. on Tuesday. In a pleasing little farewell ceremony, the President and the Prime Minister exchanged "autographed photographs," Morton tells us. A cordial message had been sent to the Russian dictator just before the final parting.

Back on the *Prince of Wales,* Churchill again telegraphed his government. "They"—the pronoun hangs in the air—"are sending us immediately 150,000 more rifles, and I look for improved allocations of heavy bombers and tanks. I hope they will take over the whole ferry service and deliver both in England and in

West Africa by American pilots, many of whom may stay for war-training purposes with us."[26] He hoped that his colleagues would feel that his mission had been "fruitful." From the King came a message of congratulation. Nine days before, Franklin D. Roosevelt had started out on what he had called a fishing trip, but it was Winston Churchill who made the big catch.

Lord Beaverbrook, the Minister of Supply, who had flown over at the Prime Minister's invitation, was now sent on by air, in the company of W. Averell Harriman, to Washington, where a local wit was quoted in *Time* as saying, perhaps with more perspicacity than graciousness, "Beaverbrook came over to see if the British had left anything."[27]

There was one point on which Roosevelt took full charge. That was the form of the Charter and the timing and manner of its release to the world. He insisted that it not be inscribed on parchment and signed and sealed as a treaty. That would have required him to submit it to the Senate for ratification, and, as Sherwood frankly states, "he was taking no chances on that."[28] It was merely to be mimeographed and released.

"Nevertheless," writes Sherwood, "its effect was cosmic and historic." Sumner Welles has written that "it was precisely as valid in its binding effect as if it had been signed and sealed,"[29] thereby introducing a new concept into the law of international compacts which might be designated, for want of any other passport, as the Welles Doctrine and which has, at least, the merit of clothing with legality, even if by sheer fiat, an ostensible agreement which the masses of the world were allowed to think was solemnly consecrated. A "Joint Declaration" presupposes a meeting of minds, i.e., an agreement or compact. As for Franklin D. Roosevelt, whether or not he considered his agreement with the Prime Minister "valid in its binding effect" in a technical, legal sense, there is no doubt that he intended the effect of its release to the world to be "cosmic and historic." It was to strike the American scene like a bolt of lightning.

He had arranged that it be released in London and Washington on Thursday, August 14, while he would still be at sea. When the conference ended, Welles was sent on to Washington with the President's instructions. Just as Welles was leaving the harbor, he received this message, which Roosevelt, with his usual finesse in such matters, had ordered Admiral Stark to send him:

> U.S.S. Augusta
> Ship Harbor, Newfoundland
> August 12, 1941

. . . .

> The President said he would like no release of the names of those who accompanied the President until Saturday on which day you may release it.
> His reasons are that he wants the press release to stand out "like a sore thumb," with nothing to detract from it or to cause any other discussion; then when it has had time to be thoroughly digested, just of itself, to go ahead and give out the names of the rest of the party—on Saturday.
>
> H. R. Stark[30]

The "sore thumb" technique was spectacularly successful. On Saturday, when the yacht *Potomac,* with the President again on board, came around the breakwater and dropped anchor at Rockland, Maine, the country was still agog, and fifty newsmen, radiomen, cameramen, and technicians were waiting for the great performer. Broadcasters babbled into microphones. He was home from the mysteries of the Atlantic, from hostile seas, from a conference that had no parallel. The mellifluous phrases of the Charter had already cast their spell. It was an extraordinary Rooseveltian coup, more dramatic than the cross-country flight in 1932 to address the Chicago convention which first nominated him for the Presidency.

In the wardroom of the *Potomac,* the President received the White House press corps. He sat calm and relaxed, with Harry Hopkins nearby. To the newsmen, who had been through thirteen days of irritating suspense, he talked informally, smoothly, and soothingly but was sufficiently evasive to allow an intriguing air of grandiose mystery to hover. He said that Anglo-American understanding was now complete as regarded developments on every continent of the world and that he and the Prime Minister had outlined a course of action for any eventuality that might develop anywhere. Some newsmen nodded knowingly at this. Manifestly, anyone who wanted war could easily read into this equivocacy a portent of imminent participation. But to the question "Do you think we are any closer to entry into the war?" the President replied cryptically that he would not say so.

Whereupon Mr. Roosevelt went to Washington by train. His first moves were to confer with Secretary of State Cordell Hull and to summon Congressional leaders to the White House for a first-hand report of the conference. But there was nothing to deliberate about. The whole affair, including the Charter of the Atlantic, was a *fait accompli.*

In Great Britain, the *London Daily Sketch* refused to believe that the Prime Minister and the President had conferred only to produce "a piece of oratory." To Britons in general, the Churchill-Roosevelt conference was worth the effort and expense only if it brought the United States deeper into the war. They were disappointed that Roosevelt had not openly committed his country to declare war, but they hoped that his understanding with Churchill was like an iceberg, the largest part of which remains invisible.

As for the Charter, that was thought to be mainly for American consumption. Its eight points were met with widespread indifference in England and Canada, where the more outspoken newspapers and magazines brushed it off with such phrases as "stale magniloquence," "a rhetorical manifesto," and "unrealistic." One London newspaper (the *Daily Express*) growled that the English people were more interested in war aims than peace aims (a fact which, unfortunately for the future, was only too true). Furthermore, English statesmen had been attending international conferences for a long time, much longer than the Americans. There was much less inclination to whoop things up over mere words. The *London Times* did manage, dutifully, to rejoice that "the world now knows beyond doubt what we are fighting for," but the *Canadian Forum,* in its next issue, ridiculed "the gushing efforts" of editors and columnists who took that tack. "None of them," it said, "professes to discuss the actual content of the eight points—and for the obvious reason that there is nothing much in them to discuss.... About the only conclusion we can reach is that Mr. Churchill must be a better sailor than President Roosevelt. He has notoriously been opposed throughout to committing his government to any war aims except the defeat of Hitler. He now concedes to the president a few pious generalities, including two of the president's 'four freedoms,' and in return he no doubt goes home with some very specific promises of American assistance."

A piece of oratory or not, the Atlantic Charter no doubt deserves a place among the memorabilia of British history. It may be trotted out by historians of the future to illustrate the fatuity, or the perfidy, of Anglo-American statesmanship in the Second World War, which is perhaps an ignoble destiny, considering its flamboyant origin. In 1941, however, its consequences were real, if devious. Viscount Samuel did bother to discuss the eight points in the *Contemporary Review* and to argue that some were meaningless and others were silly, yet he said that the Charter would always be "outstanding in the history of these times." Winston Churchill gives us the key to this paradox. He writes in his memoirs that "the profound and far-reaching importance of this Joint Declaration was apparent." But it is also apparent from his treatment of the subject in his memoirs that in his mind, the importance did not lie in any probability that the eight points would be honored at the end of the war. These had been cast off long before Mr. Churchill wrote his memoirs. It lay first, of course, in the efficacy of the proclaimed principles as soothing sirup for a gullible American public and, secondly, in the fact that President Roosevelt's very words, pronounced in the Charter, were a *casus belli*. The German government could take them in no other way. Churchill writes:

The fact alone of the United States, still technically neutral, joining with a belligerent Power in making such a declaration was *astonishing*.[31]

Mr. Churchill knew the restraints put upon neutrals by international law, and he had read the American Constitution, which gives to the Congress alone the power to declare war. So it was natural that he should consider Roosevelt's conduct "astonishing," pleasing though it was to the British and the Russians. He prided himself on having induced Roosevelt practically to declare war. "The inclusion in it," he goes on to say, "of a reference to 'the final destruction of the Nazi tyranny' (this was based on a phrase appearing in my original draft) amounted to a challenge which in ordinary times would have implied warlike action." A challenge to whom? To the existing government of Germany. A challenge to the death. (It "implied warlike action" this time, too. In September, Roosevelt announced orders to the Navy in the Atlantic to "shoot on sight," and in October, in his Navy Day speech, he said, "The shooting has started.")

The message was also plain to the heads of the Soviet government. The tyranny which President Roosevelt was going to see destroyed was the Nazi one, not their own. It was important to them to know this.

Whatever Churchill's private feelings may have been, he played the game to the end. On the Sunday evening after his return to England, at the hour when the greatest number of the American people were sitting quietly at home, he made a broadcast. It was beamed to the United States and had been widely advertised in advance. Never was his voice more sonorous, his cadences more exquisitely executed, his judging of American susceptibilities more astute. The meeting with President Roosevelt, he said, was "symbolic." It symbolized "the deep underlying unities of the English-speaking people throughout the world." This was fraternal, as befitted the occasion, but it was not grand enough for Mr. Churchill. Sure of his mastery, he rose to a higher plane. It symbolized, he intoned, "something even more majestic, namely the marshalling of *the good forces of the world against the evil forces.*"[32]

Coming from another man, such sanctimony might have evoked either disgust or laughter, but Mr. Churchill brought tears to many eyes. In the spell of his oratory, the element of self-exaltation was overlooked, and forgotten were the British Empire's long record of conquests and subjugations, her invention of the concentration camp during the Boer War, the scrapping of the Fourteen Points after Germany surrendered in World War I, the grabbing of vast territories in Africa in 1919, and other skeletons which were moldering in His Majesty's royal closet and which had contributed to the international reputation of "perfidious Albion." Also forgotten was the moral record of Britain's new ally to the east, the semi-Asiatic despotism which had only the year before been expelled from the League of Nations for aggression, at which time Mr. Churchill himself had made the historic remark that "Communism rots the soul of a nation." Not in the least abashed by any of this, Mr. Churchill put the present war up to his American listeners as a simple clash between the "good forces of the world" and the "evil forces."

Then came the shining promise. He announced that the English-speaking nations were going to lead "the broad toiling
masses in all the continents" out of "their miseries" and to "the
broad high-road of freedom and justice." If the Americans
needed a cause to fight for, what more could they want than this?
For good measure, he added this sweetener: "This is the highest
honor and the most glorious opportunity which could ever have
come to any branch of the human race!"

Surely Hitler had nothing to do with the miseries of most of
the "broad toiling masses" on the continents of the world. And
did these unfortunates include the beaten-down subjects of
Stalin, Molotov, *et al,* which notorious gentlemen now presumably came within Mr. Churchill's category of "the good forces"?
Had Mr. Churchill asked these new allies of his what their postwar plans for Europe and Asia were? On none of this was he
specific, or even articulate.

The flaws were fairly safe from detection. The Prime Minister's appeal was emotional rather than analytical, and his art was
irresistible to most Americans. Months of incessant propaganda
had predisposed them to acceptance of this type of approach.
Actually, the speech was an eclipse of fact, a sheer tour de force
of distortion, as events were inexorably to prove. But Mr.
Churchill had the sagacity to turn to religion on this Sunday eve
and, at the same time, to shroud with silence the doctrinaire
atheism of his Communist allies. He described the hymns sung
on the deck of the battleship *Prince of Wales,* good old Christian hymns familiar to his audience.

We sang "Onward Christian Soldiers," and indeed, I felt that this
was no vain presumption but that we had a right to feel that we were
serving a cause for the sake of which *a trumpet has sounded on high.*

The war had indeed been made holy.

By coincidence, Mr. Churchill's archenemy, Adolf Hitler, also had a habit of using the word "masses" with the redundant adjective "broad" preceding it. "If you want the sympathy of the broad masses," he had written in *Mein Kampf,* "then you must tell them the crudest and most stupid things." One of the few virtues found alongside the roster of Hitler's vices was the frankness to lay bare his methods for all to see and to copy if they wished. In this instance, Machiavelli had given the same counsel some four hundred years before. It had been put into practice by many illustrious figures in modern European history, who, however, unlike Machiavelli and Hitler, possessed a reticence, or delicacy, which would never have permitted such self-revelation.

If in August of 1941 one had set out consciously to compose a crude and stupid thing to say about the war then raging in Europe, one could not have done better than to say that the triumph of the Soviet military hordes, which was one of the objectives and the inevitable effect of the Allied coalition, would spread freedom and justice to the peoples who would lie in their path. It could only be more preposterous to suggest that *Onward Christian Soldiers* be the theme song.

The cynicism of Adolf Hitler should not have shocked too greatly the inhabitants of Mr. Churchill's island homeland. The Scotch novelist Henry Mackenzie had long ago given them this thought to ponder:

Mankind, in the gross, is a gaping monster, that loves to be deceived, and has seldom been disappointed.

The American people had recently heard Hitler's warmed-up version of this old aphorism quoted up and down the land to prove that Hitler was a scoundrel. Most of them were blissfully unaware that the potion he prescribed was an old recipe and that presidents and prime ministers could mix it as well as a *Führer* and often had.

Incredible as it may seem, even the House of Commons, which one would assume to have some sophistication, was to hear from the lips of Winston Churchill on February 27, 1945, and to accept docilely, this amazing statement:

I know of no Government which stands to its obligations even in its own despite more solidly than the Russian Soviet Government.[88]

Of this, the noted English naval historian Captain Russell Grenfell has said: "This must surely rank as one of the most serious political misjudgments in history."[34]

Perhaps Grenfell underrated the Prime Minister's judgment by overrating his candor. Churchill could not possibly have been speaking from conviction; for a quarter of a century he had been saying the contrary. Peremptorily, he silenced debate: "I decline absolutely to embark here on a discussion about Russian good faith." By then, Stalin had long since repudiated the Atlantic Charter pledge to seek no territorial aggrandizement, had gobbled up with the ruthlessness of a Ghengis Khan the three Baltic States of Estonia, Latvia, and Lithuania, was in the process of seizing parts of Poland, Rumania, Czechoslovakia, and Germany as permanent annexations to Russia, and had conspired, for a secret price, to violate his neutrality treaty with Japan, as Mr. Churchill, just back from Yalta, knew. The record of the Soviet government from the early days of Bolshevism had been one of chicanery, perfidy, and default because these were openly prescribed tactics of Leninism and Stalinism in the grand strategy for the Communist world revolution. The more recent moves of the Red dictatorship had demonstrated beyond cavil that it would not be deterred in its imperialistic ambitions by any moral commitments.

We can only believe that Churchill made his statement to

Commons as a gesture to which he felt committed, a sort of diplomatic obeisance which Yalta compelled. We do know that at this stage of his life he moved about, as he later wrote, "with an aching heart and a mind oppressed by forebodings."[35] Nine years later, Sir Winston, still at his euphonies as his eightieth birthday approached, was found at Blackpool, England, telling a political meeting that if the United States were to withdraw its troops and armaments from Europe, that "would condemn all Europe to Russian communist subjugation and our famous and beloved island to death and ruin."[36]

Actually, from the moment of Hitler's flaming death and the triumph everywhere of "the good forces" over the "evil forces," Europe had never been out of that mortal peril. Churchill had made his own *volte-face* publicly as far back as March 5, 1946, when in his famous Fulton speech he dolefully intoned:

> From Stettin in the Baltic to Trieste in the Adriatic, an iron curtain had descended across the continent. . . . Police governments are prevailing in nearly every case. . . . Communist parties or fifth columns constitute a growing challenge and peril to Christian civilization.*

Winston Churchill's tongue-in-cheek blurb to the House of Commons in 1945 after Yalta ("Their word is their bond," he even brought himself to say of the Kremlin masters) is one of those assertions, sometimes resorted to in desperate polemics, which in many minds defy contradiction by their very enormity. They stun the intellect by sheer audacity, and opposition freezes. It has been said that politics is the science of exigencies. In fairness to Churchill, it should be recalled that in those days he had always, in his public utterances, to take into account the wishes of Franklin D. Roosevelt, who, says Captain Grenfell, was "in

* Speech at Westminster College, Fulton, Missouri. Roosevelt was dead; Truman was now President.

a state of infatuated hallucination regarding the virgin purity of Marshal Stalin's motives." The role Churchill deigned to play was often an unenviable one.

More pleasant to perform, perhaps, though no less grotesque, was his task on that Sunday evening back in August, 1941, when, by radio, he assumed command of the forces of God on earth against Satan and graciously offered to share his generalship with the President of the United States.

Chapter IX

THE EIGHT POINTS

"SPEECH IS A FACULTY given to man to conceal his thoughts." In our day the semanticists have taken this witticism of Talleyrand and turned it into a cult. It started with the psychologists, but at the altar of Korzybski an assortment of educators, sociologists and even economists now worship, often with mixed motives. They have invented a special jargon and publish a quarterly magazine to keep the faithful up to date. Many thoughts about language which were banal to Aristotle and Cicero are now dressed up in the new esoteric vocabulary and exploited as recently discovered profundities. Then, by eschewing all objective definition and subjectivising the meaning of words as the tools of language, they propagate a kind of linguistic nihilism which, in its theoretical conclusions, would almost eradicate speech as a means of communication of ideas.

The semanticists could no doubt prove, by their methods, that such a document as the Atlantic Charter means nothing, or could mean anything. It contains words such as "aggrandizement," "freely," "right," "access," and "threaten," which, they would say, have no determinate meaning at all but are like rubber, stretchable at will. However, the moral responsibility of illustrious men, such as presidents and prime ministers, who take it upon themselves to make pronouncements and pledges to the public, cannot be dissolved by showing that they used rubber words. Obviously, they had a purpose in speaking, not to themselves, but to the public. The question we must ask ourselves is: What did they expect most of the people who would hear their message to think it meant? Or what is the minimum meaning which attaches to the words in common parlance? The words of such men beget belief and generate action. They know that. The onus of any latent ambiguity is upon them. The criteria of interpretation must be looked for in the prevailing modes of thought of the receptive public.

It appears from the eyewitness account of Sumner Welles that no little time was spent at the Atlantic Conference trying to say things in a way which would seem, on the surface, to convey a certain meaning but which would not really have that meaning. The problem was complicated by a desire to have phrases mean different things in different parts of the world. Thus Roosevelt and Welles wanted the impression to emerge, at least in the United States, that there was to be a general abandonment by all, including the British Empire, of monopolies of raw materials and trade discriminations, while Churchill, with his eye on public opinion in England and the Commonwealth, was adamant to exempt imperial preference without making the exemption so explicit that the American people would detect it.

Roosevelt wished the American people, and others, too, to feel assured that the populations to be liberated would include not only Germany's victims but all subjugated peoples everywhere, while Churchill, on the other hand, nurtured in his own mind a much narrower interpretation which it was inexpedient to spell out in the Charter but which he subsequently reported to the House of Commons. According to Elliott Roosevelt's account, the two men not only chose to give the words they adopted these two meanings respectively, but they were also quite aware of the divergence and yet allowed the fiction of complete mutual agreement to prevail. The Australian historian Chester Wilmot, in his monumental history of the war, *The Struggle for Europe,* has examined this point with care and has concluded that Elliott Roosevelt's report in this instance is accurate.[1] So we have here a curious variation on the theme of having one's cake and eating it, too.

Any man possessed of a fair wit and a facility with words can develop the art of the *double-entendre.* From Aristophanes through Shakespeare, Molière, Oscar Wilde, and Noel Coward, to the gag writers of radio and television, it has been, in varying degrees of polish, an indispensable tool of comedy. But to achieve mastery of the hidden *double-entendre* was reserved for great statesmen and diplomats. The team of Roosevelt, Welles, Churchill, Cadogan, and Hopkins, with their five heads together, was not unequal to the task. This more subtle form of wordplay is not of the stuff of comedy, however. It usually occurs in the more tragic plots.

We proceed to examine the eight points of the Charter. But first, there arises the question: Were Churchill and Roosevelt, when they brewed this potion of words, purporting to speak for their respective countries or only for themselves? In the one case they would be placing their countries' honor on the table. In the other, nothing would be committed but their own personal reputations.

Churchill's first draft of the Charter was hazy.[2] There was a one-sentence Preamble, which began: "The President of the United States and the Prime Minister, Mr. Churchill, representing His Majesty's Government. . . ." Plainly, they were present in their official capacities. The sentence went on to say that these two men ". . . deem it right to make known certain principles which they both accept for guidance in the framing of their policy and on which they base their hopes for a better future for the world." The "they" refers to the President and the Prime Minister. "Their policy" is not necessarily national policy in their democratic countries. Churchill's language was cautious.

Roosevelt changed this. The Preamble finally adopted read thus: "The President of the United States of America and the Prime Minister, Mr. Churchill, representing His Majesty's Government in the United Kingdom, being met together, *deem it right to make known certain common principles in the national policies of their respective countries* [italics added] on which they base their hopes for a better future for the world." This left no doubt. The two men were not voicing personal feelings. They were, they said, enunciating the national policies of their respective countries.

The United States of America was one of the few nations of the world which had not long since exhausted its moral credit. It had refused to ratify the Treaty of Versailles because that malignant document had violated principle and pledge; it had disassociated itself from stubborn refusal of the French and the English ever to honor the general disarmament clause of that treaty; it was not a party to the incredibly stupid policy of hatred, repression, and vindictiveness which had, in the twenties and early thirties, flaunted a cold ring of bayonets all around a disarmed Germany, stifled her trade, trampled upon her sovereignty, and humiliated her proud people, made a fiasco of the disarmament conference in Geneva in 1932, and, by the inexorable law of action and reaction, helped to assure the advent of a Hitler. Woodrow Wilson's celebrated Fourteen Points had been scrapped as soon as the Germans had laid down their arms at the end of World War I, but the United States had renounced this perfidy of the victorious nations. Furthermore, the United States, as the Poles, the Czechs, the Lithuanians, and others well knew, was, of all the great powers, the most sincere champion of the right of self-determination. So it was a shining reputation for honorable conduct, his country's esteem in the eyes of friends and foes, which Franklin D. Roosevelt was willing to throw into this new jeopardy.

The importance of this to the future of America as a moral force in the world cannot be overestimated. Sumner Welles wrote that the Atlantic Charter was "the official pronouncement of the policies of the two governments." It was "valid in its binding effiect," and it was "notice to the world by the President of the United States and the Prime Minister of the United Kingdom, that in accordance with their constitutional authority to speak for their countries and their governments, the two nations which they represented *would adhere* to the great principles set forth in the declaration."[3]

If this be so, the Atlantic Charter was a gigantic moral commitment made to a world on the threshold of enormous travail and sacrifices. Welles cited no clause of the American Constitution as giving the President authority to bind the United States in this manner. Whether he had the authority or not, Roosevelt arrogated it to himself, and the world took his words to be a pledge by the United States.

Then on September 29, 1941, in what must surely rank as one of the most macabre frauds of history, Commissar of Foreign Affairs Vyacheslav Molotov, the notorious Janus-faced collaborator with von Ribbentrop in arranging the partition of Poland, was ushered into St. James's Palace to vow allegiance, on behalf of the Soviet dictatorship, to the eight points of the Atlantic Charter. The ceremony was later repeated in Washington, D.C., for the better convenience of the American press. It would have been no more a mockery had Adolf Hitler, for a prize of fifty thousand tanks and twenty-five thousand airplanes, scribbled his signature on a paper saying that he was dedicated to the sacred Judaic laws of the Talmud. Eventually, the plenipotentiaries of more than thirty nations trooped in to subscribe to the

Atlantic Charter. It thus became a multilateral international pact.

FIRST POINT
First, their countries seek no aggrandizement, territorial or other.

This was in the original draft prepared by Churchill. This draft was handed to Mr. Welles by Sir Alexander Cadogan on Sunday morning, August 10, the day after the conference began. According to Churchill's account, President Roosevelt had told him on Saturday that "he thought it would be well if we could draw up a joint declaration laying down certain broad principles which should guide our policies along the same road." One would think the idea had not been broached before. "Wishing to follow up this most helpful suggestion," writes Mr. Churchill, "I gave him the next day, August 10, a tentative outline of such a declaration."[4]

This casual introduction is in line with Churchill's rather too obvious anxiety to play down the Atlantic Charter in his memoirs. (It was already a dead letter when he wrote them.) However, Harry Hopkins' version of the matter was different, for according to Sherwood, who had Hopkins' private notes before him, Mr. Churchill knew before he saw President Roosevelt that the issuance to the world of a joint declaration was one of the purposes, if not the only purpose, of staging such a spectacular rendezvous. On the trip across the Atlantic on the *Prince of Wales,* Harry and the Prime Minister did more than play backgammon. Sherwood records: "They discussed the phraseology of the Atlantic Charter which the Prime Minister was to present to the President."[5]

The First Point of Churchill's tentative draft was never changed. On the surface, it is unexceptionable. Territorial aggrandizement by annexation is surely covered. The more subtle kind, by the imposition of puppet rulers in nominally autonomous countries, is not specifically mentioned but should at least come under the catch-all alternative, "or other."

The basic hypocrisy of the First Point lies deeper. Costly as modern wars are, they inevitably aggrandize the victor in some ways at the expense of a powerful enemy who is utterly crushed. Surely Mr. Churchill, looking into the future, could foresee that if the German merchant marine were swept from the seas for a decade, the shipping industry of Britain would capture much of the tonnage formerly carried in German bottoms and that the Cunard and White Star lines would enjoy a more thriving passenger business if North German Lloyd and Hamburg-American were to be eliminated from the picture for many years after the war. Would not British Overseas Airways be aggrandized by the obliteration of all commercial aviation in a beaten and occupied Germany? Would Britain's markets in Asia, Africa, and South America be more secure in the years to come if the rising competition of upstart Japan were done to death, either by slow economic strangulation or by defeat in war?

Regardless of any moral posturing and pretensions of high motives, a war which eliminates, even temporarily, a strong competitor in the markets of the world and in the commerce on the seas and in the air aggrandizes the victor vis-à-vis that enemy. How had Britain won her commercial position from the fifteenth century to the twentieth? By wars in which she had knocked down each competitor who raised a head—the Spanish, the Dutch, the French, the Germans. The Germans in the twentieth century, however, would not stay down, and the Japanese were in ascendance in Asia, where British imperialism was an old story. Both were good sailors and efficient industrialists and lived in overpopulated countries. Sharp commercial rivalry with Britain was inevitable. Future historians would record that in the first half of the twentieth century, the issue was settled by war, not by fair and open competition in the market place, just as in the sixteenth and eighteenth centuries the Anglo-Spanish wars, and in the seventeenth century the Anglo-Dutch wars, had determined the commercial supremacies of those days.

President Woodrow Wilson, speaking in 1919, expressed the opinion that all modern wars are of this nature. "Is there any man or woman," he said, "let me say is there any child, who does not know that the seed of war in the modern world is industrial and commercial rivalry? This was an industrial and commercial war." Sigmund Freud would no doubt have considered this an oversimplification, for he found the seed of war deeply embedded in human psychology and probably ineradicable.[6] Nor is it likely that the economic exegesis which a distraught and disillusioned Wilson permitted himself to embrace in 1919 would have satisfied Jonathan Swift, who called war "that mad game the world so loves to play." Be that as it may, to pretend that a war involving Great Britain, Germany, and Japan, all three of them dependent on foreign trade for their standard of living and all rivals for the markets of the world, would not bring serious dislocations of economic power and aggrandize the victors in relation to the vanquished is to indulge in fantasy.

When Mr. Churchill drafted the First Point of the Atlantic Charter, he said only that his country "seeks" no aggrandizement, territorial or other. A man might just as well say, when he shakes his neighbor's plum tree, that he is not seeking the plums that by chance fall into his open basket.

SECOND POINT
Second, they desire to see no territorial changes that do not accord with the freely expressed wishes of the peoples concerned.

This was in the original Churchill draft and was not changed. It was the golden promise to peoples whose lands and homes were coveted by others. The words are: "no territorial changes."

There are no exceptions. This could only be understood to be an assurance to Germans, Poles, and all other peoples that their nations would not be forcibly dismembered.

"Freely expressed wishes of the peoples concerned." Surely this meant that countries would not be carved up by a few men sitting around a table. It meant that families would not be uprooted from the farms and dwellings which they and their ancestors had possessed for generations and set adrift on the roads. It meant that nationalities would not be put under alien domination, without even being asked their wishes. Such barbarities were renounced.

The idea of plebiscites in disputed areas is implicit. It was not the dickering of contending governments or the predispositions of such men as Roosevelt, Churchill, or Stalin that would prevail in any revision of the map of Europe, but only the wishes of the peoples concerned.

All of this was clear in the language used. It had to be, for Roosevelt could never sell this war to the American people if they were not told that this war, unlike previous wars of Europe, would not end in that fruitless shoving around of unwilling populations and callous penciling of new lines on maps which in the past had made each war but a prelude to another war. Any equivocation on this point might have been fatal to his and Churchill's purpose, so they made a solemn pledge before the world.

This war was to end in perhaps the most terrifying peace in all history. The mass deportation of millions of innocent civilians, the partitions, the spoliation and plunder, and the destruction of moral and spiritual values were to be on an unprecedented scale.[7] The world was to be left with no alternative but to prepare for a new holocaust. What took place at Teheran and Yalta, along with the procedures adopted there, we shall examine in detail later. The ancient kings of the Assyrian Empire,

from Ashurnazirpal, who ascended the throne of Nineveh in
884 B.C., to Ashurbanipal, who devastated Elam in 645 B.C., had
made mass deportation a routine procedure of conquest. Other
prototypes for the practices that were adopted at the end of
World War II, including the systematic looting, the seizure of
territory, the hanging of the leaders of the vanquished countries,
and the imposition of alien cultures and puppet officials, were
not lacking in the long annals of warfare. In the Atlantic Charter, however, President Roosevelt and Prime Minister Churchill
renounced in advance most of these excesses, which a more en-
lightened Christian civilization had come to look upon as atroc-
ities. It was an age of democracy, and—or so they solemnly proclaimed—"the wishes of the people concerned" were to be consulted.

The choice of the precatory word "desire" in the Second Point
(". . . they desire to see no territorial changes . . . .") offers no
loophole. The war was but a test of military strength. The victors would have overwhelming superiority at its conclusion, so
that their will and their desire could be the same. The only im-
ponderable was their sincerity, or the lack of it. (Actually, as we
shall see, the Second Point was thrown in the wastebasket by
Churchill, Roosevelt, and the Russians—by tacit understanding
early in the war and by firm agreement long before the war was
over.)

THIRD POINT

Third, they respect the right of all peoples to choose the form of
government under which they will live; and they wish to see sovereign rights and self-government restored to those who have been
forcibly deprived of them.

The original Churchill draft read differently:

Third, they respect the right of all peoples to choose the form of
government under which they will live; *they are only concerned to*

defend the rights of freedom of speech and thought without which
such choice must be illusory.

Why was this second clause cut out when it got into American
hands? Concern for freedom of speech and thought is at the
heart of the American political creed. Sumner Welles gives a
curious reason for the elimination. He says "it was more than
doubtful that the American Congress would at that moment
have approved a pledge by the government of the United States
to 'defend the rights of freedom of speech and thought' when
those rights were abrogated in every Axis country."[8]

Welles must indeed have been hard put to think up a respecta-
ble reason when, several years after the event, he stooped to this
bit of dissembling. In the first place, the Atlantic Charter was
not intended to be submitted to the Congress for approval, nor
was it. As Sherwood confides, Roosevelt "was taking no chances
on that."[9] In the second place, the rights of freedom of speech
and thought were not only being abrogated "in every Axis
country," as Welles chooses to put it, but had never even existed,
and were laughed at with official contempt, in Soviet Russia,
which the Roosevelt administration was undertaking to build up
to be the dominant military power in Europe. In the third place,
if the word "defend" was too strong at the moment, as implying
warlike action, such an expression as "endeavor to further," as
adopted in the Fourth Point of the Charter, could have been
substituted. Instead, Roosevelt did not permit freedom of speech
and thought to be mentioned at all.

The real reason is easy to surmise. President Roosevelt and
Welles knew that as far as the Atlantic Charter was concerned,
two of the President's much-touted "four freedoms" had to be
thrown overboard. Or, as the *Saturday Evening Post* quipped in
its September 27, 1941, issue, Roosevelt left Washington with
his four freedoms and "came back with only two." Every literate

person in the world, except the most ignorant or credulous and those blinded by an emotional affinity for Communism, knew that freedom of speech and freedom of thought were nonexistent in Soviet Russia, the new ally. Therefore, to bring the subject up at all would create an embarrassment. Too many people might be prodded to ask: "If freedom of speech and thought is what this war is all about, why was Harry Hopkins rushed over to Moscow to cuddle up to Stalin, and why are vast quantities of American weapons and supplies going to be put into the hands of this voracious dictator, who has trampled on every freedom which Americans hold dear?" The incongruity of the situation would approach the ludicrous. The hypocrisy of the pose being struck at the conference might show through, so the reference was deleted completely. That it had been included in the first draft and then cut out was never divulged by Roosevelt, and by Welles only long after the war was over.

In its place, Roosevelt himself inserted the clause "and they hope that self-government may be restored to those from whom it has been forcibly removed." The next morning, Mr. Churchill suggested putting in the words "sovereign rights and" before "self-government," and thus was the final text arrived at. The meaning was sufficiently fuzzy from the British point of view, for the conceptions of "sovereign rights" and "self government" might be quite contradictory if ever applied to such places as Hong Kong, British Honduras, British Guiana, and British Africa.

Thus did President Roosevelt eliminate language which was relatively clear but embarrassing and insert a clause which could be useful for his purposes if misinterpreted, which it would be in the United States. As we know from Hull, Hopkins, and Elliott Roosevelt, the President's mind, when he wrote the clause, was not only on Germany's successes but also on the colonial powers of the world, with their far-flung empires built upon conquest of indigenous peoples in Asia, Africa, South America, and the islands of the seas. He wanted the American people to see in it a manifesto of liberation everywhere and for all. This was essential if the war was to be sanctified in American eyes to the point of justifying an all-out effort. According to Elliott Roosevelt, his father felt very strongly about Western colonialism.[10] He knew the Prime Minister was not with him on this issue, but he did not tell that to his people at home.

The first clause of the sentence, it is to be noted, refers to "all peoples." The second clause, still within the context of "all peoples," would restore sovereign rights and self-government to "those who have been forcibly deprived of them." There are no limitations of geography or nationality or time. Yet Churchill had his own mental reservations, as Roosevelt knew. These were later confided to a worried House of Commons on September 9, when the Prime Minister said: "At the Atlantic meeting we had in mind the restoration of the sovereignty . . . of the states . . . now under the Nazi yoke." This, he insisted, was "quite a separate problem" from the question of self-government for the "regions and peoples that owe allegiance to the British Crown." This statement was for British consumption and was given little publicity in the United States.

With that breezy vagueness at which he excelled, the Prime Minister did not particularize the "we" (". . . we had in mind. . . ."). He could, of course, have meant himself and Sir Alexander Cadogan, who was with him at the Atlantic meeting, but it is doubtful that his listeners put this interpretation on his words, for he was speaking of the Charter, which was a joint declaration with President Roosevelt. But if he meant the pronoun "we" to include the President, he was stretching the fact. Sumner Welles, Elliott Roosevelt, and Harry Hopkins contradict him here by direct testimony, and the memoirs of Cordell Hull, who conversed with Roosevelt on the subject, support their recollections. Chester Wilmot's very objective history of the war states that the President "had no such limited view. . . . Roosevelt was thinking not only of the occupied countries of Europe but also of colonial peoples throughout the world."[11]

So while Churchill was singing one song in England, Roosevelt was carrying a different tune in the United States. "We of the United Nations," he said in his Washington's Birthday speech the following February, "are agreed on certain broad principles in the kind of peace we seek. The Atlantic Charter applies not only to the parts of the world that border the Atlantic but *to the whole world*; disarmament of aggressors, self-determination of nations and peoples, and the four freedoms—freedom of speech, freedom of religion, freedom from want, and freedom from fear."[12]

When he uttered these words, Mr. Roosevelt knew there was a flat disagreement between himself and Mr. Churchill with regard to the applicability of the Atlantic Charter "to the whole world." He was continuing to propagate the fiction of a sincere mutual understanding which he knew had never existed, just as Mr. Churchill had done in England. Who was trying to fool whom? Surely neither of these seasoned politicians, who had chewed over the subject together on a first-name basis in the Admiral's cabin on the cruiser *Augusta,* thought he was fooling the other. Elliott Roosevelt, who had listened in, relates, with evident relish, that each knew exactly where the other stood. We can only conclude that the Washington's Birthday speech was conceived to fool the American public.*

In this speech, Roosevelt took another extraordinary liberty.

* Sherwood states that this speech had been announced at least three weeks in advance, adding, "It had always been Steve Early's practice to build up the radio audience for the President's speeches with plenty of advance publicity and he did this extraordinarly well." *Roosevelt and Hopkins,* 950.

He spoke of freedom of speech and freedom of religion as though they were covered by the Atlantic Charter. Actually, they had been conspicuously omitted. The Charter mentioned only freedom from "fear" and "want." But by this time the United States was in the war, and in order to assure sufficient public backing for the vast gifts which the Roosevelt administration was going to make to Russia during the ensuing years, a nation-wide campaign of propaganda, or of what Aldous Huxley has labeled "emotional engineering," had been set in motion. This was to condition American thinking to the fantasy that the Soviet government was a liberal democracy which nurtured the same freedoms that all Americans treasured. By this time a Russian signature had been put on a paper saying that the Soviet Union adhered to the principles of the Charter. Mr. Roosevelt now found it expedient to pretend that the Charter contained a provision on freedom of speech and religion, which it did not.

As a matter of fact, President Roosevelt started to plow this field even before the United States was in the war. The omission of any reference to freedom of speech and freedom of thought or religion in the Atlantic Charter had proved to be a blunder. Inclusion would have caused smiles, perhaps, but exclusion left a gaping hole. No sooner had the President returned to Washington from his epoch-making conference with Mr. Churchill than a wisecrack began to reverberate and reach his ears: two of the four freedoms had got lost somewhere out in the Atlantic. Religious circles were especially shocked, and some of their spokesmen did not conceal their suspicion that the two freedoms had been dropped overboard out of tenderness for the susceptibilities of atheistic Communism.

Mr. Roosevelt was not one to let an issue of this kind dissipate his gains. His decision was a bold one, and it illustrates his extreme confidence in himself and his low opinion of the intellectual alertness of his countrymen. He would simply make believe that the Atlantic Charter covered freedom of speech and freedom of religion. He would talk that way. People not given to reading would take his word for it, while others, who read only superficially, might be bemused into some such syllogizing as this: The Charter is a good thing and looks toward a good world; freedom of speech and freedom of religion are certainly good; therefore they are covered by the Charter, especially if Mr. Roosevelt, who ought to know, says they are. Then he would follow up this verbal sleight of hand with a phantasm. He would conjure up a new Soviet Union, complete with all four freedoms, for the delectation of the American people.

Harry Hopkins, of course, was so entangled emotionally in the burgeoning Russophilism of the Roosevelt administration that he was deeply chagrined by the widespread lack of enthusiasm, in the United States, for the Soviet dictatorship. He was restless and ill humored at this period, but he considered the task ahead to be simply one of manipulating public opinion. A job of emotional engineering had to be done. Early in September, he wrote a private letter to Brendan Bracken, a member of the British cabinet, in which he said:

We are having some difficulty with our public opinion with regard to Russia. The American people don't take aid to Russia easily. The whole Catholic population is opposed to it, all the Nazis, all the Italians and a lot of people who sincerely believe that Stalin is a great menace to the world. Still I think it will come out all right in the end.[13]

By this time, the clandestine infiltration of the agencies of the federal government by the Communist party had gone far.[14] In the Party's work, everything was now subordinated to the necessities of Russian foreign policy. Borkenau describes the strategy thus:

From 1941 onwards the communists were assigned tasks such as *infiltrating at the centre into the policy-making bodies and intelligence services of America and Britain*. Even during the Popular Front phase, the communists had learned to conceal their basic political aims. Now—and this was the decisive novelty—*they proceeded to conceal, as far as possible, the political identity of their personnel.* It was the last consequence of Leninism, of the theory that a closely selected party must lead the country without allowing the masses a share in deciding upon the course to be taken.[15]

A Roosevelt intimate was Secretary of the Treasury Morgenthau, whose right-hand man and advisor on foreign affairs was Harry Dexter White. The names of Lee Pressman, David Weintraub, John J. Abt, Nathan Witt, Alger Hiss, and Victor Perlo opened many doors. Lauchlin Currie was a confidential administrative assistant of the President. He wrote his letters on White House stationery. Communist cells had been spawned in the State, Treasury, Commerce, and other departments. The burgeoning war bureaucracy brought to Washington, side by side with loyal Americans, a horde of crypto-apostates and schemers whose deepest allegiance was to a foreign power and ideology. These people, who were part of a conspiratorial network of subversion, were in positions which enabled them to advise Cabinet members and write their speeches, colonize key committees of Congress and write Congressional reports, and prepare news releases. Already the espionage rings which were to be exposed in the revelations of later years were busy. Harry Hopkins was not wrong in his prediction that the "difficulty with our public opinion with regard to Russia" would "come out all right in the end." America had her guard down.

When President Roosevelt reported the Atlantic Charter to Congress in September, his message obliquely mentioned freedom of religion, although the Charter did not. He still shied away from the embarrassing words "freedom of speech." Instead, he spoke of "freedom of information," without defining it.

His choice of this odd phrase, which is alien to American usage but which has a special significance in Marxian political terminology, escaped the attention of most commentators, but the *Saturday Evening Post,* in its September 27 issue, and certain other publications made a point of it. What did Mr. Roosevelt mean by the phrase? Why were the well-known terms "freedom of speech" and "freedom of the press" no longer good enough for him? In Communist and other totalitarian societies, the dissemination of news is controlled by the government. This output is called "information." The only freedom possessed by the individual citizen is to receive the information sanctioned by the government in its official or controlled organs of publication. This is very different from the concept of freedom of speech and press which is rooted in Anglo-American institutions.

After gingerly tossing in the expression "freedom of information" on this occasion, Mr. Roosevelt did not toy with it again. He proceeded to bear down on the subject of religion. We now know that what had been bothering him and Harry Hopkins ever since they came back from the Atlantic Conference was the problem of reconciling the facts with the pretense that the war was a showdown between what Winston Churchill had euphemistically called "the good forces and the evil forces" of the world. It would be difficult to erase from the minds of all churchmen and the devout of all faiths the revilement of religion in the writings of Marx, Lenin, and Stalin. Had not religion been called the "opiate" and the "poison" of the people?

There was only one thing to do: draw a curtain over the past and try to persuade the doubters, by reiteration and ruse, that religion was protected and flourishing in the Soviet Union. It was decided that the President would have a few carefully chosen words on the subject to drop strategically into the publicity mill at a press conference. In addition, Averell Harriman was dispatched to Moscow. His primary assignment was to discuss with Stalin the delivery of American weapons and supplies, but an important secondary purpose was to induce the Russians to make some kind of a statement, for publicity purposes in the United States, sympathetic to religion.

At his press conference of September 30, when a reporter asked about religion in Russia, Mr. Roosevelt was ready for him. "Go and read Article 124 of the Russian Constitution," he said. But he did not tell what Article 124 provided. Instead, with that facility for unobtrusive evasion which was always one of his strongest forensic assets, he went on to say that Russia's provisions concerning religion are "essentially what is the rule in this country; only we don't put it quite the same way."

A precisian might prefer to call this a *suggestio falsi* rather than a lie. One given to colloquial descriptiveness would surely call it a "whopper." Mr. Roosevelt could not have believed what he said. Not two years before, he had told the American Youth Congress how much he detested "the banishment of religion" from Russia.[16] (That was during the period of the Berlin-Moscow alliance, when it served Mr. Roosevelt's bellicose purposes to throw some mud on Hitler's ally, as well as on Hitler himself.)

However, as Mr. Roosevelt no doubt knew, not one American in ten thousand had a copy of the Russian Constitution or had access to one. Few libraries possessed it. Most newspapers printed his remarks and let it go at that. The effect was the deception of a large portion of the American public.

Some alert and courageous publications were horrified at this. The magazine *Christian Century,* which did manage to find a copy of the Russian Constitution, asked: Is Roosevelt trying to soothe the American conscience by deceiving it?[17] The Russian Constitution was known to be a dead letter. It was mere window dressing for a despotism which held individual civil rights as nothing. Furthermore, Article 124 was heavily weighted against religion, not in favor of it. Indeed, the evident objective of that amazing verbiage is the ultimate extinction of religion. First it purports to guarantee the right to perform religious rites; then it guarantees freedom to propagandize, but only against religion! Propaganda and instruction are reserved exclusively for the atheists. Even more important is the law governing "religious associations." This outlaws most of the practices considered basic in civilized countries for the cultivation of the religious life.

In Moscow, Averell Harriman had some success in getting a statement out of the Russians for publicity purposes. This was not as easy as one might have supposed. Saying nice things about religion was not on the list of recommended activities in the Soviet Union; furthermore, the whole idea of having to cater to public opinion in this way was abhorrent, if not incomprehensible. "Throughout the week in Russia," Harriman wrote in his confidential notes, "I took every occasion (and I believe covered most of the members of the Soviet delegation, including of course Stalin and Molotov) of *explaining the American political situation* and public opinion regarding Russia, particularly in relation to the religious subject, and urged that both statements and action be taken *to indicate to America* that the Soviets were willing to allow freedom of worship not only in letter but in fact."

Stalin did not tell Harriman that there was religious freedom in Russia or that he believed there should be. In fact, he said nothing. But he did nod his head, which Harriman took to mean "a willingness to see that something was done." Finally, through Oumansky, there came an assurance "that the Soviets did allow religious worship and would reduce restrictions *and would have the necessary publicity.*"[18]

This was in itself a confession. If the right to worship existed, what were the "restrictions"? And why were the restrictions only to be "reduced"? These details were irrelevant to the purpose of Harriman's assignment, which was not to reform the Soviet Union but to arrange for a publicity statement which would be useful to President Roosevelt in what Harriman had explained to Stalin as "the American political situation." He recorded his successful accomplishment of his assignment with this note: "He [Oumansky] promised the last time I saw him at the American Embassy Friday, October 3, categorically without qualification that the President's public statement on religion would be responded to by a high Soviet official *in a manner to obtain maximum publicity in the United States.*"[19]

Actually, Harriman was not taken in. He was quite aware that the pretensions about to be broadcast throughout the United States were sham. He knew a fraud was to be perpetrated on the American people, for he wrote a confidential memorandum which recorded his own disbelief. "In spite of all comments and assurances," he wrote, "I leave with the impression that all the Soviets intend to do is to give *lip service* and to create certain instances which would *give an impression* of relaxation without really changing their present practices."[20]

Apparently, Harriman made a conscientious effort to ascertain the true status of religion in Russia. He heard conflicting reports regarding the amount of worship, the percentage of churches in the villages that were open, and the attendance. However, he found everybody in agreement that worship was engaged in only by "older people," chiefly women, and never by Communists. He wrote in his memorandum: "Religion to the Communists is superstition and against the Communist philosophy, and its organized form dangerous in developing anti-Communist political groups. *It is of course a grave offense* for anyone to teach the youth under sixteen religious philosophy." He was convinced that in spite of the "lip service" to freedom which might be given for the purpose of the publicity handout to America, religious worship would continue to be tolerated "only under closest G.P.U. scrutiny." In Harriman's words: "The Communists will unquestionably continue anti-religious education of the youth up to sixteen years *without allowing reli-*

gious education. Religious worshippers will be restricted in economic or political advancement even if they are no longer persecuted. Priests or clergymen will be closely watched as will everybody with whom they have intimate contact."[21]

It was of this police regime, ideologically dedicated to the suppression of religion, that President Roosevelt was speaking when he said in his press conference that Russia's provisions concerning religion "are essentially what is the rule in this country; only we don't put it quite the same way."

There can be no doubt that the inner circle of the Roosevelt administration knew the truth from the many sources available to them. Unfortunately, the contents of the Harriman memorandum quoted above were not divulged to the American people (until many years later). In fairness to Harriman, it may be observed that his duty was to report to his chief, the President. However, no one could have compelled him to play even the least role in this business if his conscience had rebelled. *Fraus est celare fraudem.* ("It is a fraud to conceal a fraud.")

During the next two months, Mr. Roosevelt's phantasm was taking robust shape. A constant stream of propaganda went forth—to press, pulpit, school, luncheon club, radio. The Soviet Union was given a clean bill of health. It, so the line ran, allowed religious freedom, as we do. The findings of President Roosevelt's emissary, Mr. Harriman, to the contrary were, of course, kept secret, and the most was made of the prearranged publicity which emanated from Moscow, although it was known to be sham.

By December 15, Roosevelt's audacity was so unrestrained that he permitted himself to impute to the entire world, with the exception of Germany, Italy, and Japan, a tender regard for all the principles of the American Bill of Rights.[22] This must indeed have surprised many people in the far-flung magistracies of the world, in the diverse dictatorships, monarchies, oligarchies, caliphates, and lingering feudalisms which comprised the greater part of the land surface of the earth. Surely it must have brought a smile to the lips of Joseph Stalin, who, like Lenin, as Franz Borkenau tells us, always "regarded democracy as the worst enemy."[23]

It was the 150th anniversary of the adoption of the Bill of Rights as part of the Constitution of the United States. Speaking over the combined radio stations of the nation, Roosevelt said:

Indeed, prior to 1933, the essential validity of the Bill of Rights was accepted everywhere, at least in principle. Even today, with the exception of Germany, Italy and Japan, the peoples of the whole world—in all probability four-fifths of them—support its principles, its teaching and its glorious results.

On the contrary, the American Bill of Rights is grounded upon certain philosophic assumptions, concerning the relationship of Man to his God and to the State, which are in violent conflict with patterns of thought which have prevailed in most regions of the world from ancient times to the present. Mr. Roosevelt must have known that the Bill of Rights contained many principles—in limitation of the powers of the State—which were flatly rejected in many nations other than the three he mentioned. Anyone with a mediocre knowledge of the laws and mores of the peoples of the world could have named in two minutes a score of examples which would belie the President's words. But by this time, what F. J. P. Veale, in his book *Advance to Barbarism,* calls "that mental and moral paralysis" engendered by the war, had already begun to set in. Such extravagancies as this latest one of Mr. Roosevelt passed with surprisingly little challenge, even in the academic or so-called intellectual circles, where one might have expected them to arouse doubts about either the rationality or the sincerity of the speaker and to provoke an effort to set the facts straight before the people. Unfortunately, future generations were to pay heavily in blood and resources for the distortions with which Franklin D. Roosevelt was enabled to torpify the thinking of the American people at this juncture.

Just as fatuous, and indeed more reckless, was the peroration of this speech. "We covenant with each other before all the world," he intoned in a high *allargando,* "that having taken up arms in the defense of liberty, we will not lay them down before liberty is once again secure in the world we live in." If this gratuitous and unilateral commitment were to be taken literally, it could only mean that Mr. Roosevelt was sentencing his people to perpetual warfare. Of course liberty had *never* been "secure in the world we live in." It was certain not to be after this war, which was to open the floodgates of Europe and Asia to Communism.[24]

By the time of the Washington's Birthday speech in February, 1942, America was in a frenzy of wartime excitement. Few people checked Roosevelt's words when, as we have seen, he went the full way and made a palpable misrepresentation of the contents of the Atlantic Charter and the degree of mutual agreement between himself and Winston Churchill on the scope of its applicability:

We of the United Nations are agreed on certain principles in the kind of peace we seek. The Atlantic Charter applies not only to the parts of the world that border the Atlantic but to the whole world; disarmament of aggressors, self-determination of nations and peoples, and the four freedoms—freedom of speech, freedom of religion, freedom from want, and freedom from fear.

One must search far to find a Presidential utterance so lacking in integrity. Prime Minister Churchill had insisted to Mr. Roosevelt when they drew up the Atlantic Charter that it was not to apply to the whole world, and he had later emphasized this point in his report to Parliament. The Atlantic Charter did not embrace the four freedoms; Roosevelt himself had cut out two of them which were in an earlier draft. And one of the "United Nations"—one of the largest, in fact, and the one which would be the most aggrandized by victory in the war—had been virtually bribed by Roosevelt's emissary into making a fraudulent announcement of devotion to religious freedom for publicity purposes in the United States—an announcement which was known to be a sham and which had been so described by the emissary himself in his confidential report.

Thus far we have focused mainly on the tacked-together "restoration" clause of the Third Point. We have seen what was originally suggested by Churchill and eliminated by Roosevelt and what Roosevelt later pretended it contained, although it did not. The other clause, which was never changed, proclaimed "the right of all peoples to choose the form of government under which they will live."

"All peoples" must include the German people. However, the Sixth Point pledged "the final destruction of the Nazi tyranny," by which was meant the National Socialist government of the German Reich. Some English critics quickly pointed out that the majority of Germans had chosen Nazism, or National Socialism, and were loyal to it. Which point of the Charter was to prevail? Such magazines as *Contemporary Review* and *Twentieth Century* were displeased with the Third Point because it contradicted the Sixth Point; German commentators were shocked at the Sixth Point because it contradicted the Third Point. To a German or an Italian, the discrepancy was obvious. The Charter was double talk.

In fairness to Churchill, it should be emphasized that in his original draft of the Charter, he had tried to qualify the Third Point, perhaps to reconcile it with the Sixth, by adding the words "they are only concerned to defend the rights of freedom of speech and thought without which such choice [of the form of government desired] must be illusory." But Roosevelt would not have these words in the Charter. They could be brought to bear against the Soviet form of government as well as against the Nazi. The result was that both the illusion and the contradiction remained.

Their tongues "dropped manna," in Milton's phrase, "but all was false and hollow." There was no intention to ask the Tanganyikans whether British mandate was "the form of government" under which they would choose to live or the indigenous Algerians whether they were happy to be absorbed into the French Republic. Nor was it contemplated to poll the Ukrainians or the Estonians on remaining in the Soviet Union or the eastern Poles on joining it.

As their future actions proved, Roosevelt and Churchill respected the right of *some* peoples only—not "all peoples"—to choose their form of government. For millions of people in Europe and elsewhere, these two men, along with Stalin, soon presumed to make the choice themselves. But when the Atlantic Charter was "held aloft" as a "beacon"—as Sumner Welles put it—the American people were expected to take its words literally. Roosevelt's speech on Washington's Birthday demanded faith in all it said and even more. It is not surprising that a brilliant English lawyer, in a book to which Dean Inge of St. Paul's contributed the Foreword, has bluntly described the Atlantic Charter as "a collection of dishonest verbiage."[25]

FOURTH and FIFTH POINTS

Fourth, they will endeavor, with due respect for their existing obligations, to further the enjoyment by all States, great or small, victor or vanquished, of access, on equal terms, to the trade and to the raw materials of the world which are needed for their economic prosperity.

Fifth, they desire to bring about the fullest collaboration between all nations in the economic field, with the object of securing, for all, improved labor standards, economic advancement, and social security.

These are the economic points. There was a reason, especially
for the Fourth. In 1932, by the Ottawa Agreements, England
and her Dominions had shackled world trade. Sumner Welles
described them thus: "The Ottawa Agreements were designed
to force every component part of the British Empire, covering
a quarter of the globe, to trade solely within that area. Theoretic-
ally other countries would still be able to purchase what they
wished within the Empire. But, unless they were willing to come
within the sterling area, because of the hindrances otherwise
placed upon their ability to sell their own goods to the Empire,
they could not long continue so to buy for lack of sterling exchange."[26] Tariffs, quotas, and blocked currencies had become
a part of British trade policy after 1932. The Germans, under
Hjalmar Schacht, had resorted to barter; so had the Italians.
The Japanese, looking out from their meager islands, saw that
many of the raw materials and foods they needed were not
purchasable, and they had resolved to build their own empire.

The Fourth Point was meant to give the impression that all of
this was to be changed after the war, but a loophole was left.
Churchill insisted upon inserting the words "with due respect
for their existing obligations."[27] The "existing obligations" were,
of course, the Ottawa Agreements between the United Kingdom
and the Dominions.

Jeered the magazine *Catholic World*:

So that's it? Our old acquaintance reappears, the weasel word that
sucks the meaning out of a sentence. There used to be current on
Broadway years ago a bit of snappy dialogue: "You wouldn't kid me,
would you?" "I would if I could, Mister." You wouldn't trick me,
would you, Winston? You wouldn't trick me, would you, Franklin?
You wouldn't make me a fine promise about "equal access for all to
the trade and raw materials of the world," and then neutralize it with
the old diplomatic standby "due respect for existing obligations"? Or
would you?

Others took it seriously. Ralph Robey, *Newsweek*'s business specialist and its mentor on economic matters, was moved to write an article entitled "Economic Implications of the Eight Points" in the August 25 issue. This was his vision of the post-war world that Roosevelt and Churchill hoped to usher in:

> It will be a world in which the whole present system of quotas, allotments, special tariffs, barter agreements, and bilateral trade agreements will have to be junked. . . . The only system that the world has found which makes this possible is one based on hard money. . . . The whole concept of parity prices for farm products must be tossed out the window. . . . Likewise, our policy on wages would have to be reversed in order to get our cost of production down to the point where we could meet foreign competition. . . . Only in those conditions can we live and prosper in a world of the character outlined by the Roosevelt-Churchill agreement.

He concluded that such a world would be "wholly desirable."

This fantasy had a short life. What actually followed the war was the very opposite. There came an orgy of trade restrictions and blocked currencies, soft money and inflation, and as for the United States, the concept of parity prices for farm products was perpetuated, not "tossed out the window," while rising wages and costs of production became a permanent trend. As though under a heavy fine, America was to pour out her wealth during the next generation to a grasping world ridden by fear, hatreds, and militarism.

The Fifth Point was but a prayer for freedom from want "for all." The words "the fullest collaboration between all nations in the economic field" were purposely vague, if not meaningless. Similar expressions had gushed forth from the World Economic Conference in London in 1933 and on other occasions in the past. The British took a realistic view of Points Four and Five. The typical reaction was that of the distinguished magazine *Twen-*

tieth Century, which pronounced them "harmless." Bluntly, it said: "But experience has shown that aspirations expressed in terms as vague and general as these rarely come to anything."

SIXTH POINT
Sixth, after the final destruction of the Nazi tyranny, they hope to see established a peace which will afford to all nations the means of dwelling in safety within their own boundaries, and which will afford assurance that all the men in all the lands may live out their lives in freedom from fear and want.

Just as a "hope," this was as moldy as old cheese. Most men have hoped for such a peace since time immemorial. The context, however, offered more than a mere hope to the uncritical. Surely Roosevelt and Churchill knew that nations had differing ideas about what were "their own boundaries," particularly in Europe, where boundaries had been in a state of flux since the days of Charlemagne. Was this meant to restore the *status quo ante bellum?* Or to freeze forever the *status quo post bellum?* What if the latter turned out to be unjust? Or politically absurd? Or controversial? Actually, these two gentlemen, along with Stalin, were soon to draw some new and strange boundaries themselves—boundaries so wanton and anomalous that within them men could not possibly live in freedom from fear and want.

The chief hypocrisy of the Sixth Point lay in its opening phrase, which implied that "the Nazi tyranny" alone stood between mankind and the vision of a tranquil world. Tyranny was by no means an exclusive vice of Adolf Hitler. Fear and want were ubiquitous in the world. They had been before "the Nazi tyranny" and would be after its demise.

SEVENTH POINT
Seventh, such a peace should enable all men to traverse the high seas and oceans without hindrance.

Although these words sounded virtuous, nobody seemed to know their purport. In times of peace, men had no difficulty traversing the high seas and oceans without hindrance. Until the war came, the flags of Germany, Japan, Greece, Panama, Sweden, etc., flew aloft on all the sea lanes of the world. Such small nations as Holland and Denmark had enormous merchant marines. An Italian had no more trouble booking passage around the world than did an Englishman. In war, freedom of the seas was curtailed. Churchill's Royal Navy was just as busy curtailing it as was Hitler's *Deutsche Marine*.

The scholarly *Twentieth Century* was bewildered, but polite. Of the Seventh Point, it said only: "We confess we are unable to understand what this means." To this day, nobody has explained it.

EIGHTH POINT
Eighth, they believe that all of the nations of the world, for realistic as well as spiritual reasons, must come to the abandonment of the use of force. Since no future peace can be maintained if land, sea, or air armaments continue to be employed by nations which threaten, or may threaten, aggression outside of their frontiers, they believe, pending the establishment of a wider and permanent system of general security, that the disarmament of such nations is essential. They will likewise aid and encourage all other practicable measures which will lighten for peace-loving peoples the crushing burden of armaments.

This is the disarmament clause of the Atlantic Charter. Somebody is to be disarmed, but who? No names are mentioned. Sumner Welles confides that it was President Roosevelt who brought this idea to the table. There was no such clause in Churchill's draft. Mr. Roosevelt took his pen in hand and wrote that "any nation which threatens or may threaten to use force outside its frontiers" must be disarmed.[28]

When Churchill read this, the wheels in his head whirled.

Great Britain had used force outside its frontiers every generation since the time of William the Conqueror. How could he
indulge Roosevelt's little whim and yet make the clause practically meaningless? Presto! Change the words "to use force,"
which meant something, to "aggression," which meant nothing.[29] Roosevelt readily accepted this. However imprecise the
word, "aggression" was indubitably something one should be
against.

It was no compliment to the intelligence of their people at
home that the President and the Prime Minister ventured the
Eighth Point with evident confidence that it would not be widely
taken as a joke. Less than two years before, the Soviet Union had
been expelled from the League of Nations for aggression against
her little neighbor, Finland. She had, with the Nazis, marched
into Poland and wiped it off the map. She had recently overrun
the sovereign nations of Estonia, Latvia, and Lithuania and annexed them. Yet this marauder was now being made a partner
of Great Britain and America. Stalin, the strong-arm brigand of
eastern Europe, was about to be christened "Uncle Joe" and
given one of the three seats at the tables of the mighty. An arms
race unprecedented in human history was to follow this war.

PART THREE

Wastebasket Road: Casablanca to Yalta

*Those who can win a war well can
rarely make a good peace, and those who
could make a good peace would never have
won the war.*
WINSTON CHURCHILL in 1930
(In his early autobiography,
A Roving Commission)

Chapter X

CASABLANCA

In 1943, BEFORE he had ever met Marshal Joseph Stalin, President Roosevelt said to William C. Bullitt:

I have just a hunch that Stalin doesn't want anything but security for his country, and I think that if I give him everything I possibly can and ask nothing from him in return, noblesse oblige, he won't try to annex anything and will work for a world democracy and peace.[1]

Mr. Bullitt had been the American Ambassador in Moscow and in Paris and was well informed on European history and politics. He was a man of deep patriotism. One may imagine the amazement, if not dismay, with which he heard these words from the lips of the President of the United States. From that moment on, he feared for the safety of Western civilization.

Early in 1942, President Roosevelt served notice on Prime Minister Winston Churchill of his plan to ingratiate himself with Stalin and of his intention to brook no interference with this design. He served the notice in writing:

I know you will not mind my being brutally frank when I tell you that I think I can personally handle Stalin better than either your Foreign Office or my State Department. Stalin hates the guts of all your top people. He thinks he likes me better, and I hope he will continue to do so.[2]

This was a stern caveat to Mr. Churchill and all of his "top people." Throughout the war, in all the delicate and fateful decisions that were to be made, Winston Churchill had to take account of Roosevelt's attitude toward Stalin. Since his own country was in so many ways dependent upon American assistance, he was often in a position of discreet, if uncomfortable, deference to the President, who was patently a man of implacable sentiments and a capacity for vindictiveness when crossed.

During 1942, aid to Russia, by order of the President, had top priority in the beehive of activity that was Washington, D.C. Anyone who worked in the old Munitions Building in those days or in the new, sprawling Pentagon, gradually spreading its wings on the other side of the Potomac, and who had anything to do with the allocation of war supplies will remember, perhaps with a touch of irony, the sanctity that seemed to surround the "Russian requisitions." No doubt Mr. Roosevelt was right that Stalin "thought he liked him," as he boasted to Churchill. But at this point, Stalin's fondness for Mr. Roosevelt could only be based on the latter's manifold bounties to the Soviet Union, for he had never yet come face to face with the famous Roosevelt personal charm. Mr. Roosevelt, manifestly, was confident that the Russian dictator would "like" him even better if he could meet him in the flesh. Toward the end of the year, his desire for a meeting with Stalin was so ardent that Stalin could easily interpret it as a passion to be patiently nurtured.

The Russian was superbly wary. Twice he turned down what Hopkins called the President's "urgent invitations" to a Big Three conference, pleading that he was too busy directing his armies to absent himself "even for a day." Since the tide on the Russian front had already turned against the German invaders and since Mr. Roosevelt offered to fly to Khartoum or to some other place convenient to Stalin, it seems most likely that Stalin simply did not consider the timing propitious, from his standpoint, for such a conference. He was doing well as things were. American weapons, airplanes, vehicles, even machinery for factories, were pouring into the Soviet Union in prodigious quantities. He had not had to commit himself to anything specific. There is a Russian word—*vynoslivost,* "lasting a thing out"— for a quality said to be congenital in the Tartar-Slavs and which was not lacking in Joseph Stalin. Why should he risk a personal conference at this point? In a few weeks the German failure at Stalingrad would culminate in a debacle. He could stride into a later conference as a military hero, which, as he had good reason to anticipate, would only increase the President's adulation. He was in no hurry to enjoy the pleasure of Mr. Roosevelt's company, for in the middle of December, in declining for the second time, he wrote to him: "I too must express my deep regret that it is impossible for me to leave the Soviet Union either in the near future or even at the beginning of March. . . . So far I do not know what exactly are the problems which you, Mr. President, and Mr. Churchill intend to discuss at our joint conference. I wonder whether it would not be possible to discuss these problems by way of correspondence between us."[3] Mr. Roosevelt's ardor was not cooled by this rebuff. On the contrary, his assiduity to please Stalin was to grow even more feverish. Meanwhile, he decided to have a conference with Churchill in January in North Africa.

General John R. Deane, whose conclusion was based on his personal observations in dealing with the Russians during the war (he was two years in Moscow), wrote that "in Russian eyes, the war with Germany and Japan was only the first phase in the ultimate struggle between Communism and Capitalism."[4] The real enemy was the whole capitalistic world. It was, of course, the business of the President of the United States to know that also. The same conclusion was compelled by the writings of Lenin and Stalin, which could not have escaped the attention of the President and certainly not that of Harry Hopkins. These gentlemen could also have known, if indeed they did not, what Hitler plainly perceived, i.e., that the Soviet dictatorship, having consolidated its power, was, in the fourth and fifth decades of the twentieth century, inflamed with an ambition for expansion in Europe and Asia that dwarfed the ancient hopes of Ivan the Terrible, Peter the Great, and Catherine and that but bided an opening.

Joseph Stalin could hardly have done better for his cause if he had attended the Casablanca Conference in person. There, Franklin D. Roosevelt did him two favors. One was tentative, but the other was final and of historic importance. For the first time he threw cold water on the incipient British plan to strike at Germany through the Balkans and thus frustrate the postwar domination of central and eastern Europe by the Soviet Union. This issue was to arise again later.

Roosevelt pronounced "unconditional surrender" as the only condition which could bring the wars in Europe and Asia to a close. This meant that Germany and Japan, the two nations whose geographical position and historic roles made them the only bulwarks against Communist expansion, were not only to be defeated but were also to be made prostrate. This, in the words of Lord Hankey, "removed the barriers against communism in Europe and the Far East and greatly decreased the security of the whole world."[5] Hanson W. Baldwin has said that it was "perhaps the biggest political mistake of the war."[6] For the United States and many other nations, it was a calamity.[7]

If Franklin D. Roosevelt had been sent to the Casablanca Conference by Stalin as a personal envoy, he could not have served his principal more faithfully. In effect, he said so himself. According to his son Elliott, who was present at the time, he hatched up the phrase "unconditional surrender" one day while having lunch and then bared his thoughts on it in these precise words:

"Of course, it's just the thing for the Russians. They couldn't want anything better. Unconditional surrender," he repeated, thoughtfully sucking a tooth. *"Uncle Joe might have made it up himself."*[8]

There is, by common agreement, one subject on which Elliott Roosevelt had intimate, man-to-man knowledge: his father's feelings toward Stalin and the Soviet Union. We are fortunate to be given this insight.

Of course the President took Harry Hopkins with him to Casablanca. They went together by train to Miami, in the greatest secrecy, and then flew to Africa via Trinidad. En route, Hopkins wrote his usual diary-like notes. "I shall always feel," he said, "that the reason the President wanted to meet Churchill in Africa was because he wanted to make a trip. . . . He liked the drama of it. But above all, he wanted to make a trip."[9] However, there was need for a conference somewhere. A military program for 1943 had to be decided upon. As Hopkins wrote, "On the assumption that we are going to drive the Germans out of Africa it became clear to me that there was no agreed-upon plan as to what to do next. We had to strike somewhere—across the Channel, at Sardinia, Sicily or through Turkey. But where?"[10] Harry had his own ideas. They definitely excluded Turkey or any place contiguous to the Balkans.

The war was going well everywhere. In the Pacific area, the strangle hold of the Japanese navy had been broken. In the Battle of the Coral Sea in May, 1942, the American fleet sank fifteen Japanese warships, including an aircraft carrier and four cruisers. This was followed in June by the great victory at Midway, where four Japanese aircraft carriers, three cruisers, and three destroyers went to the bottom. In the naval battle off Guadalcanal in November, the Japanese lost a battleship, eight cruisers, six destroyers, and a large number of transports. In all of these engagements, American losses were proportionately small. In Washington, preference was given to the European and African theaters, and General Douglas MacArthur was obliged to beg for logistical support for his amphibious operations in the Pacific; but there was no longer any doubt that Japan's desperate gamble was doomed. She could not sustain the communications and transportation upon which her new empire depended. Her ultimate defeat was a matter of timing.

Likewise, Hitler's bold gamble in Russia looked like a failure. Napoleon's disaster of 1812 was being re-enacted, but this time the Germans were the victims of Russia's inhospitable vastness. The summers of 1941 and 1942 had passed, and the *Wehrmacht* and the *Luftwaffe* had not achieved their victory. On the contrary, it was now the Russians who were on the offensive. Churchill wrote in a military memorandum on December 3, 1942: "The Russians have not been defeated or weakened in the campaign of 1942. On the contrary, it is Hitler who has been defeated and the German Army which has been very grievously reduced. General von Thoma [a prisoner of the British in Egypt] was heard to say that the one hundred eighty German divisions on the Russian front are in many cases little more than brigades."[11] The Sixth German Army was encircled at Stalingrad, and its destruction was imminent. (On January 31, 1943, the Battle of Stalingrad ended with the capture of Field Marshal von Paulus and sixteen of his generals, together with all that remained of the surrounded forces—a German disaster which Churchill says "ended Hitler's prodigious effort to conquer Russia by force of arms and destroy Communism.")[12]

The war in the air over Europe had simmered down to a grim fulfillment of the terror-breathing words hurled by Churchill the previous June—words which surpassed, in their promise of indiscriminate horror, any precedent in the annals of human warfare:

I may say that as the war advances, German cities, harbours, and centers of production will be subjected to an ordeal the like of which has never been experienced by a country in continuity, severity, and magnitude.[13]

Neville Chamberlain, Churchill's predecessor, had shrunk from unrestricted bombing of civilian targets, as had Hitler until the R.A.F. initiated it. The *Luftwaffe* had been conceived as an instrument of tactical offensive to assist fast-moving armies. When Warsaw and Rotterdam were bombed, German armies were at their gates. As Captain Liddell Hart (Britain's foremost military analyst) points out, "Bombing did not take place until German troops were fighting their way into these cities and thus conformed to the old rules of siege bombardment."[14] A decision by the British Air Ministry on May 11, 1940, not the villainy of Adolf Hitler, originated "total war." It was this decision that instituted the mass destruction of civilian populations by aerial bombardment for its own sake. It implemented the new plan of warfare conceived by British experts in 1936 when the Bomber Command was organized. All this has been revealed in two extraordinary books by British authors of unimpeachable authority. The one book, proudly bearing the title *Bombing Vindicated,* was written by J. M. Spaight, C.B., C.B.E., former Principal Secretary of the Air Ministry. The other, written by the wartime Chief of Bomber Command, Air Chief Marshal Sir Arthur Harris, is called *Bombing Offensive.*[15]

As Spaight confirms, Hitler had been genuinely anxious to reach an agreement with Britain "confining the action of aircraft to the battle zones" and had reluctantly undertaken to retaliate not earlier than three months after the R.A.F. had commenced unrestricted bombing of the German cities. Air Marshal Harris, it seems, had only contempt for the *Luftwaffe* chiefs; they had not provided themselves with armed bomber planes designed for attacks on enemy civilian populations. They got into that game, as he puts it, "much too late in the day."[16]

In the early period of the war, Churchill fumed, not because Hitler dropped bombs on English cities, but because he did not. General de Gaulle, in his memoirs (published in 1955), describes Churchill's frustration:

> I can still see him at Chequers one August day, raising his fists toward the sky as he cried: "So they won't come!"
> "Are you in such a hurry," I said to him, "to see your towns smashed to bits?"
> "You see," he replied, "the bombing of Oxford, Coventry, Canterbury, will cause such a wave of indignation in the United States they'll come into the war."

Craftily, Churchill provoked the Germans to bomb England. "Retaliation was certain if we carried the war into Germany," Spaight writes. "There was no certainty, but there was a reasonable probability that our capital and our industrial centres would not have been attacked if we had refrained from attacking those of Germany."

By the time Winston Churchill set out for the Casablanca Conference in January, 1943, the *Luftwaffe*'s blitz on English shores had long since failed (as Spaight and Harris explain, the Germans were never prepared for such warfare). On the other hand, no German in all of the Reich could go to bed at night without a gnawing fear in his heart that British planes would drop bombs on his house before morning. At bases in England, our own air force was readying a mammoth daylight bombing campaign to pulverize whatever the British did not demolish.

In North Africa, another German defeat was almost sealed. On November 7, 1942, the British Eighth Army chased Rommel's troops 240 miles westward to the Libyan frontier. The next day, United States forces landed at Algiers, Casablanca, and Oran. They were soon joined by the British First Army in eastern Algeria, and the combined armies assaulted Tunisia. Tobruk and Bengasi fell as the pincers closed. The great expedition into French North Africa, known as TORCH and under the command of General Dwight D. Eisenhower, was achieving all of its objectives. In December, Hitler recklessly poured reinforcements into Tunisia, which slowed the Allied timetable, but in January, at the Casablanca Conference, General Eisenhower was able to give assurances that the enemy would be pushed out of all North Africa in the near future.

The question then was: "Where do we go from here?" As Hopkins wrote, "We had to strike somewhere. . . . But where?" The possible alternative that it might not be necessary to go anywhere, that a way might be sought and found to end the carnage, did not lie within his consideration at any time. The Bishop of Chichester had been approached in Stockholm by two anti-Nazi Germans who asked him to find out whether the British and American governments would negotiate for peace with a German democratic government if the Hitler regime were overthrown. As the Bishop disclosed after the war, he tried to elicit this information but was unable even to get a response. All moves toward peace were peremptorily brushed aside.

It is now known that the senior officers of the German army were ripe for rebellion.[17] There was an opposition to Hitler led by General Ludwig Beck, former chief of the German army's general staff, and Carl Goerdeler, a former mayor of Leipzig. These were men of unquestioned moral stature. Active commanders like von Kluge and von Manstein foresaw where Hitler's policy was leading Germany. Admiral Canaris, General Oster, and the valiant Count von Stauffenberg were among the long list of deeply perturbed figures who longed to kill or depose

Hitler and to end the war on some honorable terms. To succeed, they needed some encouragement from outside. This they never got.

Was there a malevolent jealousy behind the Allied attitude? A fear that the Hitler regime might be extirpated by the German people and the crusaders left too soon without a crusade? It was known in the Pentagon and in the White House that Adolf Hitler was tottering on the brink of an abyss of discontent in his own country. General Albert C. Wedemeyer, who was at General Marshall's elbow in those days and was taken to Casablanca with him, tells us: "No attempt was made by the Western Allies to divide the Germans by offering Hitler's enemies decent terms of peace—this in spite of the fact that British and American intelligence agents were aware that Hitler was faced with the opposition of men holding some of the highest appointments in the Army, Navy, and Civil Service."[18]

The handwriting on the wall was clear: Hitler had blundered into a war against three gigantic powers that he could not win. The United States had not yet had time to bring her full strength to bear, yet Germany was already losing. Stalin, Churchill, and Roosevelt were all sure of her defeat.

The men in the Kremlin had begun to scent victory months before. They were looking toward the shape of things after the war. In the early months of 1942, they had tried to get from the Churchill government an advance confirmation of title to lands they had seized in 1939 and 1940. These included eastern Poland, part of Finland, and the three Baltic States of Latvia, Lithuania, and Estonia, which they wanted to absorb outright. They also wanted a secret agreement recognizing Russia's claim to a slice of Rumania. All of this would have been revolting to public opinion in the United States, if not in Great Britain. Churchill and Eden, after hearing from President Roosevelt, explained this to Molotov in London in May, and the matter was then quickly shelved and kept out of publicity.[19] After all, in the United States people were still making orations about the Atlantic Charter.

To such men as Stalin and Molotov, it was axiomatic that the manner and timing of the inevitable defeats of Germany and Japan, respectively, would have a crucial bearing on the residua of power in the postwar world. It was not difficult to discern how the Russian bread could best be buttered. The Soviet Union and the Communist cause could best be advanced if

1. The major British and American war effort would be a frontal attack on Germany through France;
2. British and American forces would keep out of central and eastern Europe, allowing Russian armies to conquer, or "liberate," and then to plunder and Communize Poland, Czechoslovakia, the Balkan area, and as much of Germany as possible;
3. The war would not end by negotiation, either with the Hitler regime or any other German government, for such a negotiated peace would forestall the march of Soviet troops into the heart of Europe;
4. The Japanese war would be prolonged until after the collapse of Germany, so that Russia would be free to enter it at the last moment, seize as spoils all the Japanese war supplies and industrial machinery in Manchuria, and proceed to exploit to her own advantage the power vacuum which the surrender of the Japanese would leave in northern China and Korea.

In April, 1942, President Roosevelt had sent Harry Hopkins, accompanied by General Marshall, Roosevelt's Chief of the Joint Chiefs of Staff, to London to inform the British that he had come to a decision on two points. First, the main priority in the use of America's armed might was to be given to the war against Germany, with the crushing of Japan to be postponed. Second, the major military project was to be a cross-Channel invasion of Europe on a big scale in 1943 (code name ROUNDUP), to be preceded by a smaller assault on the French coast in 1942

(SLEDGEHAMMER) to draw German strength away from the Russian battlefield.

On this occasion, Hopkins said, at a meeting with Churchill and the top British military and naval people, that "if public opinion in America had its way the weight of American efforts would be directed against Japan."[20] But public opinion in America was not to have its way. It was to be cavalierly disregarded. (Yet there was prescience in the public's leaning. If the defeat of Japan had come swiftly, while Russia was engaged in Europe, the postwar fate of Asia would have been different, and millions of Chinese who were deceived into thinking that it was Russia who finally defeated the Japanese would have had a clearer view of history.)

On May 29, Molotov arrived in Washington and was whisked to the White House. After preliminary pleasantries, Mr. Roosevelt happened to mention certain Japanese naval concentrations of which he had news. Molotov hastened to say that Hitler was the chief enemy. Mr. Roosevelt got the point immediately and reassured his guest that he had brought the United States into line. Samuel H. Cross, professor of Slavic languages at Harvard, was present taking notes. According to his record of the conversation, this colloquy took place:

To Mr. Molotov's remark that Hitler was the chief enemy, the President noted his agreement and mentioned his repeated statements to the Pacific Conference that we should *remain on the defensive in the Pacific until the European front was cleared up*. It had been difficult, he added, to put this view across, but, in his opinion, it was now accepted.[21]

Naturally, this pleased Molotov.

Now Molotov had just been to London, where Churchill had told him about preparations for SLEDGEHAMMER and ROUNDUP. But Molotov had sensed a wavering which disturbed him, as though Churchill had some reservations in his mind. He wanted a commitment, so he went to work on Roosevelt. The day before Molotov's arrival in Washington, the President had received a disconcerting cable from the Prime Minister. It mentioned Norway and North Africa as possible places of operations against the Germans. This cable, says Sherwood, "provided the first danger signal to Roosevelt . . . that British thinking was beginning to veer toward diversionary operations far removed from the main point of frontal attack across the Channel."[22] Nevertheless, Roosevelt gave his approval to this public statement, which Molotov wrote and which appeared at the end of the discussions: "In the course of the conversations full understanding was reached with regard to the urgent tasks of creating a Second Front in Europe in 1942." In the context of the President's talks with Molotov, this, of course, referred to SLEDGEHAMMER, a crossing of the Channel. However, as Molotov passed through London again on his way home, Churchill, although paying lip service to SLEDGEHAMMER, was careful to hand Molotov an *aide-mémoire* saying he could not promise it.

In July, 1942, the British had decided that the time had come to "bury" SLEDGEHAMMER. Churchill confesses in his memoirs that he had never expected it to be carried out.[23] It would have been a bloody sacrifice undertaken to draw German divisions away from the Russian front. He had no stomach for this. He now informed Roosevelt that no responsible British general, admiral, or air marshal thought it practicable. In spite of this, Roosevelt sent Hopkins and Marshall to London with instructions to push for it. This time the British stood firm. Marshall reached a deadlock in his talks with the British chiefs of staff. Hopkins made a note of his own feelings on hearing this: "I feel damn depressed." The President was cabled for new instructions, and this time he capitulated and accepted the alternative plan advocated by Churchill, the invasion of North Africa (GYMNAST, later renamed TORCH).

The reason Harry Hopkins had felt "damn depressed" was that he had a premonition—as no doubt the British did also—that a large-scale adventure into the Mediterranean would mean the postponement of ROUNDUP in 1943, which would not please the Kremlin. General Eisenhower later wrote that a major factor in all American thinking at that time was a lively suspicion that the British contemplated the agreed-upon cross-Channel concept with distaste and with considerable mental reservations.[24]

In January, 1943, when the President and Hopkins left for Casablanca, they had reason to fear that the postponement of ROUNDUP might be indefinite. Churchill had sent Roosevelt a message which contained this ominous paragraph:

The paramount task before us is, first, to conquer the African shores of the Mediterranean and set up the naval and air installations which are necessary to open an effective passage through it for military traffic; and, secondly, using the bases on the African shore to strike at the under-belly of the Axis in effective strength and in the shortest time.[25]

What did "under-belly" mean? Did Churchill have any adventures toward the Balkans up his sleeve? That way of getting at the enemy would not be compatible with the Russian pattern of victory at all. General Marshall, who throughout the war was the unfailing spokesman, at the staff level, of the Roosevelt-Hopkins line of policy, was well briefed to oppose it. He had been sent to Casablanca ahead of the President to meet with British staff officers. Three weeks before, he had told Field Marshal Sir John Dill in Washington (and Dill at once tipped off Churchill) that he was "getting more and more convinced that we should be in a position to undertake a modified 'Round-up' before the summer [of 1943] if, as soon as North Africa is cleared of Axis forces, we start pouring American forces into England instead of sending them to Africa for the exploitation of 'Torch.' "[26] One of the reasons Marshall had given for such an operation was that it would be "more satisfying to the Russians." (None of the reasons was convincing to the British.)

Winston Churchill was sometimes devious in his war communications, with the result that he was not infrequently suspected of secretly favoring one course of action while paying lip service to another. But he had been in one of his more undissembling moods one night the previous November when he sat talking "the greater part of the night" with American Ambassador Winant and General Walter Bedell Smith. Foreign Secretary Anthony Eden was also present. Smith reported the conversation to General Marshall, who unquestionably passed it on to the White House. Churchill, said Smith, appeared to be cooling on the ROUNDUP plan for northern France. He was also reluctantly abandoning the idea of an expedition to northern Norway, for which the Americans had shown no inclination. However, his mind was running to the thought of getting Turkey into the war with her forty-five divisions of superior fighting men, to be armed and equipped by the Allies for an invasion of the Balkans.[27] Since it could not be contemplated that Turkey would tackle the Germans alone in the Balkans, this portended sending an Anglo-American expeditionary force to that part of Europe.

Franklin D. Roosevelt could, of course, easily see the long-range strategy behind such a gambit. He liked it not. And when he went to the Casablanca Conference in January, it was definitely not one of his purposes to help build a rampart of strength on the southwest flank of the Soviet Union. (As history would unfold, the Turks would one day have American weapons put hastily in their hands—and the Greeks, too—but that was not to be done while Roosevelt was alive.)

The American people were unaware that their President was on his way to Africa to make grave decisions there, with Harry Hopkins in constant attendance. If they had known, this latter circumstance might have caused them some concern. They were far from sure that Hopkins was the right kind of ballast for the President's mental bark on such a mission. But their anxiety might have been assuaged if they could have been told—and if it had been true—that Harry was so deeply conscious of the responsibility which his influence with the President imposed upon him that he spent the four days en route to Casablanca in careful study and humble meditation. It would have comforted them to think that he was not only fortifying his understanding of the complex forces which underlay the war but was also doing some soul-searching—to detect and expel from his own mind any impulse deleterious to his country's best interests, any error of historical perspective, or any pertinacity which might color his judgment.

Actually, it would appear from his own notes that Harry (he was Harry to everybody) was mainly preoccupied with the details of the flights, the scenery, playing gin rummy, reading detective stories, and the beverages which were made available for his and the President's consumption. He did mention, rather casually, talking once to the President "about our pending conference," but he did not bother to write down what he had said to the President or what the latter had said to him. On the other hand, he recorded—with that eccentric sense of values which permeated all his note-taking—having cocktails at Trinidad and "a first-class rum drink" in the middle of the afternoon at Belém, where he "wangled two bottles" to take along. And when they departed after this pleasant interlude, he was pleased to note that "they serve cocktails on this flying boat."

The conference was held at Anfa, a suburb of Casablanca, where a large hotel offered splendid accommodations for the British and American staffs and big meeting rooms. There was, on the grounds, a villa for the President. It was modern and had a lovely garden and a swimming pool. "The President, Elliott and I are staying here," Harry observed. Churchill had another villa some fifty yards away. Elliott's book says that Harry "went over to bring him back to our place for dinner," but Harry, shifting the emphasis, put it this way: "I went over to bring him back for a drink before dinner."

While having the "drink before dinner," Roosevelt, Churchill, and Harry—"the three of us"—"had a long talk over the military situation." The British and American chiefs of staff, in the big hotel across the road, were evidently similarly engaged, for just before dinner Harry went scouting and happily came upon them. "I found them all having a cocktail." They were invited to dine at the President's villa.

There was a distinguished and, it may be inferred, merry company at the table that night. Besides the President, the Prime Minister, Harry, and Elliott, there were General Marshall, Admiral King, and General Arnold—the heads of the U.S. Army, Navy, and Air Force—and their British counterparts, General Sir Alan Brooke, Admiral Sir Dudley Pound, and Air Chief Marshall Sir Charles Portal, plus Lord Louis Mountbatten and Averell Harriman. "There was," wrote Harry, "much good talk of war." This went on for some hours and covered a wide field of politics, diplomacy, and military subjects. Elliott only listened, but he was not idle. He later wrote: "I busied myself filling glasses."

The Casablanca Conference was lengthy. The President was there ten days. On the military problems faced, Elliott Roosevelt's book has this to say: "Still an open issue was the cross-Channel invasion, at that time referred to as ROUNDUP, the second front in 1943. As always, during all our conversations, the Americans were forcing the issue, the British holding back." This is roughly true, but a sharper focus is obtained from the memoirs of Churchill, Generals H. H. Arnold and Mark Clark, the official reports of General Marshall and Admiral King to the Secretaries of War and Navy, and Sherwood's account (based on the Hopkins papers). The Combined Chiefs of Staff had been in session three days before President Roosevelt and Harry Hopkins arrived. General Marshall was still faithfully and stubbornly arguing for the invasion of northern France in 1943. To the British, however, this was out of the question. They had brought up Sardinia, Sicily, Italy, Crete, the Dodecanese Islands, the mainland of Greece, and Turkey for consideration. And the American Chiefs of Staff were, as Sherwood observes, "by no means unanimous," for Admiral King and General Arnold balked at going along with Marshall's *idée fixe*.

More days of argument followed. The upshot was that Roosevelt yielded to the overwhelming weight of professional opinion. ROUNDUP was postponed until 1944. With respect to the Mediterranean area, he would only approve an attack on Sicily (Operation HUSKY). He refrained from any commitment beyond that. General Eisenhower was to command HUSKY, but no orders were issued to him for following it up. This solution was obviously a compromise.

Sherwood states that Hopkins was again "disappointed and depressed" by the postponement of ROUNDUP. Stalin and Molotov had been persistently calling for the embroilment of Anglo-American forces in France, and 1942 had slipped by without it, through no fault of President Roosevelt. Now there was to be another year's delay. Hopkins had been right in his premonition that TORCH, which the British had promoted so astutely, would have this consequence. However, one thing had been accomplished at the Casablanca Conference: such a splash of cold water had drenched British speculations about American and British troops heading for the mainland of Greece or Turkey and up through the Balkans that the idea was stunted in its infancy.

Mr. Roosevelt was at the high pitch of his wartime ebullience. "The Casablanca trip was grand," he bubbled in a letter to his son John, like a *bon vivant* describing a Mardi Gras ball.[28] The Sultan of Morocco, in white silk robe, came to dinner, bringing a gold dagger for the President and gold bracelets for Mrs. Roosevelt. General Charles de Gaulle, pouting because a rival Frenchman, General Giraud, was not in bad graces, was summoned from London and made to pose, shaking hands, with Giraud in front of a battery of cameras, a publicity stunt intended to conceal the enduring enmity between the two French factions. Roosevelt wrote to George VI that he wished the King could have come.[29] It all fed his tendency to be grandiose. John Gunther recalls:

He behaved in some ways like a conqueror and lord of the earth when he reached Africa, giving out decorations almost as a monarch does; he talked about the French empire as if it were his personal possession and would say things like "I haven't quite decided what to do about Tunis."[30]

The finale, on the tenth day, was the famous Casablanca press conference, which the *New York Times* called "the most informal ever held." The scene was the garden of the gleaming white villa. On two white leather chairs sat the President, smoking a cigarette in a long holder, and the Prime Minister, puffing a cigar. Correspondents and cameramen sat on the green lawn at their feet. Red flowers were in profusion. The great smile was flashed with delight when somebody presented Mr. Roosevelt with a Morocco-bound portfolio containing the signatures of all persons who had talked and visited with him at the villa. He said he would place it in his library at Hyde Park. It was on this occasion that the President announced that he and Churchill were determined to accept nothing less than unconditional surrender of Germany, Italy, and Japan. The joint communiqué had not included this.

It has always been suspected that Roosevelt pulled this card out of his sleeve. Churchill's round head was seen to nod, but four and one-half years later (July 21, 1949), in a debate in the House of Commons, he confessed:

I was there on the spot and had to rapidly consider whether the state of our position in the world was such as to justify me in not giving support to it. I did support it but it was not the idea I had formed in my own mind.

In his memoirs, he says that he heard the President's words "with some feeling of surprise."[31] He also says: "General Ismay, who knew exactly how my mind was working from day to day, and was also present at all the discussions of the Chiefs of Staff when the communiqué was prepared, was also surprised."

The subject had indeed "cropped up" before ("at meal times," Churchill recollected),[32] but, he explains, "it was natural to suppose that the agreed communiqué had superseded anything said in conversation." According to the Hopkins papers, Roosevelt himself later absolved Churchill of responsibility for the unconditional-surrender statement at the press conference. Indeed, he even suggested that it was unpremeditated on his part. These are his own words:

We had so much trouble getting those two French generals together that I thought to myself that this was as difficult as arranging the meeting of Grant and Lee . . . and then suddenly the press conference was on, and Winston and I had had no time to prepare for it, and the thought popped into my mind that they had called Grant "Old Unconditional Surrender" and the next thing I knew, I had said it.[33]

Thus, it seems, are great decisions made.

Admiral Leahy, Chief of Staff to the President, in his book *I Was There,* calls the principle of unconditional surrender "a surprising development of the Casablanca Conference." He considered it unwise.[34] The reaction of Secretary of State Hull, when he heard about it, is also revealing. He says he was told that the Prime Minister "was dumbfounded." He, Mr. Hull himself, "was as much surprised as Mr. Churchill." He opposed it, but "there was nothing we could do except to follow it. . . . It was to rise . . . to plague us."[35]

Louis P. Lochner, translator and editor of the Goebbels diaries, states that after the German defeat at Stalingrad in the winter of 1942-43, few responsible officers believed in victory and the German people regarded the war as lost.[36] Goebbels and Göring thought that Hitler had aged fifteen years since the war began; he had become a morose recluse. "He sits in his bunker, fusses and broods." (This was written on March 2, 1943.) Why did his people fight on?

The German generals have talked. So have the people. The Goebbels propaganda machine equated "unconditional surrender" with "total slavery."[37] As one English military historian has written, "Gagged by this idiotic slogan, the Western Allies could offer no terms, however severe. Conversely, their enemy could ask for none, however submissive."[38] Hitler's road to chaos was left open; all others were blocked off.

In grim fact, what did Roosevelt's demands foredoom? Many have traced, with sober analysis, the inexorable import of his words, so impetuously spoken in the garden at Casablanca.[39] In epitome, Major General J. F. C. Fuller puts it thus:

First, that because no great power could with dignity or honour to itself, its history, its people and their posterity comply with them, the war must be fought to the point of annihilation. Therefore, it would take upon itself a religious character and bring to life again all the horrors of the wars of religion.

Secondly, once victory had been won, the balance of power within Europe and between European nations would be irrevocably smashed. Russia would be left the greatest military power in Europe, and, therefore, would dominate Europe. Consequently, the peace these words predicted was the replacement of Nazi tyranny by an even more barbaric despotism.[40]

And so, for more than two years more, the Germans fought on, with the courage of despair. On the other side of the world, Roosevelt's words hung like a putrefying albatross around the necks of America and Britain. They led, in the words of Lord Hankey, to "the culminating tragedy of the two atomic bombs in Japan." By mid-1943, the Japanese knew they would lose the war and prayed for any face-saving way to accept defeat. But no; the carnage had to continue, even after Emperor Hirohito informed the Supreme War Direction Council that the war should be ended on *any* terms short of unconditional surrender.[41] The horrors of Hiroshima and Nagasaki followed.

With the garden scene, the conference at Casablanca ended. Then Churchill insisted that Roosevelt see Marrakech, which he described as "the Paris of the Sahara." They drove 150 miles across the desert to spend the night at Marrakech in "a most delightful villa." Their "entourages" were brought to Marrakech, too. This city, Churchill instructs us in his memoirs, is famous for its "gay life," including "the largest and most elaborately organized brothels in the African continent."

Harry Hopkins liked "the picnic lunch" en route. "We had plenty of wine and Scotch," his notes say. But we discover in the Churchill memoirs that this differed from the ordinary picnic in another respect: "Many thousand American troops were posted along the road to protect us from any danger, and aero-planes circled ceaselessly overhead." The cost of this merry excursion to "the Paris of the Sahara" could not have been written in less than six figures.

There was "a very jolly dinner," and "we all sang songs." The next morning, the President flew home. The Prime Minister stayed two more days, painting from the tower of the villa a picture of a sunset on the snows of the Atlas Mountains. Mr. Roosevelt had done his painting back in Casablanca. It was on the canvas of history, with ineradicable pigment.

Chapter XI

QUEBEC I

ROOSEVELT's Secretary of State was Cordell Hull, a handsome, idealistic Southerner born in 1871. Since 1933, he had brought esteem to the Cabinet and had helped to hold the "Solid South." But Cordell Hull was a frustrated man. He was not allowed to sit in on the President's war councils. "This was because the President did not invite me to such meetings," he writes plaintively in his memoirs. "I raised the question with him several times."[1] The shadow of Harry Hopkins was omnipresent. To Hull, it was obvious that scarcely any large-scale military operation could be undertaken that would not have diplomatic aspects, and he considered it a serious mistake for the Secretary of State to be left out. Even worse, he had not been taken to the Atlantic Conference or to Casablanca. Nor was he to go to Cairo or Teheran, and he was to resign before Yalta. As he puts it in his memoirs, "The President did not take me with him." He had protested this belittling treatment. "I said to him: 'I'm not looking for increased responsibilities, but I do believe the Secretary of State should attend these meetings.' "[2] Extravagant personal flattery was Roosevelt's way of smoothing the ruffled feathers.

Why was Hull left out? We know it was not age or ill health, as the public was allowed to surmise at the time; actually, Hull was to outlive Harry Hopkins nine years and the President ten

years. We have a strong clue in the fact that columnist Drew
Pearson attacked him as "anti-Russian." The *New Republic*
(September 6, 1943) said he was "notoriously" so. Other Left
Wing organs echoed this line.

The truth is that Hull fancied himself a stickler for international probity, and he was capable of being revolted by treachery
to a principle when it was plain enough for him to recognize it.
In 1942, he had blocked secret agreements Stalin had tried to
get, particularly out of the harassed British, for postwar territorial plunder which would have vitiated the Atlantic Charter
even that early.[3] In February of that year, he had rather indiscreetly sent the President a memorandum reminding him that
"there is no doubt that the Soviet Government has *tremendous
ambitions* with regard to Europe."[4] And he had shown that he
was not easily to be fooled by Stalin, for he said to Churchill in
March of 1943: "It's my opinion that if Russia should eventually
come into the war in the Pacific, it will probably be two or three
weeks before victory, during which time she can spread out
over Manchuria and other large areas and then be assured of
sitting in at the peace conference."[5]

This kind of talk did little to please Roosevelt and Hopkins.
When they went abroad to the big conferences, the Secretary
of State was left at home to putter around in Washington. Yet
Roosevelt needed Hull politically. Hull tried to resign in 1944
before the fourth-term election. "Mr. Roosevelt then asked that
I withhold my resignation at least until after the election. To
this I agreed."[6] A fortnight after the election, Hull resigned.

From Yalta, a few weeks later, Hull received a sirupy cable
signed by Roosevelt, Stalin, Churchill, Molotov, Eden, and Stettinius. "We have missed you at this conference," it said. This
gem of hypocrisy was almost too much for the patient and gentle
old man, who remembered that his presence had not been
deemed necessary at Argentia, Casablanca, Cairo, or Teheran.

In his memoirs, he hastens to add: "I should state at this point that I was not consulted by the President or anyone else on policy issues prior to or during the Yalta Conference."[7] The President saw him just before departing for Yalta, "but he did not take up any of the topics he expected to discuss with Stalin and Churchill or the decisions he might make." The undertone of irritation impels one to think that the Roosevelt brand of sirup was not sweet enough this time. The "we have missed you" was too raw to swallow. We also sense that Hull wished to assure that the judgment of history would acquit him of any guilt for the crimes of Yalta.

To only one of the Roosevelt foreign conferences was Cordell Hull invited. That was at Quebec in August of 1943. However, it was arranged that he should arrive late—after the important decisions had already been made. Nor was he ever told all that happened there.

It was another Big Two conference. Delighted by the prospect of congenial Canadian hospitality, Churchill brought his wife and daughter over from England. Stalin had again coyly declined. The American public did not know that President Roosevelt's courtship of the Russian dictator was still a one-sided romance as far as any desire for "a date" was concerned, and the press was left to speculate on whether or not Stalin had been invited. But Hull writes: "The President made his fourth unsuccessful attempt to meet with Stalin at the time of the Quebec Conference in August, 1943. He had hoped to induce the Soviet leader to attend that meeting."[8] Had Stalin come, certain people in Quebec would not have shared Roosevelt's ardor. *L'Action Catholique*, the newspaper mouthpiece of Cardinal Villeneuve, greeted the conferees with an editorial that began: "Stalin will not come to Quebec. We rejoice. His presence would have spoiled the pleasure . . . and tarnished the pride."

Italy had all but surrendered. Mussolini was out. He had been deposed in the last week of July, and the government of Marshal Badoglio was frantically trying to switch sides, a flip-flop that was complicated by the presence of German forces on Italian soil. The details of Italy's status were being worked out in Lisbon by emissaries from Badoglio and from General Eisenhower's headquarters. Italy was to surrender officially a few days after the invasion of the mainland from Sicily on September 3.

In the east, the Russians had turned the Nazi summer offensive into a rout. The Germans could hardly have been expected to perform well in view of what was happening behind their backs in their homeland. Germany was being reduced to rubble by the R.A.F. and the American Eighth Air Force. Hamburg was destroyed in six night and two day raids. Ruhr industries were almost paralyzed. On August 2, Berlin was ordered evacuated. Throughout the Reich, thousands were dying and supplies for the fighting forces were going up in flames. Desperation, whipped up by Roosevelt's "unconditional surrender" ukase, and little more, postponed the *Gotterdammerung* of the Nazi regime. At the Quebec Conference, everyone laughed at a gag credited to Churchill before he left England:

INTERVIEWER: Will you offer peace terms to Germany?
CHURCHILL: Heavens, no. They would accept immediately.[9]

In the Pacific, the Japanese were being driven out of the Solomons. Allied air superiority was assured in almost all of the Pacific and Asian theaters. The Japanese navy was to be spoken of largely in the past tense.

Churchill met with the President at Hyde Park on August 13, before the conference, and made a detour to show his daughter Niagara Falls. Roosevelt made a pompous entry into Quebec on the seventeenth. There was a parade to the Citadel, the summer home of the Governor-General, where he and Harry Hopkins were to stay and where special ramps had been built for his wheel chair. His dog, Fala, chaperoned by a Secret Service agent, had a big automobile all to himself in the parade and was visible proof to all the world that his master loved dogs and therefore had a heart of gold.

The chiefs of staff had assembled in advance on the twelfth and were lodged at the luxurious Chateau Frontenac, along with assorted conference-followers and more than a hundred news reporters. All other guests were moved out of the hotel. From all accounts, the weather was brisk after torrid Washington, the Canadian ale and whisky were superb, and there were many parties. Roosevelt and Churchill held their talks informally in their suites in the Citadel.

The big question came up, for Churchill was a bulldog on the point, even though he had lost before. Where should America and Britain hurl their military might on the continent of Europe? Into France, as Stalin had always insisted? The plan had been made, but Churchill was still against it. Roosevelt, Hopkins, and Marshall were adamant. By the time Hull arrived at Quebec on the twentieth they had prevailed again. *"Prior to my arrival,* President Roosevelt and Prime Minister Churchill had ... decided that an Anglo-American invasion of France should be made in spring of 1944. Mr. Churchill had argued—and continued to argue up to the Teheran Conference—that the invasion of Europe by the Western Allies should be through the Balkans, the 'soft underbelly of Europe.' " He wanted to "prevent a Soviet rush into that area which would permanently establish the authority of the Soviet Union there, to the detriment of Britain and incidentally of the United States."[10]

Hopkins' notes and Churchill's memoirs both confirm the disagreement, so there is no doubt that Roosevelt was untruthful when he said at a press conference on the day the Quebec Conference broke up that there had been no controversy during the conference that was in any way important. The controversy, though secret, was crucial. According to Hull, Roosevelt had his way because the United States was putting up the majority of the forces.

Churchill understood perfectly—as Roosevelt must have also —that what was involved here was not the winning of this war— that was no longer in doubt—but the geopolitics of postwar Europe. At stake was the heartland of the Continent. What Churchill was really talking about was not the war with Germany, but that other war—the hush-hush one—of militant Communism, incarnate as the new Russian dictatorship which had risen from the grave of the last Czar, against the capitalistic West, which, by the basic assumptions and written words of both Leninism and Stalinism, it was pledged to annihilate.

The busiest beaver at Quebec was Harry Hopkins. He had in his pocket an extraordinary top-secret document. It was headed "Russia's Position."[11]

If the assemblage of bigwigs at Quebec had had no other raison d'être, the opportunity it afforded Harry to pass this document around would have sufficed. The American public was to know nothing of it until after both Roosevelt and Hopkins were dead, yet it was an arrogant pronouncement of political policy of far-reaching consequence to the nation's future. Its precise authorship has never been disclosed. It claimed to be extracted from "a very high level United States military strategic estimate," so, presumably, somebody in the Army had either originated or embraced it. The words "high level" pointed to the office of the Chief of Staff; the adjective "very" seemed to put it in that office. But the "very high level" could also have been the Commander-in-Chief. In either case, it is a model of what a "military strategic estimate" should not be. So it is not surprising that its origin remains a mystery and its authorship an unclaimed honor.

Let us examine the document. One paragraph said:

Russia's post-war position in Europe will be a dominant one. With Germany crushed, there is no power in Europe to oppose her tremendous military forces. It is true that Great Britain is building up a position in the Mediterranean vis-à-vis Russia that she may find useful in balancing power in Europe. However, even here she may not be able to oppose Russia unless she is otherwise supported.

Now to anyone heedful of the future freedom of Europe, the problem presented by this intelligence was as obvious as the ribbons on General Marshall's chest. It was how to prevent the postwar domination of Europe by the Soviet Union from coming to pass. One would immediately perceive that the war should be waged and won in a manner to thwart that calamity. To Winston Churchill, this was elementary. As we have seen, he had plans to accomplish it.

But Hopkins' document made a flying leap in the opposite direction:

The conclusions from the foregoing are obvious. Since Russia is the decisive factor in the war, she must be given every assistance and every effort must be made to obtain her friendship. Likewise, since without question she will dominate Europe on the defeat of the Axis, it is even more essential to develop and maintain the most friendly relations with Russia.

In other words, give Russia "every assistance," and then, when she dominates Europe, keep flirting with her and hope for her friendship. So this was the garment being cut for America to wear. It had an unmistakable made-in-Moscow look.

One can only wonder what kind of a postwar world the writer

of this paper envisaged. The military security of the United States seems to have been the last thing in his mind, not the first, as he made this sly foray into a mystical statecraft of "friendship." If this was General Marshall expounding on the psychodynamics of nations, he was beyond his depth. If it was President Roosevelt, or Harry Hopkins, he was hiding behind a mask.

The American people, living in a thickening miasma of propaganda diffusing out from the White House, had little understanding that what Roosevelt and Hopkins were seeing in their crystal ball was the domination of Europe by Communist Russia. This grim apocalypse would have shocked the nation. Was this what the vast sacrifices were being made for? The apocalypse was not broadcast; it was a secret document in Harry's pocket, to be pulled out and shown to a chosen few. Nor was it grim to Harry and his boss, who continued, as though enchanted, to give "every assistance" to its fulfillment.

As for the Chief of Staff, his state of mind is sorrowfully described for us by an officer who had the closest prolonged contact with him in the Pentagon and on trips abroad during the war, General Albert C. Wedemeyer. Marshall, he tells us, "had little knowledge of the complexities of the world conflict" and "would seem to have failed to understand the nature and aims of communism." Wedemeyer's predicament is obvious. If this is a gentle apology for his old chief, it lets off as an ignoramus the man who had the entire intelligence facilities of the United States Army at his beck and call and those of the Navy as well for the asking, both of which services had files bulging with information on the nature and aims of Communism. Reading on, we learn of another serious flaw in the Marshall character, but it is a common and human one. Wedemeyer confesses that he revered General Marshall at one time but later came to see him as a man corrupted by power and homage: "Thus he became an easy prey to crypto-Communists, or Communist-sympathizing sycophants, who played on his vanity to accomplish their own ends."[12]

Whether or not Harry Hopkins, who was an intimate of General Marshall, had inspired this "military strategic estimate" in the first place, he took charge of putting it across as a sort of credo. Harry was not a man to dispute with at that time. For three and one-half years, he had been living in the White House, which the wits in Washington were referring to as "that two-family flat."[13] (Mrs. Hopkins had also moved in.) When the President's "man Friday" spoke to government officials or to high officers in the Army or Navy, he spoke with the authority becoming one whose address was 1600 Pennsylvania Avenue.

Slipped into his document was this mystifying clause: "Since Russia is the decisive factor in the war. . . ." (The dictionary defines "decisive" as "serving to decide; determinative.") This meant that winning or losing the war depended upon Russia. The factual absurdity of this bald assertion needs no laboring. With what motive was it implanted in this document? It was a libel against the titantic military and industrial might of the United States and Great Britain and the nations of the British Commonwealth, a force so overwhelming in the context of August, 1943, that the Axis powers were inevitably doomed even if Russia had collapsed. It exhibited a strange attitude of defeatism, almost masochistic, which somebody wished to insinuate into the American consciousness. In the postwar years, this idea —that but for Russia the Axis powers would not have been defeated—was to be one of the major propaganda weapons used by the Soviet Union throughout Europe and Asia in waging the cold war against the United States and its allies.

We know now that in Washington high naval officers were seething with suppressed dissent. Captain W. D. Puleston, the naval historian, who was a special adviser to the Secretary of

Navy at the time, writes: "Most of them were convinced that Russia needed the support of the United Nations more than they [the United Nations] needed that of Russia. The navy thought we had heard too much of Red contribution to victory and too little of the Anglo-American. They feared that if the Anglo-American representatives continued to extol Russia's efforts and apologize for their own, Stalin would demand more and more concessions."[14] Puleston mentions the document Hopkins produced at Quebec as "this almost unbelievable policy of appeasing Russia."

Anyone who went through the Army's Command and General Staff School during 1943 or 1944, as did this author, will remember the intellectual rebellion taking place there. In spite of the docility of General George C. Marshall in meshing his every thought into the Roosevelt-Hopkins pattern, his fawning attitude toward the Russians did not permeate all echelons of the Army. There was muffled grumbling in every headquarters and field camp and along the channels of supply, where Russian requisitions were usually, by order from high above, given priority. Nor was it limited to the Mark Clarks and Douglas MacArthurs. There were men of all ranks, men of independence, whose reason and patriotism could not be desensitized by any amount of politics and propaganda, in or out of the Army. They obeyed orders, as good soldiers, but with misgivings. When thousands of white sheets had to be sent to Fairbanks, Alaska, to be furnished to Red Army pilots taking delivery of free American airplanes (because they had complained of their bedding), the comments were unprintable. Such galling incidents were common.

The specter of a Soviet imperial colossus held no terror for Harry Hopkins. The anonymous, top-secret paper he flashed at Quebec was the Word. Sherwood writes that it was "of great importance as indicating the policy which guided the making of decisions at Teheran and, much later, at Yalta." Stettinius says the same. It epitomized the Rooseveltian mind.

At Quebec, Roosevelt decided to have American troops land in southern France (ANVIL), to supplement the Normandy invasion. "I never could understand why," writes General Mark Clark, who commanded the campaign in Italy. But Roosevelt and Hopkins could understand why. It diverted American strength from Italy and a push northeastward into Austria and the Balkans and was an "assistance" to Russia in becoming "dominant" in Europe. Thus it fitted in perfectly with the paper Harry Hopkins was carrying. Churchill, says Sherwood, fought "implacably" against Roosevelt's plan.

The Prime Minister induced President Roosevelt to sign one agreement at Quebec which was so secret that it lay hidden for almost eleven years. It gave Britain an equal voice in the use of the atom bomb, which the United States was soon to possess. In the first week of April, 1954, Sir Winston Churchill brought it to light in a debate in the House of Commons, causing an uproar on both sides of the Atlantic. It was at once apparent that the McMahon Act of 1946, which restricted exchange of American atomic information with foreign powers, had canceled the agreement, which few men knew anything about. Congress had abrogated a secret agreement made by the deceased President while having no inkling of it.

The secret agreement pledged that neither the United States nor Britain would ever use the bomb against the other, that neither would divulge any information to third parties without mutual consent, and that neither country would use the bomb against a third nation without the consent of the other. Actually, Roosevelt had made an unwarranted gift of power to a foreign country, however friendly at the time. It is unthinkable that the

Senate of the United States would ever have ratified a treaty conferring this veto power over weapons, strategy, and, in the dawning nuclear age, American foreign policy itself.

On this, too, the Secretary of State was kept in the dark. "I was not told about the atomic bomb," Cordell Hull's memoirs say. "I did not really know about it until it was dropped." But Klaus Fuchs and Harry Gold and David Greenglass and the Rosenbergs knew about it. People of alien and hostile backgrounds were being welcomed into installations where the newest weapons were being developed and into governmental positions. In those days, however, there were many things the Secretary of State was not permitted to know.

The Communist party knew about the development of the atomic bomb even before the F.B.I. did. The F.B.I. learned about it not from the Roosevelt administration but from undercover informants in Communist circles on the West Coast. F.B.I. men got their first information in 1943 from the Communists, who had friendly contacts with some of the scientists at a secret project at the University of California, from which it was known to be leaking, and the F.B.I. was promptly requested to discontinue its investigation of one of the scientists.[15]

Chapter XII

CAIRO

WE NOW COME to a melancholy turn in the fortunate career of Franklin D. Roosevelt. He had but seventeen months more to live when he left for Egypt in November of 1943, taking with him his physician, his masseur, his valet, six Filipino cooks from the yacht *Potomac,* Harry Hopkins, and the usual assortment of "brass." He was to confer with Churchill and Chiang Kai-shek in Cairo; but the real Mecca of this pilgrimage was beyond, under the brow of the Soviet Union, for Stalin had condescended at last to budge as far as Teheran, the Iranian capital, near the Caspian Sea, to share his company. In these next seventeen months were to be compressed a series of perpetrations which historians would judge the most ignoble of Roosevelt's spectacular life and which would forever tarnish his memory.

Now we even read it between the lines written by his adulators. He began to fumble his role. Old friends like Hull and Byrnes and Stimson and Jones saw this happening. A train of incredible blunders of policy and decision followed. And because he was now acting his part on a global stage, where every miscue could have burgeoning historic consequences, his repeated bungles at Cairo, Teheran, Quebec, and finally at Yalta, began to take on the gravity of a world catastrophe.

This is not to say there was any specific moment when the President lost his grip. And those, like Byrnes, who charitably blame his sagging health for the botcheries of the final months miss the point of the Roosevelt tragedy. The Roosevelt who wilted before the Russian dictator at Yalta was the same Roosevelt who had sent Harry Hopkins to Moscow with a blank check in 1941, who had feigned astonishment when the Japanese were provoked into "firing the first shot" in the Pacific, and who for three years had blocked Churchill's strategy in Europe every time it endangered Stalin's ambitions. The defects of personality which ambushed him when he sat down with Stalin—such as the narcissism which permitted him to gamble so heavily on his personal charm—were all there during the earlier years. It was the vertigo of unbridled world power that brought out the basic weakness of the Roosevelt character. The picture was gradually coming into focus.

His self-conceit now took on a new dimension. For beginning with the Cairo meeting with Churchill and Chiang Kai-shek, Roosevelt began to fall victim to the messianic complex which had destroyed Wilson in 1919. He began to envisage himself as the Master Builder of the shiny new postwar world. It was a role he was pathetically unsuited to attempt.

The Western powers could now reach any target in Germany with a thousand bombers by day or night. In a series of disasters, the *Wehrmacht* had been driven back from the Volga to the Dnieper. The OVERLORD Channel invasion was being prepared upon a stage so enormous that its certain success was assured. Roosevelt could now speak to his war allies as the leader of a coalition which was sure of victory. He could seriously consider the map of the world which was to follow.

In this pre-victory hour, one of the Big Four—China—was becoming weaker, not stronger. She needed a shot in the arm. That was supposedly one of the purposes of the Cairo Conference, to which Generalissimo and Madame Chiang Kai-shek were invited. China had been bled white by six years of continuous war with Japan. In its gloomy Chungking fastness, the Kuomintang government's will to fight was still strong, but its means had dwindled alarmingly.

Had Japan been her only enemy, China could have carried on and exacted a heavy toll. Unfortunately, China faced a second enemy more terrible than the first. This enemy was internal Communist rebellion. While she fought desperately on her two-thousand-mile front to expel the Japanese invaders, she was experiencing the grim sensation of seeing tens of thousands of square miles of her domain seized or infiltrated by Communist activists who were taking their orders from Moscow. What had happened was that the confusion of war had given the declining Chinese Communist Party a chance to make a sensational comeback in North China, and because he was preoccupied with the Japanese aggressors, President Chiang Kai-shek was powerless to take countersteps to check the power-hungry native Reds.

The 1943 situation stemmed back to 1937, when Chiang, just liberated from the ordeal of kidnapping by warlords at Sian, made the mistake of his life by making peace with the Chinese Communists. At that time, the Communists, who had been fighting Chiang continuously since 1927, were just about ready to quit. Confined to a small enclave around Yenan in the northwest province of Shensi, their plight was so desperate that their leaders had, even before the Sian affair, made overtures to representatives of Chiang, looking toward dissolution.[1] Their top bosses were making plans to go to Europe.

When the Japanese attack was imminent in 1937, Chiang determined that China must be unified, even at the cost of tolerating the Communists. If they could be induced to employ their Red Army to repel the Japanese, he would take them back into the fold. We now know that this failure to mop up the Chinese

Communists when he could have done so was the supreme blunder which brought Chiang down to ruin in 1948. But at the time, with Japan threatening total war, the decision seemed justified.

In an agreement which he concluded with the Communists in February, 1937, Chiang promised to discontinue his Communist-suppression policy. They, in turn, agreed to place their insurrectionary army under the authority of the National Army, to be known as the Eighteenth Group Army. The Communist forces were limited by this agreement to a strength of forty-five thousand men, later increased to sixty thousand. They were to wage guerrilla war against the Japanese in specified areas in North and Northwest China.[2] The Communists concluded this agreement with their tongues in their cheeks.

However, after Chiang was driven to Chungking, with no remaining armed force of any size north of the Yellow River, the Communists realized that their chance had come. Instead of fighting the Japanese, they withdrew from the war almost completely after Russia signed the Molotov-Matsuoka Treaty with Japan in April, 1941. With Chiang unable to halt them, they proceeded to carve out an empire for themselves in the unpoliced rural areas between the Japanese-occupied cities.

Spreading out, fanlike, through the countryside between the scattered Japanese bases, the Communists soon dominated most of the provinces of Hopeh, Chahar, Suiyuan, Shensi, Kansu, Anhwei, Shantung, and even northern Kiangsu—a vast empire of ninety million inhabitants. Disregarding the 1937 agreement with Chiang limiting the Red Army to four divisions, they increased their armed strength to more than five hundred thousand men, backed by partially armed local militia detachments.[3]

In thus defying the Chungking government, the Communists had their eyes firmly set on the date of Japanese defeat. They knew that when Japanese authority disintegrated after the surrender, control of the populous northern provinces—the heart of

China—would pass, during the interregnum of confusion, to whomever was on the ground with the largest forces. Chiang and his main forces were fifteen hundred or two thousand miles away in Szechwan and Burma and would be powerless to act in the north. By their cynical use of the war period to infiltrate and to arm, the Communists were making certain that they would be the real victors of the war. In their optimistic dreams, they envisaged Communist occupation of Nanking, Shanghai, and even Manchuria when the Japanese fell.

This was the harrowing situation which confronted Chiang Kai-shek in 1943 as he clung unhappily to his bomb-scarred Chungking capital. It was a situation which cried for bold, imaginative American intervention. It is one of the major disasters of the war that the United States, under Roosevelt, instead of bringing boldness and imagination to the Far East, brought irresoluteness and abjection.

Chiang was not naïve on the subject of Communism. "The Japanese," he had commented publicly, "are only lice on the body of China, but Communism is a disease of the heart." Politically wise, he knew that the long-range struggle in China was not between China and Japan—that war was won when the Japanese bombed Pearl Harbor—but between Chinese independence and subjugation to the international Communist revolution.

In the light of our present knowledge, the course which Roosevelt followed in China policy after the Casablanca Conference of January, 1943, seems incompatible with any conceivable pattern of American self-interest or even of plain common sense. It is the common practice of writers to blame General George C. Marshall and his 1945-46 "Mission" for the master blunders which opened China to Communism. Without exonerating Marshall in the slightest, it is only fair to point out that he was simply following the China line which Roosevelt had prescribed as early as 1943. It was Roosevelt, leaning upon such Left Wing advisers as Owen Lattimore, Lauchlin Currie and John Carter Vincent, and the now infamous Davies-Service clique in the Foreign Service, who decided arbitrarily, sometime in 1943, that it would be desirable to turn China over to Communism, at least in part, by forcing Chiang Kai-shek to take the Chinese Communists into his national government under the form of coalition.[4]

At a desk in the White House sat Lauchlin Currie, a confidential administrative assistant of the President, handling Far Eastern affairs. This man had not always been an American, and we may presume that his attachment to American citizenship was less than passionate, for the day was to come, after the war, when he would shake the soil of America from his shoes, shift his residence and activities to Colombia, South America, and see his American citizenship lapse after five years. (After the spy disclosures of 1948, in which there was testimony placing him in the Silvermaster espionage cell, Currie saw fit to depart for South America and remain there.) But during his White House interlude, under the warm wing of Mr. Roosevelt and with the benign smile of the First Lady and close contact with Harry Hopkins to give him confidence from day to day, "Lauch" (as the President called him)[5] was well placed to be of service to people.

However, Lauchlin Currie's idea of a good deed for the day was not exactly that of a Boy Scout. Joining Harry Dexter White and Nathan Witt as a reference for Nathan Gregory Silvermaster was the type of thing that appealed to him; and when Military Intelligence (G-2), outraged at seeing Silvermaster in a sensitive government post, made a secret security report on him, pointing out that he was known and listed in the files of the Seattle and San Francisco police departments, the Thirteenth Naval District, the American Legion, and the F.B.I. as a member and leader of the Communist Party and concluding that "the overwhelming . . . testimony of the many and varied witnesses and sources indicates beyond reasonable doubt that Nathan Gregory Silvermaster is now, and has for years, been a member and a leader of the Communist Party and very probably a secret agent of the OGPU," it was Currie who intervened in Silvermaster's favor, successfully, to keep him in the government. To assist himself, Currie selected one Michael Greenberg, a transplanted Britisher. Greenberg was indeed a sort of "expert" on the Far East, but it also happened to be the case that he had been a trained Communist for many years. He, too, felt enough at home in his new milieu to write letters on White House stationery.[6]

Naturally, such men had plans for China. In 1943, the gambit was "coalition." The coalition concept is now so thoroughly discredited in the free world's mind that it is difficult to recapture the almost suicidal trustfulness with which Roosevelt welcomed it. Coalition appealed to the President because it gave him the illusion that he had settled his hard problems without open collision with Stalin over postwar aims. It was an attractive device for sweeping the dust under the bed instead of cleaning it up. The fact that the coalition expedient merely postponed the showdowns into the future, while strengthening Communism in the meantime, was not the kind of thing that could keep this man awake nights. He was breathing the intoxicating incense of present glory and apparent success; the future he would leave to his successors.

It was at Cairo that Roosevelt first notified the beleaguered Chiang Kai-shek that he must take the Communists into his cabinet. No word of this historic sabotage appears in the discreetly worded communiqué which the conferees issued after the meeting. It was done clandestinely, as part of an under-the-table deal Roosevelt was attempting while Churchill was out of the room. Elliott Roosevelt, perhaps indiscreetly, reveals what was in his father's mind when he came face to face with the Chinese President; it was to wrest from Chiang a pledge to appease the Communists. "Father" confided to Elliott: "You see, he [Chiang] wants very badly to get our support against the British moving into Hongkong and Shanghai and Canton with the same old extraterritorial rights they enjoyed before the war." Elliott asked if "Father" would give that support. "Not for nothing," cried "Father." He then told Elliott he had complained to Chiang about the character of his government:

I'd told him it was hardly the modern democracy that ideally it should be. *I'd told him he would have to form a unity government,* while the war was still being fought, *with the Communists* in Yenan.[7]

It is a measure of Franklin D. Roosevelt's statesmanship and his semantics that he saw a gain for "democracy" in empowering the Communists.

With equal unreality, another *idée fixe* was germinating in Franklin D. Roosevelt's mind at this time. He was about to begin the frenzied imploration of the Russians to enter a Japanese war which only stern American opposition could have kept them out of when the time came to grab the spoils. In August, 1942, Averell Harriman had asked Stalin for a pledge of eventual entrance into the Japanese War. The shrewd Russian had put him off with a vague promise,[8] which he repeated to another Roosevelt envoy, General Patrick J. Hurley, in November.[9] Hull says that Stalin stated in October, 1943, that he would "help defeat Japan" after Germany was beaten,[10] but Stalin was not asked what his intentions would be in the Far East after Japan's defeat. Now, at the end of 1943, all the logic of the situation called for extreme vigilance to keep the Russians *out* of the Far East. Instead, President Roosevelt, egged on constantly by Harry Hopkins, was preparing to invite, entice, and even bribe them to come in. And simultaneously, at Cairo, as we have seen, he started to pull the rug out from under anti-Communist government of China.

Roosevelt, as usual, was busy thinking up ways to make Stalin happy. So at Cairo, we are informed by Averell Harriman, he proposed to Chiang that China give the Russians the use of the port of Dairen.[11] Chiang naturally dodged this blow, but it was a grim foretaste of the Roosevelt technique. It is the common impression that Dairen was yielded to Russia at Yalta under duress by a reluctant Roosevelt. The truth is even more discreditable. Roosevelt offered it. He had liked the idea at Cairo, and at Teheran he opened the door to this and all the later concessions demanded by Stalin at the expense of China.

The military discussions at Cairo concerned a project—to which Roosevelt had already committed himself—to reconquer Burma and open the Burma Road into China. The idea was that the Chinese would invade Burma from across the Salween River, and American General Stilwell would lead four crack Chinese divisions being trained in India through the jungles of northern Burma. At the same time, the British were to undertake an amphibious operation across the Bay of Bengal. It was both a romantic plan and "Vinegar Joe" Stilwell's obsession.

Prime Minister Churchill had no stomach for it. Why should British forces be sent to fight the Japanese? Japan would lose the war in due time anyway. So he talked again about Rhodes and the Balkans—or veering toward "the right" from Italy—and he wanted any available British naval strength to concentrate in the eastern Mediterranean, not the Bay of Bengal. He was not pleased that Roosevelt had invited the Chinese to Cairo. "The talks of the British and American Staffs were sadly distracted by the Chinese story, which was lengthy, complicated and minor," his memoirs moan. "All hope of persuading Chiang and his wife to go and see the pyramids and enjoy themselves until we returned from Teheran fell to the ground, with the result that the Chinese business occupied first instead of last place at Cairo."[12]

As for President Roosevelt, he was on his way to make a favorable impression on Marshal Stalin, and the last thing he wanted to talk about at this moment was an Anglo-American invasion of the Balkans. The American delegation saw plainly that the dogged Prime Minister was resuming the advocacy of strategic diversions into southeastern Europe and away from northern France. "They prepared themselves," says Sherwood, "for the battles at Teheran in which the Americans and the Russians would form a united front."[13]

"The Chinese business," which so irked Churchill, was a comedy of motives. He was opposed to ANAKIM (the Burma campaign) because he wanted to use the British strength elsewhere. Roosevelt favored ANAKIM because he did not want British strength to be sent where Churchill wanted to send it. Chiang Kai-shek took a long-range view; he perceived that the opening of the Burma Road to his stronghold in China would enhance his prestige, bring a seasoned, loyal, well-equipped army home, and reinforce his capacity to deal with the Communists as the war ended. At the same time, Roosevelt was pressuring Chiang to merge with the Communists, for a secret price, at the expense of the British.

If this seems fantastic, particularly since the Cairo Conference had the outward appearance of a love feast of dedicated allies, Sherwood's analysis gives a candid answer. In Southeast Asia, he says, *"the British and Americans were fighting two different wars for different purposes, and the Kuomintang Government was fighting a third war for purposes largely its own."*[14] This would have been a stunning revelation to the American people if it had been made while the war, or wars, were in progress.

Actually, there was a multiplicity of wars in Europe and Asia as a whole, and the pseudo-alliance of America, Britain, China, and Russia was a tissue of cross-purposes.

The upshot was characteristic. The talks produced what Sherwood calls "a semblance of agreement" that ANAKIM would be carried out. As Admiral Leahy points out, "the commitment had been made months before." He adds: "Chiang left Cairo for Chungking fully expecting his allies to make good their promises."[15] This corroborates Sherwood's assertion that when the Generalissimo and the Madame departed, their hopes were high that this time China's demands would be met with more than "mere words."

These hopes were short lived. Roosevelt and Churchill stopped at Cairo again on the way home from Teheran. They tossed the ANAKIM plan into the wastebasket. As Sherwood puts it, "Roosevelt felt impelled to renege on his own promise to Chiang Kai-shek, made ten days previously."[16]

Why? Because Roosevelt had talked with Stalin in the interval. Russia was intending to come into the Japanese War herself. (Sherwood admits that this was "the most important factor.")[17] A strengthened Chinese Nationalist government would hardly fit in with Stalin's long-term plans for China.

The consequences soon proved to be catastrophic. The Japanese, relieved of uncertainty over Burma, mounted their most formidable offensive against China in five years. It carried their troops forward on a fifteen-hundred mile front between the Yangtze and the frontiers of Indochina. It wiped out strongholds in Southeast China which had withstood the Japanese since 1938 and airfields used by the U.S. Fourteenth Air Force under General Claire L. Chennault in Hunan, Kwangsi, and Yunnan. This blow, coming in the final year of the war after seven years of agonized Chinese resistance, almost knocked Chiang out of the war. Only his stout heart, the fortunate assignment of General Albert C. Wedemeyer to Chungking, and the valor of such men as General Chennault saved the disaster from becoming total.

By inducing Chiang to focus upon Burma and then walking out on him, his allies imposed an impossible war plan upon him. His best troops were on the Burma frontier. He was drawn to the south. Yet it has always been true that he who controls the north of China controls China. The Communists were feverishly busy there. When the war ended, they were either entrenched in or contiguous to the important areas and in direct contact with the Russians. Bereft of the logistical support he had expected from his allies, Chiang was never able to recover the military advantage over Mao Tse-tung and the Red Army.

The return to Cairo, after Teheran, also concerned another neighbor of the Soviet Union. For a long time Churchill had been avid to get Turkey to join the Allies, as part of his strategy to penetrate southeastern Europe, but President İnönü of Turkey was a cautious fence-sitter. Roosevelt had never shown any enthusiasm for going into that part of Europe, so when İnönü came to see Roosevelt and Churchill at Cairo, he was friendly, but he committed none of Turkey's fifty divisions. To Churchill's bitter disappointment, Roosevelt contributed nothing but smiles to the interview, and İnönü departed.

Before he left Cairo for home, Roosevelt made one historic decision which it is generally believed pleased Churchill. He selected General Dwight D. Eisenhower to command OVERLORD. This choice was against "the almost impassioned advice" of Harry Hopkins, who preferred Marshall for the job.[18] Admiral Leahy, Admiral King, and General Arnold had all hoped that Marshall would not be appointed.[19]

We now know from the war diary of Field Marshal Viscount Alan Brooke, chief of the Imperial General Staff, that Brooke did not have a high opinion of Marshall as a strategist.[20] The

Hopkins-Marshall team had consistently bucked Churchill in favor of strategy pleasing to Stalin. It is probable that strong British pressure upon Roosevelt accounts for the unexpected appointment of Eisenhower. Marshall was placated with this Presidential compliment: "I feel I could not sleep with you out of the country."

As Chief of Staff, Marshall continued to be a powerful figure. If we are to accept Field Marshal Brooke's final appraisal, Eisenhower's skill lay in harmonizing the diverse elements which planned and carried out the invasion. "He learned a lot during the war, but tactics, strategy and command were never his strong points. . . . As Supreme Commander what he may have lacked in military ability he greatly made up for by the charm of his personality."[21]

Be that as it may, Eisenhower went on to become a national hero and the President of his country. That he owed much to Franklin D. Roosevelt's decision at Cairo in December, 1943, will never be denied. Perhaps a lingering gratitude is the reason why, in the Presidential office, he protected the Roosevelt reputation with a solicitude which is not helpful to historical research. The Teheran papers, shrouded in the State Department's files under lock and key, were to be revealed. They never were.

Chapter XIII

TEHERAN

Dr. EDUARD BENEŠ, the last and tragic president of the First Republic of Czechoslovakia, visited Moscow on December 12, 1943, eleven days after the Teheran Conference. To his nephew and close associate, Bohus Beneš, he reported his observations. "I recall," the latter relates, "how President Beneš was astonished when, visiting Moscow shortly after Teheran, he found Stalin jubilant."[1]

The Russians tickled Dr. Beneš' ethnic pride by telling him he could now be sure that the Slavs would eventually rule Eurasia. "Stalin did not tell Dr. Beneš that, at Teheran, Churchill and Roosevelt secretly consented to Red Army liberation of Czechoslovakia." Voicing the postwar bitterness of a tortured people, Bohus Beneš speaks plainly: "General Patton was stopped from liberating Czechoslovakia by General Eisenhower acting on instructions from Washington as a result of Teheran and Yalta. Patton had to stand by while Nazis were shooting Czechoslovakians until three days later the Reds came in. Can you imagine that Czechoslovakians felt for the second time they had been betrayed by decisions behind their back and lost faith in democracy? . . . President Beneš also told me how astounded he was when . . . President Roosevelt told him to advise Stalin that 'he could have his Baltic states,' though nothing should be published about it."

The Poles were especially worried about Teheran. It was inevitable that the future of Poland would be discussed, yet no Pole was invited. Stanislaw Mikolajczyk, the prime minister of the exiled government of Poland, was not granted an interview by President Roosevelt until June 6, 1944, six months after the conference. The fourth-term campaign was looming, and the Polish spokesman had to be quieted for a few months more. "I haven't acted on the Polish question because this is an election year," Roosevelt said to him.[2] He held out hope, and his manner to his visitor was one of great courtesy. "I later learned," writes Mikolajczyk sadly, "that Roosevelt had only a few months before agreed to turn over to Stalin the huge section of Poland that the Red Army had invaded while an Axis partner." When this Polish statesman came to write his book on these events, he could find no more apt title than *The Rape of Poland*.

What, indeed, did happen at Teheran? Why did Dr. Beneš find Stalin so jubilant? The basic reason is that the Russian dictator learned something at Teheran—something very joyous for him. He discovered that he had the President of the United States *dans sa poche,* as the French would say.

Some things remain hidden to this day. That the Atlantic Charter (Points One, Two, and Three in particular) was treated as so much rubbish by the three Caesars who confronted each other around the green baize table in the Russian Embassy at Teheran is known beyond conjecture or surmise. But some of the furtive military arrangements—which had grave consequences—are still being tossed about like hot potatoes by the people who had to execute them. And the precise words spoken by the triumvirate, the unguarded comments, and the air of cynicism, conspiracy, and contempt for the millions of human beings whom they were preparing to push around, which must have pervaded their discussions because it is inherent in their works, have only partially seeped through the wall of secrecy. When in April, 1953, Senator William F. Knowland demanded the opening of the official files on Teheran, the State Department promised to make them public before June 30, 1955.[8] They remain locked up. It is probable that some of the more embarrassing, if not heinous, details will not see the light of day until after the deaths of a number of people now living.

And yet, as a direction marker for what was to follow, Teheran was perhaps more important than the more publicized Yalta. It was at Teheran that the basic decisions which later took concrete and appalling form at Yalta were plotted. It was at Teheran that it first became evident that Stalin, not Roosevelt, was to shape the peace.

So closely guarded were some of the Teheran decisions during the last months of the war that even so highly placed a person as Vice-President Truman (Senator at the time of the Conference) was unaware of them and of their Yalta sequels and was hurriedly briefed on these secret agreements by Harry Hopkins when he was projected into the Presidency in April, 1945. By then, he was already a prisoner of Roosevelt's folly.

Significantly, the Communists in the United States were never in doubt about the decisive import of what had taken place. Getting their newest line through an international grapevine, they quickly announced that Teheran had changed the world. It had generated, they said, a new atmosphere in which Communists could work unreservedly with Washington. Earl Browder, then chief boss of the American Communist Party, whom Roosevelt had released from jail (for a passport fraud) on a White House pardon, arranged a Madison Square Garden mass meeting in New York on May 25, 1944, where he bellowed to fifteen thousand Communists that Teheran had supplied the pattern for the postwar world. Later, he elaborated the theme in a book *Teheran and After,* issued and widely exploited by the Communist party.

We now know that President Roosevelt maintained a secret liaison with Browder. One Josephine Adams, an artist, acted as a courier between the two men. She relayed information, and even documents, between them, conveying to each the views of the other. She saw Roosevelt between thirty-eight and forty times during the three year period preceding his death. The meetings were held either at the White House or at Roosevelt's Hyde Park home. (Years later, Miss Adams so testified under oath before a subcommittee of the United States Senate.)[4] Browder has confirmed this, taking obvious pride in the fact that he presented his "views on world events" to the President by this device and adding that the President "appreciated the service I gave him."[5]

The salient fact that emerged at Teheran was that President Roosevelt had been grotesquely wrong in his confident assurance that he could "handle" Stalin. It was easy for him to assume, in the fawning atmosphere of Washington, that he had but to meet the Russian, "turn on" his famous personality, and have his way. When they met, he was in for a rude awakening. He found Stalin, says Sherwood, "much tougher than he had expected and at times deliberately discourteous."[6] It was Stalin, not Roosevelt, who did the handling.

Stalin, with Georgian cunning, had deliberately waited until he could take a threatening tone with Roosevelt and Churchill before consenting to meet them in a summit conference. He was prepared to drive a hard bargain now. As for Roosevelt, he had already lost the psychological hour for bargaining. But that was not his technique with Stalin, and never had been.

The dramatis personae of the Teheran meeting lifted it to the eminence of high theater. There was Stalin, the mystery man, flanked by Molotov and Voroshilov. This incredible figure, who had already won a place in history alongside Ivan the Terrible, had at last stepped from the shadows. The world was to take his measure, when pitted against the West's top statesmen.

In contraposition was Winston Churchill. So deep seated was his detestation of Communism that he had once lost an election to the House of Commons by overstressing the issue. But he was an opportunist, capable of bizarre switches and turns and flights from principle when he thought it was to Britain's gain. By a sardonic twist of fate, this man, with his unsleeping awareness of the Russian peril, had been destined to be one of Moscow's saviors when Hitler stood on the brink of conquest in 1941. What unvoiced thoughts passed through his fertile mind as he sat opposite the Communist dictator at Teheran, with the unctuous American President at his side holding the balance of power, can be imagined.

The third principal was Franklin D. Roosevelt. This was his great hour, and he played his role for all it was worth. "If there was any supreme peak in Roosevelt's career," says Sherwood, "I believe it might well be fixed at this moment, at the end of the Teheran Conference." With his weakness for self-hypnosis, Roosevelt no doubt persuaded himself that he accomplished something good at Teheran. History has regretfully handed down a different verdict.

Stalin, with his unerring judgment of men, quickly sensed that Roosevelt was the weak link of the Big Two. He set about at once to establish an entente. Pleading his concern for the President's safety, he invited Roosevelt to move out of the American Legation into the heavily guarded Russian Embassy compound. Roosevelt accepted, whereupon Stalin ostentatiously turned over the main villa to him and moved with his staff to one of the smaller buildings. The President and his party were now under the Russian microscope. The servants who made their beds and cleaned their rooms were all members of the highly efficient NKVD, the Soviet secret police.[7]

Fifteen minutes after Roosevelt arrived in his new quarters, Stalin came to call. It took no perspicacity to discern that the President was fairly bursting to please him. Roosevelt talked about various parts of the British colonial empire in a way which made plain his detachment from Churchill. Then he had a new bonbon to offer. By the end of the war, he said, the American and British merchant fleets would have achieved such proportions that they would be more than two nations could possibly need and he felt that some of these ships should be made available to the Soviet Union.[8] Naturally, to Stalin, who had his own long-range plans for Communist penetration into Southern Asia, the Middle East, and Africa and inroads into world trade, all of this was music with a lovely melody. It meant that Roosevelt could be counted upon not only to help make the Soviet Union the dominant land power in Europe and Asia but also to enhance her stature as a maritime nation.

The dictator was in a mood to impress. Hopkins noted that he was dressier now, wearing a uniform with gold epaulets, each bearing a large white star fastened with a red pin. Harriman has said that Stalin, in greeting Harry Hopkins at Teheran, displayed more open and warm cordiality than he had been known to show to any foreigner.[9] This hard-shell specimen, this Tartar whose flinty eyes hinted the Mongolian admixture in his blood, this tyrant who had starved the Kulaks and cut down with callous savagery every human obstacle in his rise to power, was hardly an affectionate type, but he was shrewd enough to know a friend when he saw one. No doubt his pleasure at seeing Hopkins at Teheran was sincere.

Playing upon the President's vanity, Stalin hurried to propose that Mr. Roosevelt be chairman of the sessions. Churchill agreed. At the first plenary session, the chairman welcomed Stalin, Molotov, and Voroshilov as "new members of the family circle." After painting this weird picture of a family circle, which should have brought laughs but did not, he proceeded to predict that the three nations would work together in close co-operation "for generations to come."

When Stalin spoke, he got down to military business fast. He said it would be "unwise" for his Western allies to "scatter forces" in operations throughout the eastern Mediterranean, and he pooh-poohed the idea of their moving northward in Italy or into the Balkan area. He wanted the cross-Channel invasion of France (OVERLORD) to be the preoccupation of his allies in 1944, and he wanted some American and British forces taken out of Italy and sent into southern France to supplement it. Then he turned to the war against Japan. He said Russia would come into that one when Germany was finally defeated. He then added a remark that most Americans probably would have considered sheer impudence. "We shall be able by our common front to beat Japan," said Stalin.[10]

That night, the President was host at a dinner for Stalin, Molotov, Churchill, Eden, Kerr, Hopkins, Harriman, and three interpreters, at which the six Filipino cooks he had brought with him displayed their talents. The conversation was that of men giddy not only with the martinis, the vodka, and the champagne, which flowed profusely, but also with sheer power; for these men commanded almost all the naval forces of the world, three-quarters of its air power, and land armies numbering nearly twenty million men. Stalin set the tone. He spoke contemptuously of the French nation and of what he called its "ruling class"; he said the Germans must be given harsh treatment permanently; and he said a big chunk should be handed over to Poland. Feeling his way, he did not spell out what aggrandizement he had in mind for the Soviet Union, beyond a categorical remark that he would keep the Baltic States of Latvia, Lithuania, and Estonia, which his armies had seized.

The next day, Churchill sent a message to Roosevelt suggesting that they have lunch together preparatory to the second plenary session. Roosevelt sent back his regrets. But he did have a private confab that afternoon with "Uncle Joe." We have accounts of this tête-à-tête from son Elliott, who was present with his father, and from Sherwood, who had access to the President's logbook. If anything was needed to convince Stalin that he was fortunate enough to be dealing with an infatuated Don Quixote, this meeting must have sufficed.

Roosevelt seems to have done most of the talking. He brought nods of approval from Stalin when he told of his missionary work with Chiang Kai-shek at Cairo—how he had exerted pressure to have Communists brought into the Chinese government. As they talked about the Far East, Stalin held his cards close to his chest; he gave out nothing. Roosevelt then asked Stalin if he cared to discuss the future peace of the world. This question nonplussed the Russian, for his mind was attuned to concrete situations, not airy abstractions. He replied that there was nothing to prevent them from discussing anything they pleased, whereupon Roosevelt sprang his idea of "The Four Policemen." He conceived a United Nations organization consisting of an Assembly, an Executive Committee, and an enforcing agency which he termed "the Four Policemen." The Soviet Union, the United States, Britain, and China were to comprise this constabulary. Little nations threatening the peace would be handled by blockades and embargoes. A major threat to world peace would arise if a large power made a gesture of aggression; in this case, said Roosevelt, the Four Policemen would send an ultimatum to the threatening nation, and, if the demands were not immediately met, they would bomb and, if necessary, invade that nation.

There is no evidence of any discussion of the possibility that the offending aggressor might be one of The Four Policemen. It must have been obvious to Stalin that Roosevelt's world was a phantasmagoria. He encouraged the delusion and was quite willing to be a policeman.

Stalin went into the second plenary session later that afternoon so sure of Roosevelt's captivity that he permitted himself to be blunt toward Churchill to the point of rudeness. With his usual persistence, the Prime Minister started talking about the eastern Mediterranean area. Sharply, Stalin said he wanted to talk about OVERLORD; Turkey, Rhodes, Yugoslavia, and even the capture of Rome were not important enough. Churchill made a last, gallant effort, but Roosevelt went along with Stalin. OVERLORD, coupled with an attack in southern France; Stalin knew what he wanted and that is what he got.

It was obvious at Teheran that both Stalin and Voroshilov recognized General Marshall as a friend.[11] Marshall, it will be remembered, had plugged for a diversion into southern France at the First Quebec Conference. This was precisely what Stalin had been prescribing, for it relegated the amphibious forces in the Mediterranean to a distant corner of Europe (from the Russian viewpoint) and away from the Balkans, and it headed British-American troops away from the eastern half of Europe. The geopolitician MacKinder had written that he who rules eastern Europe commands the heartland, he who rules the heartland commands the world island, he who rules the world island rules the world. As Chester Wilmot points out, "there was a long-term political strategy behind the Russian desire for the Allies to concentrate on Western Europe and the Western Mediterranean."[12] At Teheran, Churchill was disgusted to find that General Marshall, taking his cue from Roosevelt and Hopkins, had joined forces with Stalin. The President told his son Elliott after this session: "If there's one American general that Winston can't abide, it's General Marshall."[13]

The President made another remark to Elliott, in the privacy of his apartment, which reveals how susceptible he was to Stalin's purposes:

Trouble is, the P.M. is thinking too much of the post-war, and where England will be. He's scared of letting the Russians get too strong.[14]

It was quickly apparent to the Russians at Teheran that Roosevelt, unlike the British delegation, had arrived with a supine, trust-Russia mind. Had Roosevelt stood firmly with Churchill, it would have been possible, even at this late date, to block Stalin's rapacity. The die had not yet been cast. The German army, though retreating, was still on Russian soil, five hundred miles from the borders of Germany proper. American and British military, air, and naval strength, still uncommitted, was overwhelming and could strike where it chose. But Roosevelt did not stand firm with the Prime Minister. He affected the flattering role of middleman between two contenders. Actually, he always leaned Stalin's way. Churchill, thus isolated, was forced to capitulate. At every turn, Stalin had Roosevelt's open or tacit support for his determination that on V-E Day there should be no British or American troops in eastern Europe to challenge his plot for a Communist hegemony.

(One American who soon protested vigorously was General Mark Clark, commander of the U.S. Fifth Army in Italy. He made a strong plea to General Marshall for an invasion of the Balkans, in spite of the Teheran decision.[15] It was, of course, in vain. General Clark has written:

A campaign that might have changed the whole history of relations between the Western world and the Soviet Union was permitted to fade away. . . . Not alone in my opinion, but in the opinion of a number of experts who were close to the problem, the weakening of the campaign in Italy in order to invade Southern France, instead of pushing on into the Balkans, was one of the outstanding mistakes of the War. . . . Stalin knew exactly what he wanted . . . and the thing

he wanted most was to keep us out of the Balkans. . . . It is easy to
see, therefore, why Stalin favored ANVIL at Teheran.[16])

After Stalin had bludgeoned his way through the second plenary session, he was host at dinner. Hopkins' notes record that
during this dinner, the Prime Minister asked Stalin an important
question. He wanted to know what territorial interests Russia
might have in the future. Stalin was quoted as having replied:
"There is no need to speak at the present time about any Soviet
desires—but when the time comes, we will speak."[17] This chilly
closure of the subject had ominous portent, but there is no evidence that it caused Roosevelt the slightest discomfort.

This Russian banquet was a raucous bout at which serious
subjects were discussed in a rolling gunfire of toasts as course
after course was washed down with vodka and champagne.
Harry Hopkins lasted only halfway through. Whenever tension
ran high between the British and the Russians, Roosevelt would
achieve a superficial truce by rushing in with a breezy wisecrack.

However, one of his jokes fell flat (although it has won a kind
of notoriety because both Churchill and Elliott Roosevelt saw
fit to include it in their memoirs). Stalin rose and proposed a
blood-curdling toast. The strength of the German army depended, he said, upon fifty thousand high officers and technicians. His toast was a salute to shooting them "as fast as we
capture them, all of them."

Churchill was horrified. Quick as a flash, he was on his feet;
his face and neck were red, says Elliott Roosevelt, who was present. He announced that British conceptions of law and justice
would never tolerate such butchery. Into this breach stepped
President Roosevelt. He had a compromise to suggest. Instead
of executing fifty thousand, perhaps "we should settle on a
smaller number. Shall we say 49,500?"

All the Russians at the table roared with laughter. So did the

Americans, who were obliged to show proper appreciation for their chief's humor. The Prime Minister, shocked as much by F.D.R.'s flippancy as by Stalin's barbarity, left the table. That joke—or was it a joke?—was too grim.

Amiability was restored the next day, which was Churchill's sixty-ninth birthday. It was climaxed with a dinner party to which all the military and civilian conferees were invited. "I think about a hundred toasts and speeches must have been given that night," General H. H. ("Hap") Arnold remembered.[18] Again, because of Roosevelt's attitude of deference, Stalin was accorded the right to be sarcastic and cagey and to collect valuable information while giving out none. In his mild way, General Arnold writes, "I am not so sure we were as successful in discovering what the Russians wanted as they were in finding out what our objectives were."

Actually, Roosevelt and Hopkins already knew. The secret prospectus Harry had carried in his pocket at the Quebec Conference the previous August was unequivocal. Not only was Russia to "dominate Europe," but she was also to be assisted and propitiated by the United States in every possible way. Furthermore, at Roosevelt's dinner two nights before, Stalin had made it plain that he had in mind carving up both Germany and Poland.

Perhaps that is why, the next day, before the last plenary session, at which the Polish question was to come up, the President went into a private talk with Stalin and Molotov. If he had taken a copy of the Atlantic Charter into this meeting and required Stalin and Molotov to reread it, he would have been fulfilling a pledge and duty. But such was not his purpose. It was not to plead for the Poles; it was to plead for himself. He felt it necessary to acquaint Stalin with the facts of American politics, particularly with the fact that there were six or seven million Americans of Polish extraction, and others of Lithuanian, Latvian, and

Estonian origin, all of whom had the same votes as anyone else.[19]
(This meant, in terms of practical politics, that any decisions
which would be offensive to these groups would have to remain
secret at least until after the Presidential election of 1944.) Stalin
said he understood the problem. (No doubt he did; yet a few
months later, Roosevelt, then exercising his blandishments on
the democratically minded Mikolajczyk, recounted with great
amusement: "You know, I mentioned the matter of our forthcoming American elections to Stalin, and he just couldn't understand what I was talking about."[20])

Having thus prepared Stalin, Roosevelt was now ready to re-
treat to the sidelines and pretend to look the other way while
the Polish nation was placed on the sacrificial altar—with public
announcements of the bloody deed to be withheld until he had
coasted in safely to a fourth term as President.

What was to be done about Poland was a sort of ethical test of
the Allies in this war. The British had based their declaration
of war on Germany in 1939 upon Hitler's violation of the Polish
frontier. The territorial integrity of Poland was the moral justifi-
cation for plunging into war. The war would degenerate into a
monstrous, historic fraud if the Allies themselves were to enact
a new rape of unhappy Poland. Yet this was exactly what happened.

The background of the Teheran discussions was important.
In the preceding April, Stalin had broken off relations with the
Polish government-in-exile in London, following the Polish de-
mand for an International Red Cross inquiry into the Katyn
Forest massacre. The Germans had revealed that the bodies of
fifteen thousand Polish officers had been found in the Katyn
Forest, slaughtered by the Russians. Stalin was furious at the
thought of a Red Cross inquiry and demanded that the London
Poles deny the truth of the charge. When they refused, he repu-
diated them.

Premier Mikolajczyk, realizing that the future of Poland was at stake, endeavored to enlist the support of the Americans and British for the coming struggle for freedom. Hoping to put his case before President Roosevelt before the latter met Stalin, he offered to come to North Africa to see him en route to Teheran. Roosevelt had dodged him repeatedly and now would not give him an appointment. A last, desperate wire sent to Cairo brought from Roosevelt a reply through an American chargé d'affaires. The President asked Premier Mikolajczyk to rest assured that he had made an extensive study of the Polish situation and was fully prepared to present the Polish case at the meeting with Stalin.[21]

When the discussion of Poland took place at the last plenary session, Roosevelt did not take part.[22] Neither did he utter dissent to the formula which was evolved for the dismemberment of Poland. Stalin had a cut-and-dried plan. Eastern Germany, as far as the Oder River, was to be taken from the Germans and given to Poland, and the eastern half of Poland, which had been seized by Stalin while he was an accomplice of Hitler in 1939, was to be ceded to the Soviet Union. This was a bitter potion for Churchill to swallow. However, abandoned as he was by Roosevelt, he was powerless to stand up to the high-riding dictator. The resulting agreement, a shameful betrayal of the Polish people and a clear-cut violation of the Atlantic Charter, remained a secret until at Yalta, thirteen months later, it was ratified with little change. History knows that on the afternoon of December 1, 1943, in the Russian Embassy at Teheran, the Polish Republic was secretly partitioned by a Russian, an Englishman, and an American. Forty-eight per cent of the land of Poland was to be torn away and given to the Soviet Union.[23]

No Pole was present. There was no talk of plebiscites, of the will of the people, of justice, of compensation to the inhabitants, of legal rights, of moral rights. It was a naked power deal. Roosevelt did not lift a finger to prevent it and must be deemed to have acquiesced. Reading Churchill's memoirs, one is struck by the casualness—and the callousness—with which these Moguls of the twentieth century wielded the cleaver. Ancient cities were picked off like the wings of butterflies. "I was not prepared to make a great squawk about Lvov." And "Stalin then said that the Russians would like to have the warm-water port of Königsberg."

It would seem that man, panoplied with power, is incorrigible. He mouths his pretensions of virtue and compassion, and a credulous world listens, and even believes; but with a change of time and company and mood, his natural recidivism cuts loose. So it happened at Teheran.

It was late in the afternoon at this last meeting by the time the dissevered body of Poland was hauled away. Stalin then asked: "Are there any other questions?" President Roosevelt already knew there was something else dear to Stalin's hopes; it was the permanent debilitation of Germany. Obligingly, he replied: "There is the question of Germany."[24] Stalin was ready. He said he would like to see Germany split up. Like an echo, quick agreement issued from the President's lips.

Actually, Roosevelt was ready with a proposal, which he had not shown to Churchill. He said he was throwing it on the table as a basis of discussion. It was a plan to split the German nation into five separate, autonomous states: Prussia (minus its eastern province); Hanover and the Northwest; Saxony and the Leipzig area; Hesse-Darmstadt, Hesse-Kassel, and the section south of the Rhine; and Bavaria, joined with Württemberg and Baden. The malice of the project was that the richest industrial area of Germany—the Ruhr, the Saar, the port of Hamburg, and the Kiel Canal—should be taken away outright and turned over to the United Nations. No plan was better calculated to wipe out Germany as a major nation, Balkanize the Continent, and facilitate Russian domination.

When Roosevelt started expounding this fantastic scheme, Stalin, with a grin, cut in to remark that Churchill was not listening because he was not inclined to see Germany split up. But Churchill listened, and he was staggered by what he heard. Restraining himself, he retorted: "If I might use the American idiom, I would say that the President has 'said a mouthful.'"

Churchill was historian enough to know that to do what Roosevelt was proposing would leave central Europe a festering sore. In fact, although he favored treating Prussia sternly, his mind was running toward the amalgamation of the rest of Germany with a Danubian confederation to form a large, German-led buffer power in the heart of Europe. This, he thought, would be more conducive to peace. He was, of course, conscious of the Red peril. He did not say so, but no doubt Stalin knew what was in his mind.

The President's "mouthful" was chewed over for a while, with Stalin liking it, Churchill reluctant, and Roosevelt agreeing warmly with everything Stalin said. The Russian had a secret reason to be elated. It suited his strategy to have the United States identified in the German mind as the architect of German ruin; and Roosevelt's fatuous haste to take the initiative at Teheran to design a Carthaginian peace could be used to good political advantage by Communist propagandists in the crucial years ahead.

Nothing came of it at the time. The question was referred to the European Advisory Committee in London, to Churchill's relief. The President, undismayed, continued to contemplate all-out revenge upon post-Hitler Germany, and he was to come up with an even more vindictive proposal the following September at the Second Quebec Conference.

When Churchill published his memoirs, he ended his chapters on the Teheran Conference with this wail of remorse and this prophecy:

> The Polish frontiers exist only in name, and Poland lies quivering in the Russian-Communist grip. Germany has indeed been partitioned, but only by a hideous division. . . . About this tragedy, it can only be said, "IT CANNOT LAST."

Has the importance of Teheran been exaggerated? It was a spectacular encounter of three extraordinary political personalities, but was it historically significant in the sense that the conversations of Alexander I, Castlereagh, Metternich, von Hardenberg, and Talleyrand at Vienna upon the downfall of Napoleon were significant? The balance of power they fabricated in 1815 was broadly operative in Europe for one hundred years, down to the outbreak of World War I.

The conclusion is inescapable that the Teheran Conference is not just of passing interest as part of the cacaphony of World War II. It was a calamity of historic proportions. Wilmot erred, if at all, only on the side of moderation when he wrote, in *The Struggle for Europe:*

> Even before Teheran it was inevitable that the enforcement of "Unconditional Surrender" upon Germany would leave the U.S.S.R. the dominant power in Eastern Europe, but it was by no means inevitable that Russian influence would extend deep into Central Europe and the Balkans. After Teheran, it became almost a certainty that this would happen. Thus the Teheran Conference not only determined the military strategy for 1944, but *adjusted the political balance of post-war Europe in favor of the Soviet Union.*[25]

The more indirect consequences are unfolding as each year passes. The piper has not yet been paid.

After the conference, Roosevelt admitted that he had found Stalin tough and stiff and that at first he had made "no personal headway." Back in Washington, he related to Frances Perkins that he had worked for three days to make Stalin laugh and had ended up calling him "Uncle Joe."[26] To an extrovert like Roosevelt, this was a major success, even though he had had to use the Prime Minister of Great Britain as the butt of the jokes that finally brought guffaws from "Uncle Joe." He had concluded that Stalin was "getatable," to use his term, but in the Rooseveltian sense, a man had been "gotten at" when he evidenced a liking for Roosevelt. In the case of Stalin, the recipe had been a simple one: he had sided with the dictator on every issue and had not once crossed him.

So as we contemplate the Teheran atmosphere and decisions in the light of what followed, it is easy to perceive that this conference was the point in the war where the control of events passed into Stalin's hands. The responsibility must be ascribed to Roosevelt. His psychological aberration was such that in spite of Stalin's bludgeoning tactics and cynicism and in spite of the sordidness of the price he, Roosevelt, was willing to pay, he could believe that he was purchasing a relationship from which the concomitants of genuine friendship could be expected to flow. We must either judge that he was too smug to doubt this or that he was using his high place to push a monstrous fraud when, upon his return home, he made a world-wide broadcast on Christmas Eve from Hyde Park in which he alluded to Stalin in these words:

He is a man who combines a tremendous, relentless determination with a stalwart good humor. I believe he is truly representative of the heart and soul of Russia; and *I believe that we are going to get along very well with him and the Russian people—very well indeed.*

Nobody knew the American people better than Franklin D. Roosevelt. This language—trailing off into its folksy amiability —was most carefully chosen to popularize an impression that Stalin was a good fellow ("stalwart good humor"), that he was a representative ruler who did what his people wanted him to do, and that Soviet aims for the future were compatible with the ideals for which the American people had been told the war was being fought. This was a compound of three falsehoods, yet wafted over the air by the voice of the President of the United States, it gained wide currency. The innuendo that lurked in his speech, that he, Roosevelt, by his skill at Teheran, had won the golden key to lasting friendship with the Soviet Union, would serve him decisively in the forthcoming campaign for a fourth term, for the American people would be loath to dispense with the services of an emissary who appeared to have such winning ways at the council tables of the world. Having secretly compromised himself and the future tranquility of Europe and Asia at Cairo and Teheran and having torn up the Atlantic Charter in a clandestine conspiracy to gratify a brutal, power-lusting tyrant who already had a long record of crimes, he now permitted himself to lull his countrymen, in fact the whole world, into a specious sense of security.

The biographer delving into the Teheran episode is in for a dismal experience. So unsavory a performance it was, both morally and strategically, that the mythmakers and canonizers usually shun it altogether or give an expurgated account. This first meeting with Stalin brought out in high relief the weaknesses that flawed the character of the charming Roosevelt. Stalin, the cold percentage player, took the measure of these weaknesses and moved in quickly for the kill. After Teheran, the disaster of Yalta and its galling aftermath followed with the relentlessness of a Greek tragedy.

But first there was to be another "Big Two" conference, again in the lovely Canadian city of Quebec. This one the mythmakers and the canonizers avoid as they would the pox. For here, Franklin D. Roosevelt did indeed, by almost universal recognition of those who know what happened, reach the nadir of folly, if not depravity.

Chapter XIV

QUEBEC II

WE KNOW NOW that Mr. Hull, the Secretary of State, and Mr. Stimson, the Secretary of War, were horrified by what happened at the OCTAGON Conference in Quebec in September, 1944. At that time, their "stupefaction" (to use Hull's own word) was made a White House secret, and it was quickly deemed expedient to let the conference go down in history as one of the minor decision points of the war. Actually, it was the scene of one of the most damning blunders of Franklin D. Roosevelt's career— a blunder inspired by a Svengali-like figure in the administration who was later to be identified by the F.B.I. as a key member of the Washington Communist spy ring. Although Roosevelt partially extricated himself from the blunder, thanks to the frantic rescue work of Hull and Stimson, his Quebec decision almost delivered postwar Germany entirely to Communism.

Nine months had passed since Teheran. Events had moved with dizzy speed. At Quebec, the Big Two sat down together in the realization that the war was won. OVERLORD had been a stupendous success, and the Anglo-American armies were poised at the Siegfried Line. Russia had pushed the German invaders off Russian soil, and its battle-flushed armies were now at the Vistula in Poland. It was no longer a question of victory. It had become a question of what the so-called Allies would do with their victory.

In this intoxicating climate, some of Roosevelt's most intimate advisors began to lose their heads. One of these was Henry Morgenthau, the long-time Secretary of the Treasury and the President's Dutchess County neighbor. From the beginning, Henry Morgenthau had looked upon World War II as a punitive expedition to punish Hitler and the Germans for persecuting the Jews. He was close to those powerful circles, largely centered in New York City, which were demanding a Carthaginian peace. Since Roosevelt was in the middle of his fourth-term campaign, running against Thomas E. Dewey, the governor of New York, and since New York was a pivotal state in the coming election, the moment was politically propitious for Mr. Roosevelt to evidence a special regard for the opinions of Henry Morgenthau. So when the leaders of these "groups," as Hull calls them, caught the President's ear and asked him to invite Morgenthau to the Quebec Conference, he was "induced." To the country's surprise, the Secretary of the Treasury was called to Quebec.

Morgenthau, never considered a strong figure and lightly regarded in the administration, even by Roosevelt, had come under the influence of a Treasury economist named Harry Dexter White (his parents were Jacob and Sarah Weit when they emigrated to America from Russia). White had an indefatigable drive and a facile brain. After teaching at Harvard University and Lawrence College, he had entered the Treasury Department in an obscure role in 1934. Moving up the departmental ladder, he had won Morgenthau's confidence early in the war period and was entrusted with a series of important missions. He became Assistant Secretary of the Treasury, which, under a figurehead such as Morgenthau, was a post from which he could wield influence throughout the Washington bureaucracy. On the eve of Quebec, he was in full charge of all operations of the Treasury Department pertaining to foreign affairs. With his astute mind, he had easily established intellectual mastery over his chief, and when, on the night of September 4, 1944, a week before the conference began, Morgenthau dined with Secretary of War Stimson to propound his plan for postwar Germany, he brought Harry Dexter White, who had drafted it, to dinner with him.[1] Stimson immediately saw trouble ahead. Indeed, this was the beginning of the most violent single interdepartmental struggle of Stimson's career.

The success story of Harry Dexter White is, of course, one of the bizarre phenomena of the Rooseveltian dispensation. This vulpine character, whose signature placed many men in the government and brought fat promotions to others, was a traitor. On November 8 and December 4, 1945, only a little more than a year after the OCTAGON Conference, the F.B.I. transmitted memoranda to the White House identifying him as a Soviet informant. The F.B.I. reported that he was part of the Silvermaster ring. For years he had been supplying Russia with confidential information.[2] Later, White was publicly named by both Elizabeth Bentley and Whittaker Chambers, former Soviet spy couriers, as one of their Washington contacts. While his case was being probed, he died under mysterious circumstances. Subsequent revelations verified his treachery, which is no longer an issue.

This was the man who sold Henry Morgenthau the so-called Morgenthau Plan for the pastoralization of Germany, which was to be the crowning achievement of the second Quebec Conference. That the President of the United States fell into this transparent Communist trap demonstrates the wild irresponsibility with which he was conducting American foreign policy in these final months of the war. The supple sycophants who write obeisant biographies of Roosevelt nimbly shun the episode, hoping to expunge it by silence. Sherwood, compelled at least to mention it, makes an offhand allusion to the "notorious" Morgenthau Plan, but he charitably refrains from telling his readers what it was.

Morgenthau presented his plan to President Roosevelt on September 6 at a meeting attended by Hull and Stimson. The three met again with Mr. Roosevelt on the ninth. On the eleventh, the conference was to begin in Quebec. These last few days saw a vigorous battle between Hull and Stimson on the one hand, and Morgenthau on the other, for the President's decision. Both Hull and Stimson considered Morgenthau's proposal barbaric and disastrous, and they warned the President against it in strongly worded memoranda.

The Morgenthau Plan, in brief, was to strip, pillage, and so destroy Germany that it would be permanently converted into "a country primarily agricultural and pastoral in character." Speaking of the Ruhr "and surrounding industrial areas" to a total of over thirty thousand square miles, Morgenthau (or, in reality, Harry Dexter White) had written: "This area should not only be stripped of all presently existing industries but so weakened and controlled that it cannot in the foreseeable future become an industrialized area. . . . All industrial plants and equipment not destroyed by military action shall either be completely dismantled or removed from the area or completely destroyed, all equipment shall be removed from the mines and the mines shall be thoroughly wrecked."[3]

But that was not all. Even more diabolical punishment was prescribed for the German people and their children and grandchildren. First, a list was to be made of Germans who were to be shot at once upon apprehension and identification. Second, the entire German population was to be held down to a standard of living no higher than bare subsistence.

To Hull, this was "blind vengeance." It was blind because "it was striking at all of Europe. . . . The Treasury recommendation that the German mines be ruined was almost breath-taking in its implications for all Europe, because various other countries relied upon German coal for their industries."[4] As for turning Germany into a pasture, Hull argued: "Seventy million Germans could not live on the land within Germany. They would either starve or become a charge upon other nations. This was a scheme that would arouse the eternal resentment of the Germans. It would punish all of them and future generations too for the crimes of a portion of them. It would punish not only Germany but also most of Europe."

Stimson was horrified at the idea of turning "the center of one of the most industrialized continents in the world" into a nonproductive "ghost territory." "I cannot conceive," he told the President, "of turning such a gift of nature into a dust heap."[5] The proposal to hold the German population to a bare subsistence level seemed downright immoral to him. "This would mean," he argued, "condemning the German people to a condition of servitude in which, no matter how hard or effectively a man worked, he could not materially increase his economic condition in the world."

How a plot of such pre-medieval vindictiveness could be seriously considered by supposedly "liberal" twentieth-century statesmen is not easy to understand. Even the passions of war could not, in a civilized age, rescue it from the charge of depravity. Harry Dexter White, of course, along with his Soviet prompters, wanted the Morgenthau Plan because it would wreck the economy of western Europe. This was part of the program of militant Communism.

There was another Machiavellian twist to the proposal. By inducing the Americans and the British to father this "cataclysmic plan for Germany," as Cordell Hull described it, these conspirators could turn the hate of the German people against the

Western democracies for years to come. Moscow foresaw a turn of the German masses to Communism, with the Soviet Union looming in their eyes as the lesser of two evils. From any angle, the Morgenthau Plan could bring nothing but loss to the United States.

At his meetings with Morgenthau, Hull, and Stimson before going to Quebec, President Roosevelt was noncommittal, although his remark that "Germany could live happily and peacefully on soup from soup kitchens" evinced to Stimson the shallowness of his attitude. Actually, Roosevelt was not a well man. Sherwood, who saw him in the White House just after the Quebec Conference after having not seen him for several months, writes: "I was shocked by his appearance. I had heard that he had lost a lot of weight, but I was unprepared for the almost ravaged appearance of his face."[6] Secretary Stimson was worried about the President's state of body and mind. He wrote in his diary on September 11, the day the conference began: "I have been much troubled by the President's physical condition. . . . I rather fear for the effects of this hard conference upon him. I am particularly troubled . . . that he is going up there without any real preparation for the solution of the . . . problem of how to treat Germany. So far as he has evidenced it in his talks with us, he has had absolutely no study or training in the very difficult problem which we have to decide."[7]

This entry in Secretary Stimson's diary—it is not extravagant to say—may be the most trenchant observation penned during the entire war period. He knew, as did any person informed on the ethnography and the economy of Continental Europe, that the German question would be as vital after the war as it was before, if not more so, and that to treat it either casually or emotionally would prove an expensive folly. Roosevelt was now going forth to deal with this question. And here we have a member of the Cabinet, fresh from intimate White House talks, writing sorrowfully in his private diary that the President was going to Quebec "without any real preparation" and that he had "absolutely no study or training" in the problem.

Harry Dexter White was thoroughly prepared. Through the red network of treachery, he had received his orders from Jacob Golos, a high Rusian official in America who directed a number of Communist cells in the American government and was one of the ghostly manipulators of two espionage rings which encircled the White House. The Communist apparatus knew, of course, that Henry Morgenthau was the weak reed who could be used for their purpose and that White, his "assistant," was the perfect agent for the job.

Neither Hull nor Stimson was at Quebec. Generals and admirals were in abundance, but the ball had long since passed to the statesmen. It was they who could lengthen the war and fumble the peace. Germany was on the verge of collapse, and as for Japan, Admiral Leahy, who was with the President at Quebec, writes: "By the beginning of September, Japan was almost defeated through a practically complete sea and air blockade."[8] At a propitious moment, Henry Morgenthau put before Mr. Roosevelt a paper containing the main features of the Morgenthau Plan. The President took his pen and wrote at the bottom: "O.K.—F.D.R."

At first, Prime Minister Churchill was violently opposed, but Morgenthau was armed with two weapons. One was an argument and the other was a bribe. The argument was the kind the British always find hard to resist. Britain, said Morgenthau, would inherit Germany's Ruhr business, her iron and steel markets, and would be rid of a competitor forever. The bribe, or *quid pro quo,* as Hull chooses to call it, was an offer of credits to Britain totaling six and one-half billion dollars.

Both Hull and Stimson give this explanation of Morgenthau's coup in inducing Churchill to initial the Plan, too; and in his memoirs, Churchill himself declares he did so only because "the President, with Mr. Morgenthau—from whom we had much to ask—were so insistent." He then proceeds to wash his hands of the plan. Plainly, he initialed it at Quebec with his fingers crossed, never expecting as monstrous a program as the "pastoralizing" of Germany to be carried out. But he did want—and he did get—the six and one-half billion dollars for his country.

The same two men had signed a very different document three years before. It was the Atlantic Charter, which had pronounced that the United States and the United Kingdom would endeavor "to further the enjoyment by all States, great or small, victor or vanquished, of access, on equal terms, to the trade and to the raw materials of the world which are needed for their economic prosperity." Both being opportunists, Roosevelt and Churchill were not ones to be hedged in by solemn words, even their own. The Atlantic Charter had been the expedient of its hour. Now they paid no more heed to it than they did to the rainfall in Afghanistan.

Returning to Washington after the conference, Henry "the Morgue," as the President playfully called him, came rushing to Stimson and Hull to gloat. He was, writes Hull, "wildly enthusiastic over what he had accomplished." Harry Dexter White was at his side. Hull was furious. "This whole development at Quebec, I believe, angered me as much as anything that had happened during my career as Secretary of State." He went to the White House and told the President bluntly that Morgenthau's plan would wipe out everything in Germany except the land and that this meant that only 60 per cent of the German population could support themselves on German land and that the other 40 per cent would die. He added that he was satisfied the British had acquiesced at Quebec only to get Morgenthau's help in obtaining the six and one-half billion dollars Morgenthau had dangled before them.[9]

Mr. Roosevelt, skilled tightrope-walker that he was, said little during this conversation, but he pricked up his ears when Hull hinted that it would injure him politically, in the middle of the election campaign, if it became known to the country as a whole that he espoused such a plan. His refuge was to play dumb. He told Hull that he had not actually committed himself to Morgenthau's proposals. "In fact," Hull records, "he did not seem to realize the devastating nature of the memorandum of September 15 to which he had put his 'O.K.—F.D.R.' "[10]

Hull's conclusion was that Roosevelt "had not understood the meaning of what he had agreed to at Quebec." This is doubtful, and Churchill's account fails to bear it out. The document they initialed was short, simple, and clear. Hull had taken Roosevelt's remarks to him at face value, a mistake which the trusting Secretary of State made frequently. Dismayed by the President's insouciance, Hull saw an immediate danger. His memoirs explain his worry: "If the Morgenthau plan leaked out, as it inevitably would—and shortly did—it might well mean a bitter-end German resistance that could cause the loss of thousands of American lives."[11]

Mysteriously, the press got wind of what had happened. The reaction was hostile, with many newspapers violently attacking Morgenthau and the President for reportedly backing him. Only the Communist organ, the *Daily Worker,* leaped to praise them. Mr. Roosevelt, reaching the conclusion that he had made a false step, kept the actual document, with its "O.K.—F.D.R.," out of the hands of the press. Excitedly, he telephoned Secretary Stimson (who had, "to preserve his self-respect," as he put it, sent the President a strong message of protest) and began to backtrack. He told Stimson that he "didn't really intend to try to make Germany a purely agricultural country" but that England was "broke" and he wanted to get her "more business" after the war.[12] Naturally, this did not mollify Stimson, who could read plain English.

Stimson lunched with Mr. Roosevelt on October 3 and brought the subject up again. The President "grinned and looked naughty and said 'Henry Morgenthau pulled a boner.' " He then rambled on about Germany in a way which he evidently thought would be pleasing to Stimson. To the latter, he appeared "very tired and unwell," and he seemed not to know, or was pretending not to know, the import of the paper he had initialed at Quebec. Finally, Stimson, in exasperation, read to him verbatim from the document itself: "This programme . . . is looking forward to converting Germany into a country primarily agricultural and pastoral in its character." Right after these words came the sentence "The Prime Minister and the President were in agreement upon this programme." Roosevelt and Churchill had taken their pens and placed their initials within an inch of this affirmation of their accord. Nothing could have been clearer or more serious.

Although Roosevelt had been over the same ground with Secretary Hull a few days before, he feigned surprise when Stimson finished reading and looked up. Stimson's diary describes this incredible performance thus:

He was frankly staggered by this and said he had no idea how he could have initialed this; that he had evidently done it without much thought.[13]

This was the man who fancied himself indispensable to represent his country at international conferences at this critical moment in history and who was running for a fourth term as President.

As a result of the entreaties by Hull and Stimson, the Morgenthau Plan was temporarily shelved. The President did not publicly repudiate it, just as he had never publicly announced it, but on October 20, he privately ordered that detailed planning for the treatment of Germany be halted. Careful to give no affront to Morgenthau and the latter's political confederates, in his campaign speeches he did not commit himself beyond promising that the German people were "not going to be enslaved." "Enslaved" was a word one could take as one chose.

As Hull feared, the leakage to the press was disastrous, for nothing could have been more ill timed, in its psychological impact upon the German people, than Morgenthau's devilish coup at Quebec in September of 1944. Up until then, there was a fair chance, supported by intelligence reports, that Germany might discontinue its resistance to the Americans and British while holding the Russians at bay in the east in order to avoid the frightful fate of a Russian occupation. This could have shortened the war by months and could have averted the spawning of a malignant Communist East Germany that was to plague Europe for years into the future.

Once the Anglo-Americans allowed themselves to be cast as destroyers more vengeful than the Russians, however, this hope went glimmering. As Eisenhower's troops lunged at the Siegfried Line, Herr Goebbels used the Morgenthau Plan as a rallying cry to the German people to put up a last-ditch resistance. This they did, for seven more months of horror—months in which American airmen flattened and burned hundreds of German plants and factories, cities and towns, which American taxpayers would one day be called upon to help rebuild in order to correct the imbalance in Europe which, by a monumental miscalculation, their "victory" had achieved.

Morgenthau persisted, and in 1945, he wrote a book, with White's aid, expounding the Plan. White earned new laurels, and power, by playing the leading role in the Bretton Woods Conference, which set up the International Monetary Fund, and he was slated to be the first executive director of the Fund when the F.B.I. revelations wrote finis to his career.

As events transpired, the fetid breath of the Morgenthau Plan polluted the air of central Europe for about three years of abortive, partial implementation, which proved to be as costly as it was absurd. Harry Dexter White's triumph in the capture of Roosevelt's mind was by no means short lived, for the spirit of Quebec prevailed at Yalta, too. And the momentum of hate and destruction was hard to stop.

By 1948, the U.S. Military Government reported that 767 factories in the British, French, and American zones of Germany had been dismantled and sent away to the victorious countries, mostly to Russia, some to Britain and France, and none to the United States.[14] During this time, the United States was spending six billion dollars on food, clothing, shelter, and care for destitute, conquered people and the uprooted hordes who had fled westward in the path of the Red Army. With one hand we were destroying central Europe's means of subsistence; with the other we were supporting it at the expense of the American taxpayer. This farce stemmed back through Roosevelt to Morgenthau and Harry Dexter White. The Truman administration eventually gathered the courage to confess that it was suicidal, and the dismantling ground to a halt in 1949.[15] Not only was Germany helped to rise from the rubble, but the time was soon to come when she would be implored to rearm and American weapons would be pressed into German hands.

This was the sequel, ironic though it was. If excuses are looked for, they are hard to find, for there is nothing of the fortuitous, the incalculable, in this chain of happenings. The concatenation of events was grounded in the attitudes which dominated the White House until the day Franklin D. Roosevelt died and which spilled over, as an inescapable legacy, into the early days of his successor's administration. Yet in the fall of 1944, Roose-

velt would have excoriated any reporter who might have had the
temerity to ask him at a press conference if he thought it possible
that within a decade we would be laying the foundations for a
new German army to help save western Europe from the threat
of conquest by Russia. Hitler had already predicted this more
than once, and each time, Roosevelt had fumed with anger.

"A prudent man foreseeth the evil," says the Bible. Franklin
D. Roosevelt was preoccupied looking for something pleasant
in his crystal ball. He saw it. It was his own re-election. No
other President had had a third term, much less a fourth. He
was lucky, in that his young opponent in this campaign, Thomas
E. Dewey, fatuously hoped to coast into the Presidency on the
slogan "It's time for a change!" and hardly attacked him at all.
While frustration and a feeling of disfranchisement gripped millions in the electorate, the seasoned old trouper, his physical
deterioration concealed and his long series of diplomatic blunders
magnanimously spared from public debate, managed to win
again in November. Thus he came to the last lap on his road to
Russia.

Chapter XV

YALTA

FRANKLIN D. ROOSEVELT's fourth inauguration was held on January 20, 1945. Three days later, the President boarded the cruiser *Quincy*. For several months his fondest dream, next to his re-election, had been another love feast with "Uncle Joe" Stalin, but now the Russian dictator had made it plain that if the President of the United States wanted to see him, he would have to trek to Russia to do it. The conference would be on the soil of the Soviet Union or nowhere.

General John R. Deane, head of the American Military Mission in Moscow, had seen Americans, under White House policy, licking the Russians' boots *ad nauseam* for three years, but this troubled him more than anything. "No single event of the war irritated me more," he wrote in *The Strange Alliance,* "than seeing the President of the United States lifted from wheel chair to automobile, to ship, to shore, and to aircraft, in order to go halfway around the world as the only possible means of meeting J. V. Stalin."

All of the President's advisers except Harry Hopkins opposed his going.[1] Cocksure, ill-prepared, and, as at Teheran, with no strategy beyond his old obsession that the important thing was for Stalin to "like" him, he ignored them and went across the world to engage in an ostentatious spectacle of personal vanity and power which was to be his last. The Crimean, or Yalta, Conference was held in February. On April 12, Roosevelt died.

Just before he left for Yalta, he received some momentous news at the White House. Secretary of War Stimson and General Leslie R. Groves, the director of the Manhattan Project, which was secretly developing the first atomic bomb, informed him that the success of the A-bomb was "a 99 per cent certainty," that it "would probably be ready in August," and that it would be "extremely powerful."[2]

If there were any lingering doubts that the United States, un-aided, and without storming the Japanese homeland, would be able to blast Japan out of the war, this intelligence would probably have dissipated it. But there was no doubt in the minds of those best able to know, and Mr. Roosevelt knew this. Six months before, he had made a trip to Honolulu. There, on July 27 and 28, 1944, he had discussed the war in the Pacific for many hours with General Douglas MacArthur, who had flown up from Australia, and Admiral Chester W. Nimitz, commander of the naval forces in the Pacific. MacArthur and Nimitz, in the presence of Admiral William D. Leahy, had told him that "Japan could be forced to accept our terms of surrender by the use of sea and air power without an invasion of the Japanese home-land."[3] Since then, what was left of the Japanese fleet had been crushed in the Battle of the Leyte Gulf in October, the Philippines had been retaken, B-29's were bombing Japan from Guam, Tinian, and Saipan, and Japanese peace feelers had been put out.

When Roosevelt went to Yalta, he kept MacArthur and Nimitz far away. He asked them nothing, told them nothing. In view of what he did at Yalta, this would seem an incomprehensible neglect on his part to avail himself of the counsel of the two men most qualified to give it. The only explanation that makes any sense is that he already knew what their advice would be, that it was not compatible with his plans, and that he did not welcome having their opinions—overwhelmingly authoritative as they would be—presented. At this stage, elementary statesmanship, for the security of American interests in the Far East, required that the Soviet Union be, at almost any cost, dissuaded, discouraged, and forestalled from entering the war with Japan. Roosevelt went to Yalta and secretly did just the opposite.

Millions of words have been written about Yalta. In a sense, the Teheran Conference was more critical, for there, Stalin and Roosevelt stacked the deck with which the game was played out at Yalta. But when they came together on the Russian shore of the Black Sea in February of 1945, they finalized decisions so malodorous—for slave labor, forcible repatriation of refugees, the uprooting of millions of human beings from their homes and lands, the breaking of pledges of the right of self-determination, and similar brutalities—that Yalta has become, more and more as each year passes, a symbol of international immorality. The reams of apologetics which the Roosevelt cultists have poured forth in an attempt to prevent the damage to their hero's reputation from becoming too devastating have had only a sparse and ephemeral success. Too much is known. The verdict of history is inevitable.

The Yalta Papers, which the State Department at last released in March, 1955, are voluminous, but expurgated. Two department historians who worked on the compilation have exposed the pressure they were put under to "pretty up" the record and delete certain discreditable details in order to "shield" the Roosevelt administration;[4] and Sir Winston Churchill opposed the publication in its entirety. But in one form or another, the story of Yalta, in all its essentials, is in the open. There are the notes of four of the American participants, Edward R. Stettinius, James F. Byrnes, Admiral Leahy, and Harry Hopkins, as well as the Bohlen transcripts, the Churchill memoirs, the Alan-brooke diary, and other sources, which, cumulatively, put the salient facts beyond challenge. No amount of varnish can alter the picture.

It has been said, with some truth, that when Woodrow Wilson entered the cockpit of the peace conference at Versailles after World War I, he was a sheep among wolves. But if Wilson was sometimes naïve, he was a meticulous scholar and was never casual. Roosevelt approached Yalta as if he were on a vacation. In fact, the Hopkins notes are frank enough to say: "I was sure the President would wind up by going to the Crimea, the primary reason being that it was a part of the world he had never visited and his adventurous spirit was forever leading him to go to unusual places and, on his part, the election being over, he would no longer be disturbed about it for political reasons."[5] He rested much of the time on the *Quincy*'s voyage across the Atlantic. James F. Byrnes, who was on board, was amazed at his lack of preparation for the forthcoming conference, although stacks of pertinent reports and data were on the ship. This worried Byrnes.

Illness may have played a part. According to Stettinius, the President was in a bad state when he made his inaugural address on the porch of the White House on January 20. "That day he had seemed to tremble all over. It was not just his hands that shook, but his whole body as well."[6] Stettinius found him "cheerful, calm, and quite rested" when the ship arrived at the island of Malta on February 2, or so he says in his book. But Admiral King later told Harry Hopkins that when he went aboard the *Quincy* that day and saw the President, he was "alarmed" at the state of his health and noted a deterioration since the inauguration.[7] Even so, Sherwood assures us that Mr. Roosevelt was "as always buoyant and excited at the prospect of new adventures as he left the *Quincy* to make the rest of his journey by air."

Churchill was already at Malta. Transport planes wafted the President and the Prime Minister and their entourages of some seven hundred people across the Aegean and Turkey and the Black Sea to Saki Airfield in the Crimea. Roosevelt flew in his luxurious new four-engine plane, the *Sacred Cow,* which was equipped with elevators.

This, indeed, was the purple path of adventure. But a member of a U.S. Navy interpreting team at the Yalta Conference, who watched Roosevelt there and on one occasion acted as his personal Russian interpreter, was one American who had to smother his disgust. He felt, he tells us, that President Roosevelt "had no business" at the conference. His layman's diagnosis was a simple one: "He looked sick, he acted sick and he talked sick."[8]

The President's daughter, Mrs. Anna Boettiger, was on this trip, and Sarah Churchill accompanied her father, as did Mr. Harriman's daughter, Kathleen. Back in Washington, Mrs. Eleanor Roosevelt was knee deep in Left Wing politics. As a post-election whimsy, the President had made one of the most anomalous nominations ever sent to the Senate for confirmation, that of Henry A. Wallace to be Secretary of Commerce. Wallace had become so closely entangled with pro-Communist elements in the country that resistance to his appointment was strong even within the Democratic party. This so moved Mrs. Roosevelt that she sent two urgent messages to her husband (he was on the *Quincy* at the time) advising him what steps he should take to get the Wallace nomination through a reluctant Senate. By the time Admiral Leahy published his memoirs in 1950, he felt free to divulge this confidence and to add ruefully that the attitudes of Mrs. Roosevelt and Mr. Wallace "were at that time not very different" and appeared to him to be "about equally impracticable." Obviously, five thousand miles did not put Mr. Roosevelt out of the indefatigable First Lady's range.

Yalta had been a favorite watering place of the aristocracy in the days of the Czars. Wooded slopes drop down from the Crimean highlands to the beaches of the Black Sea. President Roosevelt and his retinue were domiciled in Livadia Palace, built as the summer home of Nicholas II. The British were housed in Vorontsov Villa at Alupka, twelve miles away, and the Russians occupied the Koreis Palace, which once belonged to Prince Yusupov, midway between. Churchill was not going to pop in on Roosevelt in his bathrobe this time. It was a hard and circuitous drive from Alupka to Livadia. One had to go through Koreis.

The Soviet secret police (NKVD) were everywhere and were under the personal command of the notorious Commissar L. P. Beria, who was destined to be denounced as a monster and executed after Stalin's death. Beria's duties at Yalta were, no doubt, exacting but not unpleasant. For example, he had the opportunity to jolly up with Roosevelt, Mrs. Boettiger, Secretary of State Stettinius, and the others at a dinner, at the Russian headquarters, which included twenty courses and forty-five toasts.[9] Also draining vodka at this wassail were Andrei Y. Vishinsky, the grisly public prosecutor at the liquidation purge trials Stalin had staged from 1935 to 1939, and V. M. Molotov, who in August of 1939 had contrived with Hitler's von Ribbentrop the unholy pact which signalled the start of World War II. Such a feeling of fraternity welled up in Mr. Roosevelt, in the company of Marshal Stalin and Messrs. Beria, Vishinsky, and Molotov, that he offered a particularly saccharine toast in which he observed that the atmosphere at the dinner was "that of a family."

The plenary sessions of the conference were held in the ballroom of Livadia Palace. The ownership of this palace had changed since it was built by the Romanovs, but did the aims and ambitions of the new owners differ much from those of its former masters? Wilmot remarks that the only significant difference was that the men who now sought to fulfill Russia's imperial destiny were more ruthless and more powerful. Elliott Roosevelt tells of his father's private tirades against British "colonialism," but there is not a word to suggest any fear of or distaste for international Communism. In fact, among the dramatis personae of Elliott's book, *As He Saw It,* Churchill is more of a villain than Stalin. This is virtually the theme of the book. Stalin comes through an unscathed hero; Churchill is badly tarnished.

This is vital to an understanding of Yalta. President Roosevelt, and, of course, Harry Hopkins, too, cherished an implacable fixation that the Bolsheviks who ruled Russia were men of good will and that their expansionist aspirations, which were plainly evident, boded no evil for Europe and the world. Whether this was a sincere conviction based on a rational process, or a "peculiar aberration," as Wilmot calls it, or sheer hypocrisy, may be a Freudian puzzle. However, that these two men knew that the Soviet Union was winning its battle to become the "dominant" power in Europe and that they embraced this concept with complete equanimity is not open to question. As we have seen, this was down in black and white as early as the First Quebec Conference in 1943.

Throughout the war period, Roosevelt deliberately put on blinders when any fact derogatory to the Russians turned up. Thus in April, 1943, he had scoffed when John Franklin Carter presented him a special intelligence report casting upon the Russians the guilt for the massacre of fifteen thousand Polish officers in the Katyn Forest, and he had shown acid displeasure in May, 1944, when former Governor of Pennsylvania George

H. Earle, who had been Minister to Austria and Bulgaria and Special Envoy to Turkey, brought to the White House documents and photographs attesting Russian guilt in that cold-blooded atrocity. On March 24, 1945, two weeks before he died, Roosevelt wrote a letter to Earle, then a commander in the Navy, expressly forbidding him to publish an article contending that Russia was a greater menace than Nazi Germany. He suppressed the article and had Earle shipped off to Samoa.[10]

The pro-Russian atmosphere in Washington—so hard to combat because the President himself, his wife, and his most intimate friend were at the center of it—was galling to many, including the frustrated Secretary of the Navy, James Forrestal. His diaries reveal that in September, 1944, he had written to a friend that "if any American suggests that we act in accord with our own interests, he is apt to be called a . . . Fascist or imperialist, while if Uncle Joe suggests that he needs the Baltic provinces, half of Poland, all of Bessarabia and access to the Mediterranean, all hands in Washington agree that he is a fine, frank, candid and generally delightful fellow." Such was the frame of mind Roosevelt took to Yalta.

Roosevelt also took Harry Hopkins. Harry was ill and missed some of the festivities, but the President consulted him on everything. He prompted Roosevelt with scribbled little messages at the conference table.

As we examine the opinions Hopkins entertained about the motherland of Communism, we find a quagmire of wild nonsense. He had lost all objectivity; the words seem childish. His mirage stayed bright in his eyes until his death a year after Yalta. It seems incredible that in August, 1945, any informed man could have written this: "We know or believe that Russia's interests, so far as we can anticipate them, do not afford an opportunity for a major difference with us in foreign affairs." Germany had surrendered in May, Stalin had dishonored his Yalta promises before the ink was dry, and the black shadow of a new and ghastly tyranny had descended over eastern Europe. Yet this palpable absurdity was dictated to a stenographer by the man who for several years had been the chief adviser of the President of the United States.[11] And of the Russian people, whose minds had been drugged by the Bolsheviks for twenty-eight years and who had no traditions of freedom nor experience in democracy in their entire national history, he added that they "think and act just like you and I do." Any college freshman should have known better.

James F. Byrnes was a new face in the American delegation. He had resigned from the Supreme Court to aid in the war effort and was Director of Mobilization when the President invited him to go "on this trip to the Crimea." As for affecting the outcome, he might just as well have stayed home. In fact, he was sent home before the important last day of the conference, on which the agreements were drafted and signed.

Byrnes was kept in the dark about many things that happened at Yalta. Although in his book, *Speaking Frankly,* he makes a half-hearted attempt to lift his old chief out of the mire (for Roosevelt had honored him with high appointments), he takes pains to dissociate himself from the sordid aspects. Thus he did not know of the agreement condoning slave labor. That relapse into the barbarism of past ages was not discussed when he was present. "Had I known it," he writes, "I would have urged the President to oppose the inclusion in the protocol of any provision for the use of large groups of human beings as enforced or slave laborers." Nor was he let in on the secret agreement which bribed Russia, with Japanese and Chinese territory, to enter the war in the Pacific. "When the President returned, he did not mention it to me and the protocol was kept locked in his safe at the White House."

There was another new face at Yalta. It was the handsome face of the new Secretary of State, Edward R. Stettinius. Unfortunately, Mr. Stettinius, whose tenure was not long, will not go down in history as one of the strong incumbents of that office. In fact, as Sherwood explains, Hopkins had instigated his appointment for the very reason that he would be a willing nonentity. Byrnes had been passed over because Roosevelt wanted to be his own Secretary of State, with Hopkins at his side, and it was doubted that Byrnes would fit into the role of "a mere mouthpiece."[12]

Three State Department "experts"—H. Freeman Matthews, Alger Hiss, and Wilder Foote—had been assigned to accompany Stettinius. Whittaker Chambers had tried to warn the government against Hiss, but in vain. (The F.B.I. was to learn, in the Canadian espionage cases that grew out of the disclosures of Igor Guzenko, that it was known in the office of the Soviet military attaché in Canada that the Russians had an agent who was an assistant to Secretary of State Stettinius in the early part of 1945. In 1949, Hiss was convicted of perjury, for denying that he had supplied secret State Department documents to a Communist spy ring. Unmasked at last, he was sent to prison.) Alger Hiss himself testified before a Congressional committee that "it is an accurate and not immodest statement to say that I helped formulate the Yalta agreement to some extent." Indeed he did.[13] Some of his handwritten notes at the Yalta Conference went back and forth between President Roosevelt and himself.[14] At the plenary sessions, the three heads of state and the senior officials sat at a great round table. Where was Alger Hiss? He sat with Harry Hopkins behind the President.[15]

En route to Yalta, Secretary Stettinius, with Hiss, Matthews, and Foote, made a little side trip. Lured perhaps by the ideal North African winter climate, they flew from the Azores to Marrakech, Morocco, where the sumptuous Villa Taylor was at their disposal. There they went over all the questions that might arise at Yalta and decided what they would recommend to President Roosevelt. The treatment of Germany, the boundaries of

Poland, the future of the Balkan States, the revision of Turkish control of the Dardanelles to insure Russian access to the Mediterranean, the admission of Communists into a coalition government in China—all of these topics were explored in the warm sunshine, and concise answers were written down for the President's convenience. After four days devoted to reformation of the world, they flew to Naples to meet Harry Hopkins before proceeding on their trip to Yalta. After all, one did not tinker with the future of mankind without checking in frequently with Harry. Thus briefed, with the tutoring of Alger Hiss and Harry Hopkins fresh in his ears, the neophyte Stettinius was now considered ready to go through his act, as the American opposite number to crusty, crafty Russian Foreign Minister Vyacheslav Molotov. It was never intended that he should have much to say, but at least he would not say the wrong thing. The rubber stamp was well inked.

(There has been a studied attempt to cleanse the Yalta Conference of the Hiss taint. His notes are still suppressed, and from reading what the State Department has published, one would suppose that Hiss was there only to carry the Secretary's briefcase. Such, of course, is far from the truth. Byrnes saw him "frequently consulted by Mr. Hopkins and Mr. Stettinius" in the conference room. "Hiss performed brilliantly throughout . . . the Yalta Conference," wrote Stettinius. This is not the way one compliments a mere flunky. This particular praise, moreover, was not undeserved. Alger Hiss was, indeed, quite a performer.)

Yalta, of course, was Stalin's show. He was the star. At the conference table, he was at once the most blunt and the most subtle. As a host, he overwhelmed his impressionable guests with lavish care, so that Churchill telegraphed home that the Russians' "prodigality exceeds belief." On one occasion somebody said casually that there was no lemon peel in the cocktails. The next day, a lemon tree, loaded with fruit, was in the hall, brought from far away by air. Mesmerized from the start, Roosevelt presented a spectacle that can only be described as pitiful—this fading President, floating slowly out of this life, outmatched and outwitted at every point, mouthing meaningless clichés, and dripping with flummery in the presence of the dictator.

How did the host of Yalta look in the flesh? "He has got an unpleasantly cold, crafty, cruel face," wrote Alanbrooke in his diary, "and whenever I look at him I can imagine his sending off people to their doom without turning a hair. On the other hand, there is no doubt he has a quick brain."

To call the Yalta Conference "one of the biggest drunken brawls I ever saw,"[16] as did one of the American interpreters, who observed more than one participant helped out, in a stupor, from the banquet table, is no doubt an extravagance. To say that an alcoholic atmosphere pervaded it is more felicitous. Stalin, and even Molotov, and the square-faced, stubble-topped generals and commissars in the Russian contingent could be genial when it served their purpose, even to the British, about whom they always had some reservations. Certainly they were more accomplished consumers of vodka and champagne than their British and American guests, who, by all accounts, brought to the festivities of this eight-day Saturnalia a do-or-die spirit, if inadequate preparation for such rugged competition.

On these occasions the toasts proposed by Churchill and Roosevelt were long, windy speeches, Churchill's being excruciatingly eloquent and Roosevelt's alarmingly rambling. Stalin could easily see that the Americans present, taking their cue from the President, were eager to lap up his every word and exalt him. Naturally, he played on this credulity. Sly and disarming, he was an expert at the Communists' forensic device of giving special emphasis to an assertion of which the exact opposite was the real truth. "I am talking as an old man; that is why I am talking so much," he said at a dinner at the Yusupov Palace on the eighth.

"But I want to drink to our alliance. . . . In the history of diplomacy I know of no such close alliance. . . . In an alliance the allies should not deceive each other. Perhaps this is naïve? Experienced diplomatists may say, 'Why should I not deceive my ally?' But I as a naïve man think it is best not to deceive my ally even if he is a fool." Yet no man at the table could have doubted that Stalin would make an alliance with the Devil, or with angels, if it would be to his advantage, or break it whenever it suited him. Even at this moment, he was scheming with Roosevelt to pounce on the Japanese, with whom he had agreed in writing not to do so and was bound by a treaty of friendship.

Drinking-bout diplomacy had served the Russians well. They had discovered the American weakness for conviviality and had been exploiting it with consummate skill. General Deane, as American attaché in Moscow, had seen enough. Fed up at last, he had written to Washington two months before Yalta as follows:

I have sat at innumerable Russian banquets and become gradually nauseated by Russian food, vodka, and protestations of friendship. Each person high in public life proposes a toast a little sweeter than the preceding one on Soviet-British-American friendship. It is amazing how these toasts go down past the tongues in the cheeks. After the banquets we send the Soviets another thousand airplanes, and they approve a visa that has been hanging fire for months. We then scratch our heads to see what other gifts we can send, and they scratch theirs to see what else they can ask for.[17]

General Deane had also learned from experience that to a Communist, "the party of the second part is either a shrewd trader to be admired or a sucker to be despised." He had so reported to Washington, with the warning that the Americans should get off the sucker list. But at Yalta, the Russians were still playing the old game, and the Americans were still straining to show what uncritical, trusting, jolly fellows they were.

At the end, there was, as usual, a communiqué. Who drafted it? Admiral Leahy says the draft was "prepared by Secretary of State Stettinius." Stettinius does not say that, but we do learn in his book that Alger Hiss was his expert in "wording." We also learn that "while the communiqué was being drafted, the Prime Minister gave a dinner." That was on the night of February 10, the last night. Since Stettinius himself was at the dinner, it must be presumed that Mr. Hiss was hard at work.

By Stettinius's appraisal, the dinner was "excellent" and the evening "historic." Stalin had his guards posted at the Vorontsov Villa hours ahead. Churchill staged the affair with pomp and opulence, from the cocktails before a glowing fire in the fireplace to the inevitable succession of toasts. Lest it be thought that no serious business was transacted in the alcoholic milieu of these banquets, Stettinius reveals that Stalin, who had been rebuffed that afternoon on the reparations question, brought the subject up again at this dinner party and won an important concession.

The President seems to have been in a rather garrulous mood that night, touching on a wide range of subjects, including constitutions. Chiding Churchill for "always talking about what the British Constitution allowed and what it did not allow," he informed the Prime Minister that actually there was no constitution and added that an unwritten constitution was better than a written one.[18] No doubt this dissertation was amusing, if academic, to "Uncle Joe," to whom nothing could have been less restraining than a constitution, written or unwritten.

The Big Three and their advisers met briefly at noon the next day in Livadia Palace to go over the public communiqué and the secret protocol which embodied their conclusions. After making slight revisions, they all repaired to the dining room. "While the formal papers were being prepared," Admiral Leahy relates, "the final luncheon was held." The historic documents, which were to have an impact upon the balance of the twentieth century and which condemned millions of human beings to home-lessness and other millions to slavery or death, were signed as a luncheon *divertissement* in an atmosphere perfumed with rich gravy and wine. "During the meal, the formal papers were brought in and the final report and communiqué signed by the three principals."

The German nation was to be dismembered. The details were referred to a committee, but this much was settled: a huge chunk was to be torn off and given to Poland as a sop for the mayhem to be performed on that unhappy country; some choice morsels, such as the city of Königsberg, were to be donated to the Soviet Union outright; and the rest of eastern Germany was to be spread-eagled for forced Communization by Russian masters, since occupation by the Red Army meant nothing less than that. How and when this nightmare would ever end was too unpleas-ant a subject to be faced at Yalta. Technically, the exact western Polish boundary was to be fixed at "the Peace Conference." This was a way of deferring the blame. Actually, the present Oder-Neisse line was, roughly, the demarcation contemplated at Yalta.

Ten million Germans were doomed to be turned out of their homes and set out on the roads to flee westward, for all of the territories to be detached were ethnically German. East Prussia, Pomerania, and Brandenburg had never in six hundred years even been under dispute, with the exception of the Marienwerder and Allenstein districts of East Prussia, in which, in plebiscites held in 1919 in accordance with the Treaty of Versailles, the population had voted, by large majorities, to remain with Ger-many. Königsberg had never been Russian. Founded by the Teutonic Order in 1255, it was sentimentally revered as a foun-tainhead of German learning and the birthplace of Germany's greatest philosopher, Immanuel Kant. The city of Breslau, in Silesia, had won independence from Poland in 1163, had been destroyed by the Mongols in 1241, had risen from the ashes as a

Germanic city, and had remained such ever since. Its cathedral, its Kreuzkirche, its church of St. Elizabeth, with its fine stained glass and Cranach's portrait of Martin Luther, are part of Germany's heritage of religion and art, while its Schweidnitzer Keller has been celebrated in the lore and song of German-speaking people since 1355. As big as San Francisco, it was the chief industrial center of eastern Germany. It is not extravagant to say that Königsberg and Breslau had been Germanic cities almost as long as London had been English.

What followed Yalta was a mass expulsion which Churchill himself was impelled to allude to as "tragedy on a prodigious scale." Actually, never in history, even in the worst of pagan times, has there been such a millionfold uprooting of human beings. By the fall of 1945, shocked voices in England were heard to say that it was the most enormous official atrocity in all of the world's history, and Churchill admitted in the House of Commons in August that the land grab, "comprising as it does one-quarter of the arable land of Germany, is not a good augury for the future of Europe."

Reparations were to be exacted from the rest of Germany "in kind," said the communiqué. This meant factories, locomotives, goods, etc. The secret protocol added that reparations were to include human labor. This was, as Byrnes said when he learned of it, an authorization for forced or slave labor, which it was known the Russians intended to impose but which was, of course, abhorrent to the American people. Franklin D. Roosevelt had always taken pains to pose as a humanitarian, so it is not surprising that no inkling of this item of the Yalta agreements was allowed to creep into the public announcements.

Poland also was to be dismembered. Some eleven million people who lived east of the so-called Curzon Line in prewar Poland were to be surrendered to the Soviet Union without any semblance of a plebiscite. Thus Roosevelt, Stalin, and Churchill decreed Soviet annexation of almost half of Poland's territory and about one-third of her population. Roosevelt weakly proposed that Stalin allow Poland to keep Lwów and the nearby oil fields. He was as aware as Stalin was that the Drohobycz oil region was essential to the Polish economy, but he showed his hand too quickly. "He pointed out," says Stettinius, "that he was merely suggesting this for consideration rather than insisting on it." Naturally, the dictator scooped up all the chips.

The Polish government-in-exile, under which whole regiments of Poles were fighting valiantly for the Western powers in Italy and on the western front, was now betrayed, and the Lublin Committee, a group of Polish Communists domiciled for years in Moscow, where they had been trained in Stalin's tough school for the task of administering Poland, was described in the communiqué as "the present Provisional Government of Poland." This meant the surrender of Poland to Communism. For four days Churchill fought against this faithlessness, but his American colleague would not stick to his guns with him. Sharp differences between Churchill and Stalin came to the surface on the first day this subject was discussed. That evening, the President made a fatal move. He compromised his independence by sending a letter to Stalin in which he announced: "I am determined there shall be no breach between ourselves and the Soviet Union." With that statement he admitted that if Stalin made an issue of Poland, the United States would give way.

Thus fortified, Stalin tossed to the Prime Minister and the President only some high-sounding words to take home. He agreed that the puppet provisional government would be "reorganized" by the inclusion of "democratic leaders from Poland itself and from Poles abroad," but he refused to mention names. Since in Communist diction Communists were "democratic," this was a hollow promise. He also agreed that "free and unfettered elections" would be held. If, as we suspect, the men at the conference table—who were, surely, not insensitive to the incongruous—found it necessary to suppress smiles at this, the fact is not recorded; yet the scene is not without humor. Such elections had never been held by the Communists in Russia or elsewhere, and it could not have been seriously expected that they were about to be held in Poland under Stalin's hand-picked cabal and the occupying Red Army, particularly since it was specified that only "democratic and anti-Nazi parties" would have the right to put up candidates, and, in the Marx-Lenin-Stalin tradition of interpretation, only pro-Russian, pro-Communist, anti-capitalist political elements could possibly merit that description.

The British demanded that the elections be under the supervision of the American, British, and Soviet Ambassadors. Stalin bluntly rejected this, arguing that it would be an affront to the pride and sovereignty of the Poles! When, at the end, Eden, knowing that an unsupervised election would be a mockery, endeavored to insist upon this safeguard, Stettinius announced that Roosevelt was willing to eliminate it, saying "the President was anxious to reach agreement and that to expedite matters he was willing to make this concession." Freedom in Poland was doomed. Admiral Leahy quickly recognized the loosely worded Polish formula as a "phony." He spoke up before it was signed. "Mr. President," said Leahy, "this is so elastic that the Russians can stretch it all the way from Yalta to Washington without ever technically breaking it." Roosevelt said he knew that.[19]

One Russian coup at Yalta which would have titillated Machiavelli was the wording of the "Declaration on Liberated Europe." Surely a deft hand was at work here. The net result was to liberate Russia from the restrictions of the Atlantic Charter. The Third Point of the Charter had declared for the right of all peoples to choose the form of government under which they will live. Its solemn wish was "to see sovereign rights and self-government restored to those who have been forcibly deprived of

them." Now this language did not please Stalin at Yalta. What
about Latvia, Lithuania, and Estonia, which independent countries he had already swallowed up? And Poland, Czechoslovakia, Bulgaria, and Hungary? He had his own plans for them
as his Red forces clenched their talons on the frightened populations of eastern Europe.

> They should take who have the power,
> And they should keep who can.

These words of the poet were more congenial to Stalin than
the Golden Rule. So when Point Three was lifted out of the
Charter and put into the new Declaration on Liberated Europe,
a remarkable grafting operation was performed. There is strong
circumstantial evidence that Dr. Hiss had something to do with
the plastic surgery, with Dr. Hopkins and Dr. Molotov as con-
sultants. Be that as it may, the final product, a subtle transforma-
tion, emerged as part of the Yalta version of the Frankenstein
monster. The words "by the aggressor nations" were inserted
after the clause "to those who have been forcibly deprived of
them." And it was made clear by the context that "the aggressor
nations" were Germany and Italy, period. This neatly excluded
all Russian depredations, past and future.

Then there followed some unctuous phrases about assisting
the "liberated" states to hold free elections and establish democratic governments, but these things were to be done in "concert" and "jointly" and only when "in the opinion of the three
governments" (U.S., U.K., and U.S.S.R.) conditions "make such
action necessary." The loophole nullified the whole Declaration,
as far as it might ever circumscribe the Russian "liberators." In
effect, the Western powers were agreeing not to lift a finger for
freedom in eastern Europe without the consent of the Soviet
Union.

It was also arranged that the permanent "United Nations"

body would be impotent to interfere effectually with the incipient Communist empire. At Yalta the veto was agreed upon, and Roosevelt acceded to Stalin's preposterous demand that the Soviet Union have three votes in the General Assembly. The State Department's "specialist" on setting up the United Nations was none other than Alger Hiss. In fact, he was slated to become the sparkplug and presiding officer at its organizing convention in April. To a man of Stalin's foresight, the potentialities which this new polyglot conglomeration of nationalisms and basically disunited world factions would furnish to Soviet tacticians for propaganda and mischief were obvious. (Its very name was fraudulent from the beginning. The world has since split into old-fashioned military alliances, such as NATO, SEATO, the Warsaw Pact and the Baghdad Pact.)

As for Roosevelt, he was floating in a cloudland of self-delusion. Intoxicated with the name "United Nations," he actually professed to believe that alliances, military pacts, and balances of power were things of the past. Slyly, the Russians encouraged this fantasy, all the while making sure that the balance of power in Europe and Asia would be well tipped in Russia's favor.

A dark moral blot upon the Yalta record was the promise to Stalin that the Russian nationals rounded up by the Americans and British in Germany, France, and Italy would be deported to Russia, by force if necessary. There were about two million of these. Some had been captured by the Germans; others had voluntarily fled from Communism early in the war. Many were found in German uniforms, but others were civilian escapees who wanted only to find freedom. Most of them begged not to be sent back to Russia, knowing their fate would be the firing squad or Siberian slave camps.

The State Department had decided to disallow forcible repatriation and abide by the provisions of the Geneva Convention on the treatment of prisoners of war, but a message was dis-

patched to Washington from Yalta overruling this decision. As
a consequence, when the war ended, a sickening drama was en-
acted. All the Russians were herded indiscriminately—scream-
ing, in tears, at bayonet point or dragged bodily—into boxcars
and sent to Russia. Not the slightest attention was paid to the
Geneva Convention, the doctrine of asylum, or the humane regard for individual choice which had ameliorated man's cruelty
in less barbarous years. The gruesome spectacle was singed in
memory, but not until ten years later, when the State Department published the so-called "Yalta Papers," was it known for
sure that this unholy crime against humanity had been connived
at Yalta. The contemporary publicity was silent about it.

It was also silent about any furtive promise by Roosevelt to
Stalin to let the Russian army reach Berlin and Prague first. Yet,
as we have seen, President Beneš of Czechoslovakia was convinced there was one. So was General George S. Patton, who
was ordered to halt his troops only a dash from the Czech capital
to allow the Russian army time to "liberate" the city and seize
two of the biggest prizes in Europe: the vast Skoda munitions
works and the uranium deposits at Jáchymov.

Patton's deductions were not likely to be erroneous on a point
so tender to him. However, the full details of the humiliating
checkrein put on Patton at Pilsen and Bradley's strange sit-down
at the lightly defended Elbe River, with Berlin only fifty-three
miles away and his own American patrols in its suburbs, remain
obscure to this day. Eisenhower's utterances on the subject have
been guarded and divergent. It is definitely known that Churchill considered the capture of Berlin and Prague by the Western
Allies to be a matter of transcendent postwar importance and
that his stern pleas struck no spark in Roosevelt. Eisenhower's
final battle plans were drawn up in March, the month after
Yalta. They left Berlin and Prague to the Russians. Without getting British approval or even mentioning the subject to Air

Chief Marshal Tedder, his deputy, he sent his plans by a direct telegram to Stalin for clearance on March 28.[20] Naturally, Stalin approved them with alacrity. It is hardly plausible that Eisenhower would have followed such a course and made such a decision without word from the highest level. Churchill was furious and protested at once to both Eisenhower and the President, but in vain. Churchill's messages to Roosevelt on April 1 and April 5 were pathetic entreaties, serious warnings.[21] It was "a pity," he said, that Eisenhower had sent the telegram to Stalin. "I say quite frankly that Berlin remains of high strategic importance." He might as well have been shouting at a tree.

Of this period, Churchill writes in his memoirs:

The United States stood on the scene of victory, master of world fortunes, but without a true and coherent design. Britain, though still very powerful, could not act decisively alone. I could at this stage only warn and plead. Thus this . . . was to me a most unhappy time. I moved amid cheering crowds . . . with an aching heart and a mind oppressed by forebodings.[22]

Churchill knew the secret, too—the secret in the White House closet, the face of reality which Roosevelt and Hopkins had kept in murky banishment through three years of artifice and propaganda. Three wars were raging, not one. One of them was the expansionist onslaught of Communist imperialism, the Juggernaut of the twentieth century, the rapacious destroyer which Selwyn Lloyd has described as "a horse of strange parentage, by Karl Marx out of Catherine the Great." It was in this war that Roosevelt refused to man the ramparts, leaving Churchill a lonely figure, impotent to act alone. Thus the paradox: the moment of "victory" was for Churchill "a most unhappy time." Veiled by the temperance of his words is a branding accusation which history will not overlook. The discretion of a statesman permitted him to say no more at the time.

After lunch on the afternoon of February 8, Stalin and Roosevelt, like two archconspirators slinking off to hatch the direst plot of all, vanished behind the locked doors of a room in Livadia Palace. At the President's request, Churchill was not there. Roosevelt knew what to expect: the Russian dictator was to state his price for entering the war against Japan at some time in the future. An old-fashioned, ante bellum secret deal, like those that had turned the stomach of Woodrow Wilson when they came to light at Versailles after World War I, was about to be made. Roosevelt brought only Averell Harriman, and Stalin brought Molotov. Two interpreters were present.

Why Harriman? It happened that he was one of the few Americans who knew of Roosevelt's resolve not only to allow Russia to intrude into the Pacific war at the eleventh hour, which would have been injudicious enough, but even to coax her—yes, bribe her—to do so. Roosevelt had made him Ambassador to Russia after Ambassador Standley, a retired admiral, had been recalled for blurting out to American reporters the embarrassing fact that the Soviet government was keeping from the Russian people the knowledge that it was receiving vast quantities of aid from America.[23] The suave New Yorker was not likely to commit such an indiscretion.

One of Harriman's assignments had been to act as messenger in the business of selling the Japanese War to Stalin. So in October, 1944, he had called upon the dictator in Moscow, bringing him a portrait of Roosevelt as a present, and he had conceived this a fitting occasion to broach the subject. Since Stalin had already, at Teheran and before, given his firm assurance that he would come in after Germany was defeated, this too-eager salesmanship on the part of the American Ambassador no doubt had opened up in the Russian's mind a green vista of grandiose profit and loot. "These simpletons," we can imagine him thinking as he listened to the Ambassador's cultivated cadences and observed his deferential manner, "are actually entreating me to say I will do what I have three times promised to do, and what I would be a fool not to do when the time comes, for the simple reason that it will be to my own advantage to do it. Here is my chance to make hay." For then he had blandly asked that the United States furnish supplies and equipment for a Russian Far East force of 1,500,000 men, including 3,000 tanks, 75,000 motor vehicles and 5,000 airplanes. Harriman, who had been given his instructions, had smilingly agreed on the spot, and Stalin had said he would enter the war against Japan about three months after the German surrender (well knowing, as they must all have, that by that time, Japan would have little or no fight left in her). In the following months, 860,410 tons of dry cargo and 206,000 tons of liquid cargo were extracted from American arsenals and depots to build up Soviet military power in the Far East, and this flow, to be transported in a hundred American ships, was just starting when Roosevelt sat down with Stalin at Yalta.[24]

Here, sensing Roosevelt's mood, Stalin quickly perceived that the time was ripe to make more hay. Why be bashful? He would not only demand some Japanese territory, but he would, more importantly, ask for the key to the political and economic mastery of Manchuria, the industrialized powerhouse of China. In short, he would present a preliminary blueprint for the Communist conquest of China, which, following the familiar tenets of Lenin and himself, meant the eventual mobilization of her manpower and resources for war against the capitalist democracies. To give a farcical twist to America's war with Japan, he would insure that its only results would be the reversal of the Russo-Japanese War of 1904 and the replacement of a Japanese hegemony in China by a Russian one, all paid for by the blood and money of the childlike Americans, who knew not what they were doing.

So, although he had at least three times previously promised to enter the Japanese War, Stalin now, for the first time, laid down his conditions. Behind the closed doors of the room in Livadia Palace, he named his price to the President of the United States. It was high. At the expense of Japan, Russia was to annex South Sakhalin and the Kurile Islands. At the expense of China, Russia was to gain possession of Dairen as an "international" port and the naval base of Port Arthur under a long-term lease; the Manchurian railroads were to be put under a "Soviet-Chinese Company" which was to safeguard "the pre-eminent interests of the Soviet Union"; and "the status-quo in Outer Mongolia" (which by infiltration and pressure had been turned into a puppet of the Soviet Union) was to be preserved. Obviously, no part of this price was Roosevelt's to give. And such back-room trading was a butchery of the Atlantic Charter.

The President of the United States might have withdrawn from the room, stung by the insolence of Stalin's presumptions. Or he might, at the least, have politely demurred on grounds of principle and changed the subject. But Mr. Roosevelt did neither. He agreed to everything. He guaranteed that the price would be paid. Stalin agreed only that "in two or three months after Germany has surrendered . . . the Soviet Union shall enter the war against Japan." (She entered it six days before Japan surrendered and two days after the atomic bomb was dropped on Hiroshima. Her contribution to Japan's defeat was nil.)

It had been known since the days of Theodore Roosevelt that whoever controls the Chinese Eastern and South Manchurian railroads dominates Manchuria. Surely Franklin Roosevelt knew it. Whether he was also aware that the United States Navy had its eye on the Kuriles as the site for a base to shield both Japan and North America from Russia in the uncertain future is not known,[25] but a glance at a map would have told him why Stalin wanted them. They stretch, like a giant armada, from Hokkaido into the North Pacific. They lie athwart the shortest route between Japan and Alaska. Yet on that Thursday afternoon at

Yalta, Roosevelt lightly handed them to Stalin. "I like this man," he had said to Frances Perkins, "and I want to keep on good terms with him." (The Kuriles are now Russian submarine bases.)

After the secret came out, a predecessor of Harriman's as Ambassador to Russia, William C. Bullitt, who, like Standley, had tried in vain to dispel Roosevelt's hallucinations about the Soviet regime, wrote a chilling article entitled "How We Won the War and Lost the Peace."[26] In it, he held up the Yalta deal so that it could be seen in perspective:

At Yalta . . . President Roosevelt broke the pledge which he had made to the Chinese government at Cairo and—secretly, behind the back of China—signed . . . an agreement by which the vital rights of China in Manchuria were sacrificed to Soviet imperialism. By this secret agreement Roosevelt gave to the Soviet Union not only "pre-eminent interests" in the great Manchurian port of Dairen and full control of the great naval base which protects it, Port Arthur, but also "pre-eminent interests" in the railroads which lead from the Soviet Union to Dairen and split Manchuria from the northwest to the south.

In view of Roosevelt's Cairo pledge that Manchuria would be restored to China this secret agreement was entirely dishonorable. It was also potentially disastrous not only to China but also to the United States, because it gave Stalin a deadly instrument. . . .

As an additional payment for this repetition of his promise to fight Japan, Stalin persuaded the President at Yalta to agree that the Communist state which he had set up in the Chinese province of Outer Mongolia should be permanently detached from China, and that the southern part of Sakhalin, and the Kurile Islands, which cut the great circle airplane route from Alaska to Japan, should be annexed by the Soviet Union.

The agreement . . . was kept secret from the American people . . . not even Mr. Byrnes knew it existed. And the exhausted President returned from Yalta to Washington amid the almost unanimous applause of his bamboozled fellow countrymen.

The stunning thing is that Roosevelt's action was utterly willful. There was no *force majeure* pressing on him. He faced no

Hobson's choice. He should have spurned what he was bargaining for even if it had been tendered as a gift.

It has been said, and uncritically repeated, that Roosevelt acted on General Marshall's advice in order to save American lives in a house-to-house invasion of Japan by inducing the Russians to engage Japanese forces in Manchuria. That is the Stettinius version, for example. After the war, Stettinius tossed the hot potato to Marshall. Washing his own hands, he wrote: "The Far Eastern agreement was not handled by the State Department. ... The President ... in signing ... acted on the advice of his military advisers." But when Marshall was called to testify before the House Foreign Affairs Committee, he dropped the hot potato. Of the Yalta "arrangements," he said, "I personally was unaware of them." Then, according to the stenographic report:

REPRESENTATIVE WALTER H. JUDD: Was it considered necessary ... that we promise her [Russia] control of the ports and railroads in Manchuria ... ?
GENERAL MARSHALL: As I say, I never saw those things. I never saw them and they were never published.[27]

It is true that in earlier months Marshall had given lip service to the propaganda theme, nurtured by the White House and Left Wing groups, that America needed the Soviet Union in the Pacific war. Admiral Ellis M. Zacharias, who was Deputy Director of Naval Intelligence, was amazed, when he came to Washington in the fall of 1944, to find a lack of disposition there, particularly in the Office of War Information, to depart from the "line" that Japan was capable of prolonging the war for several more years. He explains: "It was due undoubtedly to directives and instructions received from other and higher quarters that this line was taken."[28] It was because of these political undercurrents that nothing was done to exploit the opportunities to bring about a quick Japanese surrender.

In the summer of 1944, the cabinet of the bellicose Hideki Tojo had fallen. His successor, Kuniaki Koiso, for the first time brought the army and navy heads into a responsible relationship with the civilian authorities. The progressive decline of Japan's stocks of aircraft, oil, steel, and coal made the end just a question of time. U.S. Naval Intelligence saw the situation clearly: the Japanese had lost their gamble, they knew they had lost, and they longed for a way to quit, if only they could keep their emperor. The secret branch of the Navy which operated under the code name of OP-16-W, which had intelligence reports from all over the world, was "frankly opposed," as were all echelons of the Navy, to Russian participation in the Pacific war.[29] The same thinking was prevalent in Military Intelligence as well, regardless of whatever posture General Marshall may have assumed.[30]

Although an irreverent fellow-officer has said that Marshall would have prescribed an invasion of Patagonia if Roosevelt and Hopkins had wished him to, it should be said, in fairness to Marshall, that it has never been proved that at the time of Yalta he believed or advised that American soldiers would have to storm the beaches of Japan itself to force a surrender. It is incredible that he could have been guilty of such a miscalculation.

A gross miscalculation it would have been. The United States Strategic Bombing Survey, after studying the effects of aerial warfare on Japan, reported the following conclusions to the War Department in 1946: "Based on detailed investigation of all the facts, and supported by the testimony of the Japanese leaders involved, it is the Survey's opinion that . . . Japan would have surrendered even if the atomic bombs had not been dropped, even if Russia had not entered the war, and even if no invasion had been planned or contemplated." Significantly, the report was entitled "Japan's Struggle to End the War." As Professor David Nelson Rowe declares in the Introduction to Tochikazu

Kase's memoirs, "It now becomes even more difficult than before to understand the heavy price paid to Stalin at Yalta to
bring the U.S.S.R. into a war which, as this book shows, was
already won by us and lost by the Japanese at the time of the
Yalta meeting."[31]

The senior staff officer at Yalta was Admiral Leahy. Did
Roosevelt consult with him before his fateful talk with Stalin?
"I was of the firm opinion," Leahy records, "that our war against
Japan had progressed to the point where her defeat was only a
matter of time and attrition. Therefore, we did not need Stalin's
help to defeat our enemy in the Pacific."[32]

Certainly Admiral King, Chief of Naval Operations, was asking no Russian help. General Arnold, head of the Air Force,
whose Superfortresses were now sweeping the skies over Japan
from island airfields, was not at Yalta, but his thinking at this
time coincided with Leahy's;[33] and he had sent General Lau-
rence S. Kuter to represent the Air Force and to present a strategic report which concluded that Russian entrance would be
inimical to American interests at this late stage. Kuter reached
Harry Hopkins; he was not consulted by the President. Mac-
Arthur and Nimitz, who knew more about the Pacific war than
any two men alive, were not summoned to Yalta. They had, as
we have seen, already advised the President that "Japan could be
forced to accept our terms of surrender by the use of sea and air
power without an invasion of the Japanese homeland." Mac-
Arthur has said:

Neither directly nor indirectly did I have the slightest connection
with the Yalta Conference. My views on the advisability of Soviet
Russia entering the war at that late date were never solicited. Neither
I nor any member of my command was present at the Yalta Conference and I personally did not even know it was being held. The imminent collapse of Japan was clearly apparent. . . .

Had my views been requested with reference to Yalta I would

most emphatically have recommended against bringing the Soviet into the Pacific war at that late date. To have made vital concessions for such a purpose would have seemed to me fantastic.[34]

The evidence is overwhelming. Roosevelt's generosity to Stalin that afternoon at Yalta was a willful caprice of his own. The Russophilism which possessed his mind at this time blinded him to all other considerations. The claim that he acted under military advice has always been a sham.

Roosevelt accepted one more dishonorable role in the betrayal of China. He agreed to coerce the Chinese government to accept the terms, the plain implication being that if Chiang Kai-shek resisted, the United States would join with Russia to compel Chinese compliance, by force if necessary. Stalin was a practical man. He was not disposed to allow his American benefactor to leave the scene without giving an airtight commitment. So before Roosevelt left the room, he had promised Stalin not only to get Churchill's acquiescence but to guarantee that the Russians would receive their booty whether the Chinese liked it or not. We therefore find in the secret pact this extraordinary sentence: "The Heads of the three Great Powers have agreed that these claims of the Soviet Union shall be unquestionably fulfilled after Japan has been defeated." Surely this will long stand as a monument in the history of international turpitude. It reduces the plot to the level of gun-point banditry.

It is interesting that even the faithful Sherwood condemns this. He calls it "the most assailable point in the entire Yalta record," for, as he correctly interprets it, "if China had refused to agree to any of the Soviet claims, presumably the U.S. and Britain would have been compelled to join in enforcing them." But he does not let his hero down without providing a soft cushion. Mr. Roosevelt, it seems, meant no harm; he was just worn out. Sherwood gives it as his belief that "Roosevelt would not have agreed to that final firm commitment had it not been that the Yalta Conference was almost at an end and he was tired and anxious to avoid further argument."

Stettinius bridles up at this opinion and asserts that "the Far Eastern agreement was carefully worked out and was not a snap decision made at Yalta." It would seem that in his mind, malice aforethought is a lesser charge than impulsiveness or tired dereliction. "Carefully worked out" by whom? Was Stettinius perchance recalling those preparatory talks with Alger Hiss back at Marrakech? Or the preliminary American meeting in Livadia Palace on February 4, to brief the President on the agenda and procedure for the conference, when Hiss was one of the two officials called in?

We do know that the British were aghast when they learned what Stalin and Roosevelt had cooked up. Anthony Eden and others in the delegation did all they could to dissuade the Prime Minster from setting his signature to the discreditable agreement;[35] but he concluded that he must sign, for he felt that if he angered Roosevelt on this issue, "the whole position of the British Empire in the Far East might be at stake." He was not forgetting that Roosevelt had often made serious hints that Britain should hand over Hong Kong to China. And, like Leahy, he may have foreseen that the United States would have a poor case to push the British out of Hong Kong while inviting the Russians into Dairen and Port Arthur.

In *Triumph and Tragedy,* Churchill takes pains to point out that Roosevelt, not he, was the architect of the China sellout. It is as though he is beseeching History to clear his name of the political crime that was perpetrated:

I must make it clear that, although on behalf of Great Britain I joined in the agreement, neither I nor Eden took any part in making it. It

was regarded as an American affair and . . . we were not consulted
but only asked to approve.

Rightly or wrongly, he felt his own country's interests compelled him to acquiesce rather than isolate himself by a lonely
dissent and risk retaliation.

Months passed before the Chinese government even knew
what had happened. At Stalin's insistence, Roosevelt agreed that
they should not be told until the Russians were ready to march.
This denied Chiang Kai-shek any opportunity to initiate moves
in advance to thwart the stripping of Manchuria by the Russians
and their seizure of the arms and supplies of the surrendering
Japanese forces at the moment of victory. In the end, of course,
the hapless Chinese had to go through the form of consenting
to the deal. They were bereft of choice. But the coerced stroke
of a pen could not expunge the iniquity of the Yalta conspiracy.
Those whom it pleases to believe that it did might well heed the
words of Plato: "That is the greatest wrong, which is accomplished in the form of right."

The eventual consequences, as the world now knows, were
catastrophic. The vast stores of the Japanese Kwantung Army,
denied to the government of China, which had been fighting
the Japanese for twelve years, were in time presented by the
Russians to the Chinese Communists, who were invited to infiltrate the towns and cities of Manchuria under the protection of
Russian troops. Thanks to the Kwantung arms, the Communist
army for the first time became a well-equipped force capable of
challenging Chiang Kai-shek's trained troops. With Manchuria
a subjugated domain, the Chinese Communists were able to
sweep down upon the Yellow River Valley and prepare the
doom of the Chinese Republic. The Soviet Union, with the concessions agreed to by Roosevelt, had a strangle hold on the railroads and ports, the lifeblood of North China.

Those writers who hold to the sacrosanctity of Franklin D. Roosevelt at any intellectual cost usually fall back, in moral desperation, to a final line of defense on the Yalta issue. "What, with the possible exception of the Kuriles," asks Stettinius, "did the Soviet Union receive at Yalta which she could not have taken without any agreement?" Better a bad excuse than none at all. A burglar's accessory, it would seem, is absolved if the burglar could have done the job without any accessory.

The factual assumption is dubious at best. The United States at that time stood on a summit of power rarely scaled by any nation. When the war ended, her army was overwhelmingly superior in equipment of all sorts, including the atomic bomb. Her navy and air forces were supreme everywhere. Her industrial machine was intact, while Russia's was backward, damaged, and, to a large degree, dependent upon the bounty of others and the plunder she could seize in occupied countries. As Bullitt says, "We held power to enforce our will throughout the earth." Would Stalin have violated the sovereignty of China if Roosevelt, at Yalta, instead of handing out vital concessions, had said firmly that Manchuria must and would remain inviolate? We shall never know, but it can be argued persuasively that he would not. Furthermore, fantastic as it seems, in the six months after the Yalta Conference, the United States actually equipped the army with which Russia snatched Manchuria.

In either case, Stettinius' last-ditch question, which he probably hoped would remain rhetorical, has provoked devastating replies of another sort. For example, Professor John A. Lukacs asks in return: "But is it not the aim of war and diplomacy to avoid such situations (especially at the threshold of victory)?" And William Henry Chamberlin: ". . . what a mockery this makes of our professed war objectives. Was it worthwhile to fight a costly and exhaustive war merely to give Poland and other east European countries Russian rather than German gauleiters,

to substitute the Soviet Union for Japan as overlord of China?"
And from Chester Wilmot:

That question [Stettinius'] does not pose the real issue which surely
was: What did the Soviet Union receive at Yalta which she could not
have taken without flagrantly violating the fundamental principles
of the Atlantic Charter and the United Nations to which she had
subscribed? The real issue for the world and for the future was not
what Stalin would or could have taken but what he was given the
right to take. This agreement provided Stalin with a moral cloak for
his aggressive designs in Asia, and, more important, with almost a
legal title enforceable at the Peace Conference to the territories and
privileges which he demanded.[36]

As Wilmot points out, that Thursday afternoon tête-à-tête of
Stalin and Roosevelt was the turning point of the Yalta Conference. "If this was not realized by the Western delegations at the
time, it seems to have been fully appreciated by Stalin."[37] Having
abandoned principle in Asia, Roosevelt could hardly expect to
apply it in Europe the next day; not against a realist like Stalin.

During the rest of the conference, Roosevelt was a broken
drum. This man, who had just crossed the dictator's palm with
the tarnished silver of old-fashioned, nineteenth-century-style
imperialism in China as a bribe to induce him to break a treaty
of non-aggression with Japan, could only appear ludicrous, in
this company, prattling about "sovereign rights" and "the freely
expressed wishes of the people concerned." He had betrayed
himself to Stalin as a consummate windbag to whom the tub-
thumping of the Atlantic Charter had never been more than a
politician's expedient. It did not require the acumen of a Tolstoy
or a Dostoevsky to perceive this. Stalin was no fool. He correctly
concluded that Roosevelt would be satisfied with a few fine
phrases with which to cover himself at home. That is all he
spared him.

En route home, the President paused near the Suez Canal to

be visited on his cruiser by King Farouk of Egypt, King Ibn-
Saud of Saudi Arabia, and Emperor Haile Selassie of Ethiopia.
In a note, Harry Hopkins sized up this interlude as "in the main,
a lot of horseplay."[38] It was no surprise to him that Mr. Roosevelt
was just the one "to thoroughly enjoy the colorful panoply of
the sovereigns of this part of the world." Smooth talk flowed,
and costly gifts were exchanged.

Back in Washington, the President addressed a joint session
of Congress sitting in a wheel chair. He had not been ill "a single
day" since leaving Washington, he bragged; it was just that the
braces on his legs weighed ten pounds and it was "a lot easier"
sitting down. Those in the front rows listened incredulously, for
what they were looking at was an obviously failing man. However, a man is surely entitled to his own appraisal of his own
health, and perhaps a cheerful one is salutary. We could hardly
expect Mr. Roosevelt to report, as did one of his observers at
Yalta, that he "looked sick, he acted sick and he talked sick."
Nor need it be blameworthy that his statement to Congress does
not jibe with the observations of Churchill, who writes that at
Yalta "the President was ailing. . . . His face had a transparency
. . . and often there was a far-away look in his eyes" and that
when they said good-by at the end of the conference, "the President seemed placid and frail. I felt that he had a slender contact
with life."[39] In any event, in the carefully staged performance
on Capitol Hill, an admirable show was put on, all photographs
were screened, and only the authorized ones were ever published. This was before the days of television.

If the robustness of earlier years was gone, the old habit of prevarication was undiminished. "This Conference concerned itself
only with the European war and the political problems of Europe, and not with the Pacific war," he swore. This was, of
course, a deliberate falsehood, for he had in his safe the secret
agreement signed at Yalta concerning the Pacific war. He had,

it is true, promised Stalin to keep the secret, but had he also promised to perjure himself before the Congress of the United States?

The partition of Poland and the acceptance of the Communist clique known as the Lublin Committee as the provisional government were glossed over with the phrases he had imported for the purpose. All this, said he, had been "agreed to by Russia, by Britain and by me." Intimate, rambling, and disarmingly optimistic, the speech went far to hide the grim future which now was certain. Yet we know that Admiral Leahy, who was close to the President, came home from Yalta in a different mood. In his words, "the proposed peace seemed to me a frightening 'sowing of dragon's teeth.' " He did not share the "exultation" of some members of the American delegation because he realized the decisions of the conference would make Russia "the dominant power in Europe." It seemed elementary to Leahy that this spelled trouble. "That in itself, in my opinion, carried a certainty of future international disagreements."[40]

There was no hint of this in Roosevelt's speech. "The Crimea Conference . . . spells—and it ought to spell—the end of the system of unilateral action, exclusive alliances, and spheres of influence, and balances of power. . . . I am sure that—under the agreement reached at Yalta—there will be a more stable political Europe than ever before." This may well rank as the most blustering, the most reckless—and the most wrong—prediction ever made within the walls of the National Capitol. That very evening, in Bucharest, Russia's Vishinsky, unilaterally and with Red troops to back him up, issued an ultimatum to the King of Rumania demanding that he appoint as prime minister Petru Groza, the choice of the Rumanian Communists.[41]

By this time, American public opinion was so drugged and fooled by wartime propaganda that it was possible for the President to make such a statement and be believed by millions. There were strong voices of critical dissent, too, and widespread uneasiness in the country, but people believed because they had made great sacrifices for—they hoped—something and because they desperately wanted to believe. To a large extent, the radio commentators, the newspaper and magazine writers, and the academic community failed them, supinely echoing the fashionable inanities and platitudes which flowed in a torrent from Communist-front organizations and the Roosevelt administration. To question the wisdom or veracity of Franklin D. Roosevelt was, for these, a kind of sabotage; to be suspicious of Joseph Stalin showed want of soul.

For years, Mrs. Eleanor Roosevelt had been effusing her quaint homilies throughout the land in a popular daily column in which she cleverly interlarded her views on domesticity with her and her husband's attitudes toward the Soviet Union and its "great leader," Stalin. Her influence in conditioning the American mind was immense. Such writers as David Lawrence, who promptly attacked Yalta and accurately prophesied its consequence, were, in such competition, offering unpalatable fare to the more than half of the population who were living in a fog of clichés and for whom wishful thinking had become the exclusive mental process. Even *Time* magazine abdicated its proper function so far that it permitted itself blithely to assert that "all doubts about the Big Three's ability to cooperate in peace as well as in war seem now to have been swept away." Autosuggestion is, indeed, a powerful force, yet it seems impossible that the magazine's own staff could have been without doubts. However, in fairness to those who were carried away on a wave of optimism, it should be remembered that some of the most fetid details of the Yalta Conference were still under wraps.

After the Yalta Conference, it became harder to keep the secret in the closet. The Russians were running roughshod over all the mealymouthings President Roosevelt had boasted about. As Wilmot summarizes it, "Before the end of March the Yalta Agreement had been broken or disregarded by the Russians in every important case which had so far been put to the test of action." Even Harriman was now alarmed in his messages from Moscow. Roosevelt was "vacationing" in Georgia. Churchill was on the edge of despair, as much because of the President's equanimity as because of the Russians' truculence.[42]

To the last, Franklin D. Roosevelt clung to the pretense. Finally, Churchill consulted him about what he should say to the House of Commons about the deteriorating situation in Poland. Resting at Warm Springs, Roosevelt was having his portrait painted again. On the morning of April 12, he drafted a cable in reply. In this cable he said:

> *I would minimize the general Soviet problem as much as possible* because these problems, in one form or another, seem to arise every day and most of them straighten out.[43]

An hour later he suffered a stroke. That afternoon he died.

On February 12, General Marshall, coming from the Crimea, met General Anders, the leader of the fighting Polish forces, in Florence, Italy. Anders did not know it yet, but he and the majority of his fellow-officers would never be able to return to their homes in Poland because the land on which their homes stood would no longer be Polish. The issuance of the Yalta communiqué was only a few hours away. It vitally concerned Poland, yet the American Chief of Staff refused to say a word to his Polish colleague about what had happened there. And when the emotional Anders painted a dark picture of Europe's future, an irritated and weary Marshall answered him: "We continue to march with Soviet Russia against the Germans; what will happen afterwards, God alone knows."[44]

Whether General Marshall grasped the real meaning of his admission is not known. "Who," asks Professor Lukacs, "had let

the Second World War reach that total, dead, political impasse?"
Who, indeed, had let a war in which millions had fought and
died sink to such a nadir of aimlessness and futility? Did God
alone know? General Marshall underestimated his fellow-mor-
tals. Many people knew. The logic of cause and effect is as inexorable in the field of human action as it is in the realm of
physical science. As a matter of fact, there was an unsavory character in Berlin who knew. Hitler's mouthpiece, Herr Goebbels,
had made many turgid predictions which were wide of the
mark, but this time he knew whereof he spoke. The following
words were penned by him about the same time that Marshall
made his statement to Anders. They were printed in his February
23 editorial in *Das Reich:*

If the German people should lay down their arms, the agreement
between Roosevelt, Churchill and Stalin would allow the Soviets to
occupy all Eastern and South-Eastern Europe, together with the major
part of the Reich. An iron curtain would at once descend on this territory, which, including the Soviet Union, would be of tremendous
dimensions. Behind this curtain there would begin a mass slaughter
of peoples. . . . All that would remain would be a type of human
being in the raw, a dull, fermenting mass of millions of proletarian
and despairing beasts of burden who would know nothing of the rest
of the world except what the Kremlin considered useful to its own
purposes. Without leadership of their own, they would be at the
mercy of the bloody dictatorship of the Soviets. The rest of Europe
would be engulfed in chaotic political and social confusion which
would only represent a preparatory stage for the coming Bolshevization.

Geographically, the shadow of immediate doom was slightly
overdrawn. Otherwise, all but the last sentence has become history. The fulfillment of Herr Goebbels' last black prediction is
still in doubt—thwarted, or at least postponed, by the retention
of American troops and airfields in Europe and Africa since the
end of the war, the pouring in each year of billions of dollars of

military and economic aid, and the feverish preparation for a war of survival.

"A preparatory stage"—these are Goebbels' words. The last chapter has not been written. Will a ghastly new holocaust be the price that must be paid to avert "the coming Bolshevization"? Prayerfully, men hope that the follies and crimes of World War II may be atoned for some other way. It is a hope that flickers low. Optimism is now a pleasant indulgence which there is little in human experience to justify. For Yalta was more than the unhappy culmination of Roosevelt's long series of blunders in *Weltpolitik*. It was a moral debacle of unimaginable evil to the world.

Not the least calamity was the dissipation of mankind's faith in America. Disillusionment and cynicism are the dross that remains where a high reputation for integrity once flourished. In their present bewilderment and frustration, the American people have too quickly forgotten that their dazzling wartime President gave away more than the lands and freedoms of people in Europe and Asia; he tossed away something, just as precious, that was theirs alone. Perhaps in the long run that was Franklin D. Roosevelt's most tragic disservice to his fellow countrymen.

Notes

NOTES

INTRODUCTION

1. Thomas A. Bailey, *The Man in the Street* (Macmillan, 1948).

CHAPTER I

1. This is the way the speech was verbally delivered before the Congress and heard over the radio. However, there is reason to believe that President Roosevelt ad-libbed the pronoun "me" and perhaps also the "I." See Bert Andrews, *New York Herald Tribune,* March 11, 1945. Robert E. Sherwood says, "He was extremely casual in this speech, ad-libbing a great deal of it." (Robert E. Sherwood, *Roosevelt and Hopkins: An Intimate History* [Harper, 1948], 874) Some newspapers, in printing the speech on March 2, 1945, the day after it was delivered, did not contain the "by Russia, by Britain and by me" phrase in any form whatever, probably because they were using the prepared text which had been issued to the press and which did not contain the President's extemporaneous remarks. An example is the *San Francisco Chronicle* of March 2, 1945. However, the text of the speech as printed in the *New York Times* of that date, as recorded and transcribed by the *New York Times,* includes the words "by Russia, by Britain and by me" and also the "as far as I wanted" phrase.

The words "and by me" were evidently too much for Samuel Rosenman when he came to editing the 1945 volume of *The Public Papers and Addresses of Franklin D. Roosevelt* (hereafter referred to as *Public Papers*), so he changed the "by me" to "by the United States." This version is faithful neither to the orginal text nor to the speech as actually delivered. Roosevelt very likely shied away from calling the Polish settlement an agreement by the United States, for that might have caused some eyebrow-raising on the part of the Senators whom he was addressing. Actually, the "and by me" was the more ludicrous. Perhaps that is why editor Rosenman discarded it *ex post facto* and adopted the words "and by the United States" as the lesser of two embarrassing alternatives. It will be recalled that Rosenman was for years one of Roosevelt's favorite ghost writers and was a trained expert at shuffling words and phrases in a politic manner.

2. He did say in his speech to Congress that the Charter of the United Nations would have to be approved by the Senate, making particular mention of the fact that he was "aware of" the Constitution of the United States. He was at that point talking about what had been done at Yalta concerning the about-to-be-born United Nations Organization. According to some newspaper accounts, as, for example, in the *San Francisco Chronicle* of March 2, 1945, the text included the following words: "as will some of the other arrangements made at Yalta." Such accounts were probably based on a prepared text, but Roosevelt did not utter those words in delivering the speech. Accordingly, they are not found in the "recorded and transcribed" text printed the following day in the *New York Times* (March 2, 1945). Nor are they in the version published in *Public Papers*. The paragraph referred to is somewhat casual in style, as though Roosevelt, in reading it, may have revised it on the spot by eliminating a vague reference to the necessity of Senate ratification of "some of the other arrangements made at Yalta." It is obvious that he did not intend to throw those "arrangements" open to questioning by the Senate; they were a *fait accompli* in his mind, and agreement "by me" ended the matter.

Furthermore, although he said the limits of the western boundary of Poland would be fixed in the final "peace conference," there was nothing tentative about the eastern boundary or about East Prussia, Danzig, and the other areas affected. Said the President: "I think Danzig would be a lot better if it were Polish." So it had been made Polish. The people of Danzig, 95 per cent of whom were German speaking, were not to be asked if they agreed with the sage of Hyde Park that they would be better off if their city were Polish. (*Public Papers* [1945], 582.)

3. Arthur Bliss Lane, *I Saw Poland Betrayed* (Bobbs-Merrill, 1948).

4. William C. Bullitt, "A Report to the American People on China," *Life* (October 3, 1947).

5. Sherwood, *op. cit.,* 835.

6. Winston Churchill, *The Hinge of Fate* (Houghton Mifflin, 1950), 686: "It was with some feeling of surprise that I heard the President say at the press conference on January 24 that we would enforce 'unconditional surrender' upon all our enemies."

7. Hanson W. Baldwin, *Great Mistakes of the War* (Harper, 1950).

8. Henry L. Stimson and McGeorge Bundy, *On Active Service in War and Peace* (Harper, 1947), 580, 581.

9. See the discussion of this question from the military and political points of view in Baldwin, *op. cit.* See also Note 15, *post.*

10. Edward R. Stettinius, *Roosevelt and the Russians: The Yalta Conference* (Doubleday, 1949), and "What F.D.R. and Stalin Really Did at Yalta," *Look* (June 21, 1949).

11. James F. Byrnes, *Speaking Frankly* (Harper, 1947), 42, 43.

12. Press statement, August 7, 1949. See also Don Lohbeck, *Patrick J. Hurley* (Regnery, 1956).

13. Sherwood, *op. cit.,* 867.

14. Joseph C. Grew, *The Turbulent Era* (Houghton Mifflin, 1955).

15. Baldwin, *op. cit.* This highly respected military analyst explains why the invasion of Normandy was, in his view, one of the blunders by which the United States lost the peace. The United States, he says, had no peace aims, and American policy was based on false premises and psychological delusions. Prime Minister Churchill was concerned over the postwar political repercussions which might ensue from current military decisions, only to be overruled repeatedly by President Roosevelt.

This difference in approach between Roosevelt and Churchill is reflected throughout the latter's war memoirs. Elliott Roosevelt, in his book *As He Saw It* (Duell, Sloane & Pearce, 1946), tells of the sharp cleavage between the thinking of the two men with regard to Russia. Frequently quoting from private conversations with his father, he records that Churchill fought an unceasing battle to avoid a cross-Channel invasion into Europe and constantly struggled to force a change in Allied strategy in order to prevent a situation which would find the Red Army dominating the Balkans as well as eastern Germany. (pp. 184, 185, 231, 253). Franklin D. Roosevelt adamantly opposed any strategy which was objectionable to Stalin, whom he "liked," Elliott writes (p. 176), and whom he referred to as "Uncle Joe."

16. William C. Bullitt, "The Strength of Our New Foreign Policy," *Readers Digest* (June, 1947).

17. John R. Deane, *The Strange Alliance* (Viking, 1947).

18. For a detailed report of the celebrated Alger Hiss case, see Ralph de Toledano and Victor Lasky, *Seeds of Treason* (Funk & Wagnalls, 1950).

19. David J. Dallin, *Soviet Russia's Foreign Policy* (Yale University Press, 1943).

20. Nicholas J. Spykman, *America's Strategy in World Politics* (Harcourt, Brace, 1942).

21. Deane, *op. cit.,* 90.

22. Joseph E. Davies, *Mission to Moscow* (Simon & Schuster, 1941).

CHAPTER II

1. James F. Byrnes, *All in One Lifetime* (Harper, 1958), 281.

2. Albert C. Wedemeyer, *Wedemeyer Reports!* (Holt, 1958), 340.

3. Franz Borkenau, *European Communism* (Harper, 1953), 72.

4. *Ibid.,* 493-94.

5. See Chapter XII.

6. In addition to Borkenau, see Stephen King-Hall, *The Communist Conspiracy* (Constable [London], 1953), and J. Edgar Hoover, *Masters of Deceit* (Holt, 1958).

7. Don Whitehead, *The FBI Story* (Random House, 1956), 267. See also Hoover, *op. cit.*

8. *Year-End News Report,* United Press Associations, January 6, 1941 (Hoover Institute and Library, Stanford University). So strict was the censorship that Henry Shapiro, the U.P. reporter, had a section of the Russian Constitution stricken from one of his dispatches. Censorship was also childishly arbitrary. Virgil Pinkley had a personality sketch of Stalin so ridiculously mutilated that he withdrew it. In it he had said that Stalin's hair was worn in pompadour style. When he asked why this harmless detail was removed, K. Palgunov, the chief of the Soviet press bureau, replied, "Mr. Pinkley, it is not permitted to compare Comrade Stalin with Madame Pompadour."

9. See dispatch of L.S.B. Shapiro, *New York Times,* March 19, 1946. Mr. Shapiro reported:

> The key to Russia's expansion program in Europe and the Near East has fallen into the hands of the State Department in Washington. Captured German documents detailing the final conversations between Russian Foreign Minister Vyacheslav Molotov and German Foreign Minister Joachim Ribbentrop in the spring of 1941 have been collated and compared with the reports of American envoys and military attaches in European capitals at that time, with the result that Washington now possesses exact pictures of the aims

and desires that lie behind the current Soviet troop movements and
diplomatic pressures.

A few weeks before Germany attacked Russia in June, 1941, Mr.
Molotov travelled to Berlin. . . . The transcript of these last conversations . . . became, in 1945, the chief objective of intelligence teams
of every victorious nation scouring the ruins of the Third Reich.

This correspondent has learned, on reliable authority, that the
prized transcript was in a batch of captured German documents
that were dispatched to Washington during the winter. From
sources in an indisputable position to know the facts, I have learned
that the salient points of the transcript are as follows:

. . . The Soviet emissary arrived with authorization from the
Kremlin to offer to Germany full military alliance in return for certain territorial concessions after victory, which were permanent
possession of all Polish territory then occupied by Soviet forces;
incorporation of Lithuania, Estonia, Latvia, and the Karelian Isth-
mus, Bessarabia and Bukovina into the Soviet Union; complete
control of the Dardanelles, a free hand in Iraq and Iran, and enough
of Saudi Arabia to give the Soviets control of the Persian Gulf and
the Gulf of Aden guarding the approaches to the Red Sea.

. . . After numerous conferences with Hitler, Ribbentrop arrived
at certain private conclusions. The first was that Russia's territorial
demands were too great for acceptance. Secondly, Ribbentrop felt
that even if these were suitable, he could not accept Russia's friendly
assurances at face value and that Germany would still require a
huge force on her eastern frontiers to watch Russia's every move.

These decisions were put to Mr. Molotov in an extremely stormy
final session and the conference broke up shortly thereafter.

In the light of current Russian moves, this transcript has now
assumed importance.

After a delay of three years, the State Department finally acknowl-
edged its possession of this telltale transcript. See *Nazi-Soviet Relations, 1939-1941* (Department of State, 1948).

10. Harry Hopkins, "The Inside Story of My Meeting with Stalin,"
American magazine (December, 1941).

11. Byrnes, *All in One Lifetime,* 320.

12. Russian guilt was firmly established. See Jan Ciechanowski,
Defeat in Victory, (Doubleday, 1947); Stanislaw Mikolajczyk, *The
Rape of Poland* (McGraw-Hill, 1948); Stanislaw Mackiewicz, *The
Katyn Wood Murders* (Hollis & Carter [London], 1951), with
Foreword by Arthur Bliss Lane; *Report of the House Committee to*

Investigate the Katyn Massacre (U.S. Government Printing Office, 1952); F. J. P. Veale, *Advance to Barbarism* (Nelson, 1953).

13. *Stalin's Correspondence with Churchill, Attlee, Roosevelt and Truman, 1941-1945* (Lawrence & Wishart [London], 1958).

14. First described in an obviously White House–inspired article, "Roosevelt's World Blueprint," by Forrest Davis, in *Saturday Evening Post* (April 10, 1943).

15. Demaree Bess, "What Does Russia Want?" *Saturday Evening Post* (March 20, 1943); see also Dallin, *op. cit.*

16. John T. Flynn, *The Roosevelt Myth* (Devin-Adair, 1948).

17. Sherwood, *op. cit.*, 71.

18. Frances Perkins, *The Roosevelt I Knew* (Viking, 1946), 43.

CHAPTER III

1. Sherwood, *op. cit.*, 80.
2. *Ibid.*, 690.
3. *Ibid.*, xii.
4. *Ibid.*, 191.
5. *Ibid.*, 201.
6. *Ibid.*, xvii.
7. *Ibid.*, xvii.
8. *Ibid.*, 212.
9. *Ibid.*, 26.
10. *Ibid.*, 92.
11. *Ibid.*, 94-98.
12. *Ibid.*, 112.
13. Cordell Hull, *The Memoirs of Cordell Hull* (Macmillan, 1948).
14. Sherwood, *op. cit.*, 179.
15. *Ibid.*, 529.

CHAPTER IV

1. Associated Press report in the public press, September 4, 1950.
2. William Henry Chamberlin, *America's Second Crusade* (Regnery, 1950).
3. Winston Churchill, *The Gathering Storm* (Houghton Mifflin, 1948), Preface.
4. This is no longer open to question. How Roosevelt planned American involvement in war in Europe and Asia and goaded Japan into attacking Pearl Harbor has been thoroughly documented in the following books: Charles A. Beard, *President Roosevelt and the*

Coming of the War, 1941 (Yale University Press, 1948); Chamberlin, *op. cit.;* George Morgenstern, *Pearl Harbor* (Devin-Adair, 1947); Tochikazu Kase, *Journey to the Missouri* (Yale University Press, 1950); Frederick R. Sanborn, *Design for War* (Devin-Adair, 1951); Charles Callan Tansill, *Back Door to War* (Regnery, 1952); Admiral R. A. Theobald, *The Final Secret of Pearl Harbor* (Devin-Adair, 1954); Grew, *The Turbulent Era;* Admiral H. E. Kimmel, *Admiral Kimmel's Story* (Regnery, 1955); Wedemeyer, *op. cit.,* Chapter I. See also the Introduction to this volume.

5. *Public Papers* (1941), 557.
6. *Ibid.* (1939), 1-12.
7. Charles A. Beard, *Giddy Minds and Foreign Quarrels* (Macmillan, 1939), 54.
8. *Public Papers* (1940), 93.
9. A good discussion of Article 124 of the Russian Constitution appeared in the magazine *Christian Century* on October 15, 1941. This was one of the few publications that made more than a superficial examination of it for the information of the American public.
10. *Vital Speeches,* Vol. VII, 583.
11. See Note 4, *supra.*
12. Quoted in *Nation* (December 5, 1942).

CHAPTER V

1. Sumner Welles, *Where Are We Heading?* (Harper, 1946), 3.
2. H. V. Morton, *Atlantic Meeting* (Methuen & Company, Ltd. [London], 1943), vi-vii.
3. Sherwood, *op. cit.,* 362.
4. Winston Churchill, *The Grand Alliance* (Houghton Mifflin, 1950), 441.
5. Elliott Roosevelt, *op. cit.,* 44.
6. *Ibid.,* xiv.

CHAPTER VI

1. Ray Brock in the *Baltimore Sun,* July 22, 1941, from Ankara (Copyright 1941 by the *New York Times*); Preston Groves, Associated Press correspondent in Istanbul, *Baltimore Sun,* July 28, 1941.
2. Sherwood, *op. cit.,* 342.
3. William C. Bullitt, *The Great Globe Itself* (Scribner's, 1946), 11.
4. Sherwood, *op. cit.,* 327-44.

5. The Jewish community, powerful in the motion-picture industry, was understandably incensed by Hitler's anti-Semitism.

6. See Note 4 of Chapter IV, *supra*.

7. Careful documentation of the pre–Pearl Harbor story, with specific references to the transcript of the hearings of the Joint Congressional Committee on the Investigation of the Pearl Harbor Attack (hereafter referred to as Joint Congressional Committee), as well as other documentary evidence, is to be found in the sources cited in Note 4 of Chapter IV.

8. *Foreign Relations, Japan 1931-1941* (U.S. Government Printing Office, 1943), II, 266, 267.

9. Stimson and Bundy, *op. cit.*, 373.

10. *Pearl Harbor Attack* (Hearings of the Joint Congressional Committee), Part 5, 2293/ff.

11. *Pearl Harbor Attack*, Part 5, 2121.

12. Stimson and Bundy, *op. cit.*, 373.

13. *Pearl Harbor Attack*, Part 16, 2175.

14. The testimony of Grand Admiral Karl Doenitz at the Nürnberg Trials in 1946 concerning orders to the German navy sheds light on Hitler's anxiety to avoid conflict with the United States. *New York Times*, May 9, 1946.

15. See an account in *Newsweek* (November 10, 1941).

16. *Pearl Harbor Attack*, Part 16, 2210.

17. *Ibid.*, Part 5, 2382-84.

18. See Note 8, *supra*.

19. *Pearl Harbor Attack*, Part 5, 2379-80.

20. *New York Times*, August 1, 1941.

21. *Ibid.*, August 2, 1941.

22. *Ibid.*, August 2, 1941.

23. *Newsweek* (July 28, 1941). See also *Pearl Harbor Attack*, Part 14, 1343, and Part 15, 1849.

24. *Newsweek* (July 21, 1941).

25. *Foreign Relations, Japan 1931-1941*, II, 645-50.

26. Hull, *op. cit.*, 1025.

27. For a well-documented discussion of the circumstances pertaining to the proposed Konoye-Roosevelt meeting, see Chapter XII of Sanborn, *op. cit.* See also Tansill, *op. cit.*, and Grew, *The Turbulent Era*.

28. Hull, *op. cit.*, 1025.

29. Basil Rauch, *Roosevelt: From Munich to Pearl Harbor* (Farrar, Strauss and Cudahy, 1954).

30. *Ibid.*, 447.

31. Jesse Jones, *Fifty Billion Dollars* (Macmillan, 1951).

32. Bailey, *op. cit.*

33. *Pearl Harbor Attack,* Part 12, 17.

34. Churchill, *The Grand Alliance,* 606.

35. Churchill's address of February 15, 1942, in the *New York Times,* February 16, 1942.

36. Associated Press dispatch from London, June 21, 1944.

37. Eleanor Roosevelt, *This I Remember* (Harper, 1949), 233.

38. Perkins, *op. cit.,* 379-80.

39. *Pearl Harbor Attack,* Part 6, 2837.

40. The intercepted, decoded messages from Tokyo to the Japanese Ambassador in Washington are given in detail in *Pearl Harbor Attack,* Part 12, 1-316. The advance information Roosevelt and his inner circle had concerning the Japanese attack is documented in the Tansill, Sanborn, Morgenstern, Grew, and Kimmel books. (See Note 4 of Chapter IV, *supra.*)

41. Forrest Davis and Ernest K. Lindley, *How War Came* (Simon and Schuster, 1942), 4.

42. *Pearl Harbor Attack,* Part 11, 5433.

43. *Ibid.,* Part 2, 570; see also Joseph C. Grew, *Ten Years in Japan* (Simon and Schuster, 1944), 493, 497.

44. John Chamberlain, "The Man Who Pushed Pearl Harbor," *Life* (April 1, 1946), 94.

45. Sidney Rogerson, *Propaganda and the Next War* (Geoffrey Bles [London], 1938).

46. For a study of British and German propaganda drives in World War II, see Harold Lavine and James Wechsler, *War Propaganda and the United States* (Yale University Press, 1940).

CHAPTER VII

1. *Time* (July 21, 1941).

2. *U.S.-Soviet Relations, 1933-1939,* a collection of hitherto unpublished documents released by the State Department on May 24, 1952.

3. Radio address reported in the daily press, October 18, 1951.

4. Lord Lloyd, *The British Case* (Macmillan, 1940).

5. *New York Herald Tribune,* February 24, 1940.

6. *New York World-Telegram,* February 5, 1940.

7. A thorough and objective discussion of propaganda in the early period of the war is to be found in Lavine and Wechsler, *op. cit.*

8. *New York Herald Tribune,* October 23, 1939.

9. Norman Pounds, *An Historical and Political Geography of Europe* (Harras [London] and Chanticleer [New York], 1947), 303.

10. *Vital Speeches,* Vol. VII, 583.

11. *Time* (August 18, 1941).

12. Statement released to the public on August 5, 1941.

Chapter VIII

1. The statements and impressions given to the press and the public during the first few days of Mr. Roosevelt's trip, as referred to in this and succeeding paragraphs, are drawn from the daily reports in the *New York Times* and the *New York Herald Tribune* and the weeklies *Time* and *Newsweek.*

2. Morton, *op. cit.,* xi.

3. Sherwood, *op. cit.,* 311.

4. Hull, *op. cit.,* 974.

5. Sherwood, *op. cit.,* 313.

6. Churchill, *The Grand Alliance,* 427.

7. Hull, *op. cit.,* 974.

8. Elliott Roosevelt, *op. cit.,* 39.

9. Welles, *op. cit.,* 6.

10. Elliott Roosevelt, *op. cit.,* 27.

11. Sherwood, *op. cit.,* 353.

12. Elliott Roosevelt, *op. cit.,* 30.

13. Morton, *op. cit.,* 101.

14. *Ibid.,* 119.

15. H. H. Arnold, *Global Mission* (Harper, 1949), 253.

16. *Ibid.,* 231.

17. *Ibid.,* 253.

18. *Ibid.,* 254.

19. Elliott Roosevelt, *op. cit.,* 33, 41.

20. What transpired at this meeting is gleaned from Welles, *op. cit.,* 11-15; Churchill, *The Grand Alliance,* 434-42; Elliott Roosevelt, *op. cit.,* 39; Sherwood, *op. cit.,* 356-60; and the record of the Congressional investigation of the Pearl Harbor attack.

21. Sherwood, *op. cit.,* 362.

22. See Chapter VI.

23. Churchill, *The Grand Alliance,* 438.

24. *Ibid.,* 441.

25. Churchill's address of February 15, 1942. *New York Times,* February 16, 1942.

26. Churchill, *The Grand Alliance,* 447.

27. *Time,* August 25, 1941.
28. Sherwood, *op. cit.,* 362.
29. Welles, *op. cit.,* 17.
30. *Ibid.,* 17.
31. Churchill, *The Grand Alliance,* 444.
32. *New York Times,* August 25, 1941.
33. *London Times,* February 28, 1945.
34. Russell Grenfell, *Unconditional Hatred* (Devin-Adair, 1953), 152.
35. Winston Churchill, *Triumph and Tragedy* (Houghton Mifflin, 1953), 456.
36. *London Times,* October 11, 1954.

<h2 style="text-align:center">CHAPTER IX</h2>

1. Chester Wilmot, *The Struggle for Europe* (Harper, 1952), 633.
2. The drafts were disclosed in Welles *op. cit.* Churchill's original draft also appears in *The Grand Alliance.*
3. Welles, *op. cit.,* 16, 17.
4. Churchill, *The Grand Alliance,* 433.
5. Sherwood, *op. cit.,* 350.
6. See Freud's letter to Albert Einstein, written in Vienna in September, 1932, in *Readings in World Politics* (American Foundation for Political Education, 1952), II.
7. See Veale, *op. cit.,* and the Foreword by The Very Reverend William Ralph Inge, Dean of St. Paul's; Freda Utley, *The High Cost of Vengeance* (Regnery, 1949); Austin J. App, *History's Most Terrifying Peace* (Boniface Press, 1946); Montgomery Belgion, *Victors' Justice* (Regnery, 1949).
8. Welles, *op. cit.,* 7.
9. Sherwood, *op. cit.,* 362.
10. See Elliott Roosevelt, *op. cit.,* Chapter II.
11. Wilmot, *op. cit.,* 633.
12. *Public Papers.*
13. Sherwood, *op. cit.,* 372.
14. See *Interlocking Subversion in Government Departments,* Report of the Subcommittee to Investigate the Administration of the Internal Security Laws, to the Judiciary Committee, U.S. Senate, July 30, 1953 (Government Printing Office); documentation of the House Committee on Un-American Activities; James Burnham, *The Web of Subversion* (John Day, 1954); Whitehead, *op. cit.;* Hoover, *op. cit.*

15. Borkenau, *op. cit.,* 279.
16. February 10, 1940. See *Public Papers* (1940), 93.
17. *Christian Century* (October 15, 1941).
18. Sherwood, *op. cit.,* 391-93.
19. *Ibid.*
20. *Ibid.*
21. *Ibid.*
22. *Public Papers* (1941), 557.
23. Borkenau, *op. cit.,* 72.
24. See Harry Elmer Barnes (ed.), *Perpetual War for Perpetual Peace* (Caxton 1952).
25. Veale, *op. cit.*
26. Welles, *op. cit.,* 8.
27. *Ibid.,* 14; Churchill, *The Grand Alliance,* 437.
28. Welles, *op. cit.,* 10.
29. *Ibid.,* 14.

CHAPTER X

1. William C. Bullitt, "How We Won the War and Lost the Peace," *Life* (August 30, 1948).
2. Churchill, *The Hinge of Fate,* 201.
3. Quoted in *ibid.,* 667.
4. Deane, *op. cit.,* 295.
5. Lord Hankey, *Politics: Trials and Errors* (Regnery, 1950), 38-55.
6. Baldwin, *op. cit.,* 14.
7. This becomes less disputable each year as grim events unfold. In addition to Baldwin, *op. cit.,* and Hankey, see Major General J. F. C. Fuller, *The Second World War* (Eyre & Spottiswoode [London], 1948), 258-59, 264-65, 275, 311, 312, 355, 365, 379, 391, and 392; Barnes, *op. cit.;* Admiral William D. Leahy, *I Was There* (Whittlesey, 1950), 145; Grenfell, *op. cit.;* Veale, *op. cit.;* Wilmot, *op. cit.;* B. S. Liddell Hart, *The German Generals Talk* (Morrow, 1948); F. O. Miksche, *Unconditional Surrender: The Roots of a World War III* (Faber & Faber [London], 1952).
8. Elliott Roosevelt, *op. cit.,* 117.
9. Sherwood, *op. cit.,* 669.
10. *Ibid.,* 671.
11. Churchill, *The Hinge of Fate,* 657.
12. *Ibid.,* 713.
13. *Hansard* for June 2, 1942.

14. B. S. Liddell Hart, *The Revolution in Warfare* (Faber & Faber [London], 1946), 72.

15. J. M. Spaight, *Bombing Vindicated* (Bles [London], 1944), and Sir Arthur Harris, *Bomber Offensive* (Collins [London], 1947). See also Hart, *The Revolution in Warfare,* and Grenfell, *op. cit.*

16. See his article in *The Star* (England) of December 12, 1946.

17. Hart, *The German Generals Talk,* and *The Other Side of the Hill* (Cassell [London], 1951); Milton Schulman, *Defeat in the West* (Seeker & Warburg [London], 1947); Fuller, *op. cit.;* Hans Rothfells, *The German Opposition to Hitler* (Regnery, 1948); Wilmot, *op. cit.;* Grenfell, *op. cit.;* F. H. Hinsley, *Hitler's Strategy* (Cambridge University Press, 1951); *Nürnberg Trial Proceedings.*

18. Wedemeyer, *op. cit.,* 96.

19. Churchill, *The Hinge of Fate,* Chapter XIX.

20. Hopkins' words were recorded and are quoted in Churchill, *The Hinge of Fate,* 318.

21. Quoted in Sherwood, *op. cit.,* 557.

22. *Ibid.,* 556.

23. Churchill, *The Hinge of Fate,* 324.

24. Dwight D. Eisenhower, *Crusade in Europe* (Doubleday, 1948), 90.

25. Sherwood, *op. cit.,* 674.

26. Churchill, *The Hinge of Fate,* 658.

27. Sherwood, *op. cit.,* 657.

28. Elliott Roosevelt (ed.), *F.D.R.: His Personal Letters* (Duell, Sloan & Pearce, 1950), III, Part 2, 1400.

29. *Ibid.,* 1394.

30. John Gunther, *Roosevelt in Retrospect* (Harper, 1950), 54.

31. Churchill, *The Hinge of Fate,* 686.

32. *London Times,* November 18, 1949.

33. Sherwood, *op. cit.,* 696; quoted in Churchill, *The Hinge of Fate,* 687.

34. Leahy, *op. cit.,* 145.

35. Hull, *op. cit.,* 1570-71.

36. Louis P. Lochner (ed.), *The Goebbels Diaries, 1941-1943* (Doubleday, 1948), 34, 232.

37. Allen W. Dulles, *Germany's Underground* (Macmillan, 1947), 122-23.

38. Fuller, *op. cit.,* 355.

39. See Notes 7 and 17, *supra.*

40. Fuller, *op. cit.,* 258-59.

41. *Ibid.,* 391-92.

CHAPTER XI

1. Hull, *op. cit.*, 1109.
2. *Ibid.*, 1110.
3. *Ibid.*, Chapter LXXXV.
4. *Ibid.*, 1169.
5. *Ibid.*, 1249.
6. *Ibid.*, 1716.
7. *Ibid.*, 1720.
8. *Ibid.*, 1252.
9. *Time* (August 30, 1943).
10. Hull, *op. cit.*, 1231.
11. Sherwood, *op. cit.*, 748.
12. Wedemeyer, *op. cit.*, 370, 376.
13. Sherwood, *op. cit.*, 752.
14. W. D. Puleston, *The Influence of Force in Foreign Relations* (Van Nostrand, 1955).
15. Whitehead, *op. cit.*, 355. (Foreword by J. Edgar Hoover)

CHAPTER XII

1. Hollington K. Tong, *Chiang Kai-shek* (China Publishing, 1953), 214.
2. *Ibid.*, 323 ff.
3. T. H. White and Annalee Jacoby, *Thunder out of China* (Sloane, 1946), 199.
4. John T. Flynn, *The Lattimore Story* (Devin-Adair, 1953), 53; see also the documented account in Lohbeck, *op. cit.*, Part IV.
5. Sherwood, *op. cit.*, 284.
6. On Currie and Greenberg, see references to Senate and House committee evidence and reports collected in Burnham, *op. cit.*
7. Elliott Roosevelt, *op. cit.*, 164.
8. Deane, *op. cit.*, 226.
9. Leahy, *op. cit.*, 147.
10. Hull, *op. cit.*, 1309.
11. U.S. Senate, 82nd Congress, 1st Session, *Military Situation in the Far East,* Part III, 1845.
12. Winston Churchill, *Closing the Ring* (Houghton Mifflin, 1951), 328.
13. Sherwood, *op. cit.*, 776.
14. *Ibid.*, 773.

15. Leahy, *op. cit.*, 202.
16. Sherwood, *op. cit.*, 800.
17. *Ibid.*, 802.
18. *Ibid.*, 802.
19. *Ibid.*, 767.
20. General Sir Alan Brooke, *The Turn of the Tide* (Doubleday, 1957).
21. *Ibid.*, 430.

CHAPTER XIII

1. From the text of address delivered to the Commonwealth Club in San Francisco on April 17, 1953.
2. Mikolajczyk, *op. cit.*, 59.
3. See *U.S. News & World Report* (November 4, 1955), 60.
4. Proceedings of Internal Security Subcommittee, released to the press on February 26, 1957.
5. Statement to the press (International News Service), February 26, 1957.
6. Sherwood, *op. cit.*, 798.
7. *Ibid.*, 776.
8. *Ibid.*, 777.
9. *Ibid.*, 781.
10. *Ibid.*, 779.
11. *Ibid.*, 783.
12. Wilmot, *op. cit.*, 140.
13. Elliott Roosevelt, *op. cit.*, 184.
14. *Ibid.*, 185.
15. General Mark Clark, *Calculated Risk* (Harper, 1950), 358.
16. *Ibid.*, 348-50.
17. Sherwood, *op. cit.*, 790.
18. Arnold, *op. cit.*, 469.
19. Sherwood, *op. cit.*, 796.
20. Mikolajczyk, *op. cit.*, 59.
21. *Ibid.*, 47.
22. Sherwood, *op. cit.*, 797.
23. Mikolajczyk, *op. cit.*, 96.
24. The discussion on Germany is described in Churchill, *Closing the Ring,* and Sherwood, *op. cit.*
25. Wilmot, *op. cit.*, 142.
26. Perkins, *op. cit.*, 70, 71.

CHAPTER XIV

1. Stimson and Bundy, *op. cit.,* 569.
2. For a résumé of the F.B.I. disclosures, see the *New York Times* of November 18, 1953. See also Burnham, *op. cit.,* and Whitehead, *op. cit.*
3. Stimson and Bundy, *op. cit.,* 574.
4. Hull, *op. cit.,* 1606.
5. Stimson and Bundy, *op. cit.,* 572.
6. Sherwood, *op. cit.,* 821.
7. Stimson and Bundy, *op. cit.,* 575.
8. Leahy, *op. cit.,* 259.
9. Hull, *op. cit.,* 1617.
10. *Ibid.,* 1618.
11. *Ibid.,* 1614.
12. Stimson and Bundy, *op. cit.,* 580.
13. *Ibid.,* 581.
14. Utley, *op. cit.,* 64.
15. Eugene Davidson, *The Death and Life of Germany* (Knopf, 1959).

CHAPTER XV

1. Sherwood, *op. cit.,* 845.
2. U.S. Senate MacArthur Hearings, 1951 (Transcript, Part 4, 3119).
3. Leahy, *op. cit.,* 251.
4. Donald M. Dozer's statement to press on the doctoring of State Department records, International News Service dispatch, October 22, 1955; Bryton Barron, *Inside the State Department* (Devin-Adair, 1957).
5. Sherwood, *op. cit.,* 845.
6. Stettinius, *op. cit.,* 72.
7. Sherwood, *op. cit.,* 849.
8. Statement of Andrew Sawchuk to International News Service, March 20, 1955.
9. Stettinius, *op. cit.,* 218.
10. Testimony of Carter and Earle before the House committee investigating the cover-up of the Katyn affair, November 13, 1952.
11. Sherwood, *op. cit.,* 922.
12. *Ibid.,* 835.
13. See de Toledano and Lasky, *op. cit.,* 108.

14. Testimony of Dr. Edna Fluegel before U.S. Senate Internal Security Subcommittee, February 20, 1952. Dr. Fluegel had access to the Hiss notes while in the State Department.

15. Stettinius, *op. cit.*, 103.

16. See Note 8, *supra.*

17. Deane, *op. cit.*, 84.

18. Churchill, *Triumph and Tragedy,* 392.

19. Leahy, *op. cit.*, 316.

20. Churchill, *Triumph and Tragedy,* 458; Eisenhower, *op. cit.*, 440.

21. Churchill, *Triumph and Tragedy,* 464, 468, 511.

22. *Ibid.*, 456.

23. Sherwood, *op. cit.*, 705, 733.

24. The Moscow episode is related by General Deane in *The Strange Alliance.*

25. *Yalta Papers* (Blakeslee memorandum).

26. *Life* (August 30 and September 6, 1948).

27. Quoted in the *New York Daily News,* June 10, 1949.

28. Ellis M. Zacharias, *Secret Missions* (Putnam, 1946), 334.

29. *Ibid.*, 334, 341.

30. For example, see the G-2 document known as "The Colonels' Report," written by area specialists of Military Intelligence. U.S. Senate Armed Services Committee Hearings, 1951, Vol. IV, 2916-17.

31. Kase, *op. cit.*

32. Leahy, *op. cit.*, 293.

33. Arnold, *op. cit.*, and Deane, *op. cit.*

34. MacArthur's public statement to the press, March 23, 1955.

35. A passage in the *Yalta Papers* reveals that Eden had enunciated the British position, at Malta, that it was unnecessary to make concessions to Stalin to induce him to enter the Japanese War.

36. Wilmot, *op. cit.*, 654.

37. *Ibid.*, 655.

38. Sherwood, *op. cit.*, 871.

39. Churchill, *Triumph and Tragedy,* 397, 477.

40. Leahy, *op. cit.*, 323.

41. Wilmot, *op. cit.*, 659.

42. Churchill, *Triumph and Tragedy;* see also Byrnes, Sherwood, Leahy, and Wilmot.

43. Churchill, *Triumph and Tragedy,* 454.

44. John A. Lukacs, *The Great Powers and Eastern Europe* (American Book, 1953), 655, and sources referred to.

Index

INDEX

Abt, John J., 144
Adams, Josephine, 212
Afghanistan, 16
Africa, North: campaign, 168–69, 174, 179
Air Force, U.S. *See* Chennault, General Claire L.; Germany; Japan
Alanbrooke (diary), 244. *See also* Brooke, Field Marshal Viscount Alan
Allen, Robert S., 84
ANAKIM, Operation, 205, 206. *See also* Burma
Anders, General Wladyslaw, 278, 279
ANVIL, Operation, 194, 219
Argentia. *See* Atlantic Conference
Arkansas, U.S.S., 103
Army, U.S., 9, 69, 74, 189, 191, 192, 193. *See also* ANAKIM; ANVIL; Eisenhower, General Dwight D.; Germany; Japan; OVERLORD; ROUNDUP; SLEDGEHAMMER; TORCH
Arnold, General H. H. ("Hap"): at Atlantic Conference, 100, 105, 107, 109–10; at Casablanca Conference, 177, 178; on Teheran Conference, 220; mentioned, 207, 269
Atlanta Constitution, 55
Atlantic Charter: as propaganda, 51, 55–61, 112–13, 117–21, 123–24, 128–30; subscribed to as international pact, 57, 132–33; fate of, 59–61; drafting of, 111–15, 133–58; text, 114–15; release of, 117–19; legal and moral nature of, 117, 130–32; Churchill's reservations on, 121, 129–31, 139–41, 151–52, 154, 157–58; and freedom of speech, thought, religion, 138–39, 142–53; contradictions within, 152–53; violations of, 155, 158, 185, 210, 222, 227, 235, 258–59, 265, 274; mentioned, xii, 8, 28, 30, 45, 47, 104, 119, 171, 220, 274

Atlantic Charter (continued)
——— analysis of: First Point, 133–35; Second Point, 135–37; Third Point, 135–53; Fourth and Fifth Points (economic), 60, 153–56; Sixth Point, 156; Seventh Point, 156–57; Eighth Point, 157–58
Atlantic Conference; 57–59, 96–117; 129–31, 133–58; participants, 100, 105; mentioned, xii, 45, 184, 186. *See also* Atlantic Charter
Atomic bomb, 45, 182, 194–95, 242, 265, 273
Attlee, Clement, 98
Augusta, U.S.S., 100, 103, 106, 110, 111, 114, 141
Austria, 194

Badoglio, Marshal Pietro, 187
Baghdad Pact, 260
Bailey, Thomas A., xiv, 80
Baillie, Hugh, 24
Baldwin, Hanson W., 4, 164
Balkans: proposed invasion through, 8, 164, 174–75, 178–79, 188, 215, 217, 218; mentioned, 4, 194, 251. *See also* Churchill, Sir Winston; Roosevelt, Franklin D.; Second Front
Baltic States: Russian annexation of, 7, 15, 16, 125, 170, 171, 210, 215, 220–21, 259; mentioned, 29, 158, 248
Barnes, Harry Elmer, 89
Beard, Charles A., xiv, 18, 47
Beardall, Captain John R., 97, 105
Beaverbrook, Lord (Minister of Supply), 105, 110, 117
Beck, General Ludwig, 169
Belgium, 91
Benes, Bohus, 209
Benes, President Eduard, 209, 261
Bentley, Elizabeth, 230
Beria, Commissar L. P., 246
Berlin, 27, 187, 261–62